AIRCRAFT DESIGN
of
WWII
A Sketchbook

AIRCRAFT DESIGN
of
WWII

A Sketchbook

LOCKHEED AIRCRAFT CORPORATION

DOVER PUBLICATIONS
GARDEN CITY, NEW YORK

Bibliographical Note

This Dover edition, first published in 2017, is an unabridged republication of the work originally compiled and published by the Lockhead Aircraft Corporation, Burbank, CA, in 1940, under the title *Aircraft Design Sketch Book*. The page numbers in this Dover edition are sequenced by section number and page number, following the original format.

International Standard Book Number
ISBN-13: 978-0-486-81420-9
ISBN-10: 0-486-81420-3

Manufactured in the United States of America
81320307
www.doverpublications.com

★ PREFACE ★

Less than a half century ago the pioneers of aviation were struggling with the principles of controlled flight. Before they had finished and flown one model, they were beginning to visualize the improvements for their next. ● The engineers of today are still putting into practice some of the ideas and theories laid down by their early brothers; and like them, are dreaming of the "Plane of Tomorrow" as they ponder on the problems of today. It is because of this that aviation has advanced as rapidly as it has, and we are still trying to accelerate its production. ● During the preparation of the "Aircraft Design Sketch Book" there has been but one purpose in view — to give to the designer a collection of ideas, in sketch form, that will stimulate his own creative and inventive mind. It must be remembered that the ideas as sketched in this book should not be bodily lifted, because by so doing the purpose of the book is defeated, and we would find ourselves not only standing still but actually going backward as far as design is concerned. However, if enough improvements and new features are added, it can safely be said that we are progressing in our designs. ● Therefore, it is hoped that, by the proper use of this book, the "Plane of Tomorrow" will spend less time on the design and drafting boards of today. ● Grateful acknowledgments are made by the Company to the following magazines and books for their contributions: "Aeroplane," "Flight," "Aviation," "L'Aeronautique," and Jane's "All the World's Aircraft," and in particular for the work of the Standards Group. ● To be continually useful, this book must be kept "up to date." Therefore, comments, suggestions, and new material for the book are more than welcome and should be forwarded to the Standards Group.

LOCKHEED AIRCRAFT CORPORATION

Hall L. Hibbard

VICE PRESIDENT AND CHIEF ENGINEER

★ TABLE OF CONTENTS ★

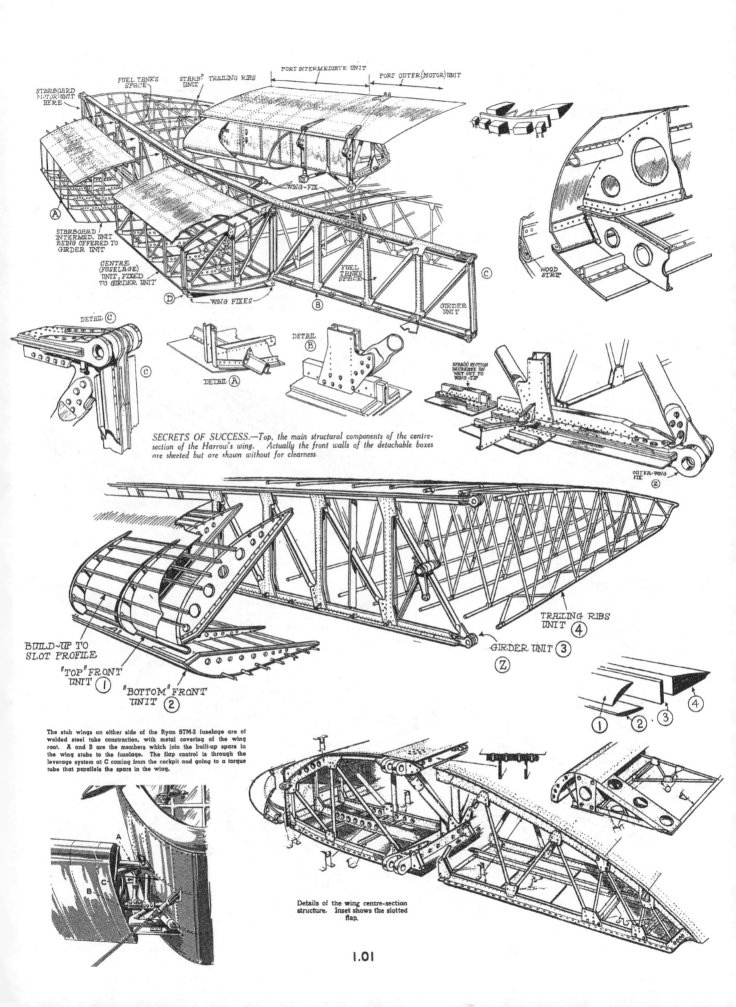

STARBOARD MOTOR UNIT HERE

FUEL TANKS SPACE

STARB.ᵈ UNIT

TRAILING RIBS

PORT INTERMEDIATE UNIT

PORT OUTER (MOTOR) UNIT

WING~FIX

Ⓐ

STARBOARD INTERMED. UNIT BEING OFFERED TO GIRDER UNIT

CENTRE (FUSELAGE) UNIT, FIXED TO GIRDER UNIT

Ⓓ

WING FIXES

Ⓑ

FUEL TANKS SPACE

Ⓒ

GIRDER UNIT

WOOD STRIP

DETAIL Ⓒ

Ⓒ

DETAIL Ⓐ

DETAIL Ⓑ

SPAR(S) SECTION DECREASE ON WAY OUT TO WING~TIP

SECRETS OF SUCCESS.—Top, the main structural components of the centre-section of the Harrow's wing. Actually the front walls of the detachable boxes are sheeted but are shown without for clearness.

OUTER-WING FIX

Ⓩ

BUILD~UP TO SLOT PROFILE

"TOP" FRONT UNIT ①

"BOTTOM" FRONT UNIT ②

TRAILING RIBS UNIT ④

GIRDER UNIT ③

Ⓩ

① ② ③ ④

The stub wings on either side of the Ryan STM-2 fuselage are of welded steel tube construction, with metal covering of the wing root. A and B are the members which join the built-up spars in the wing stubs to the fuselage. The flap control is through the leverage system at C coming from the cockpit and going to a torque tube that parallels the spars in the wing.

Details of the wing centre-section structure. Inset shows the slotted flap.

1.01

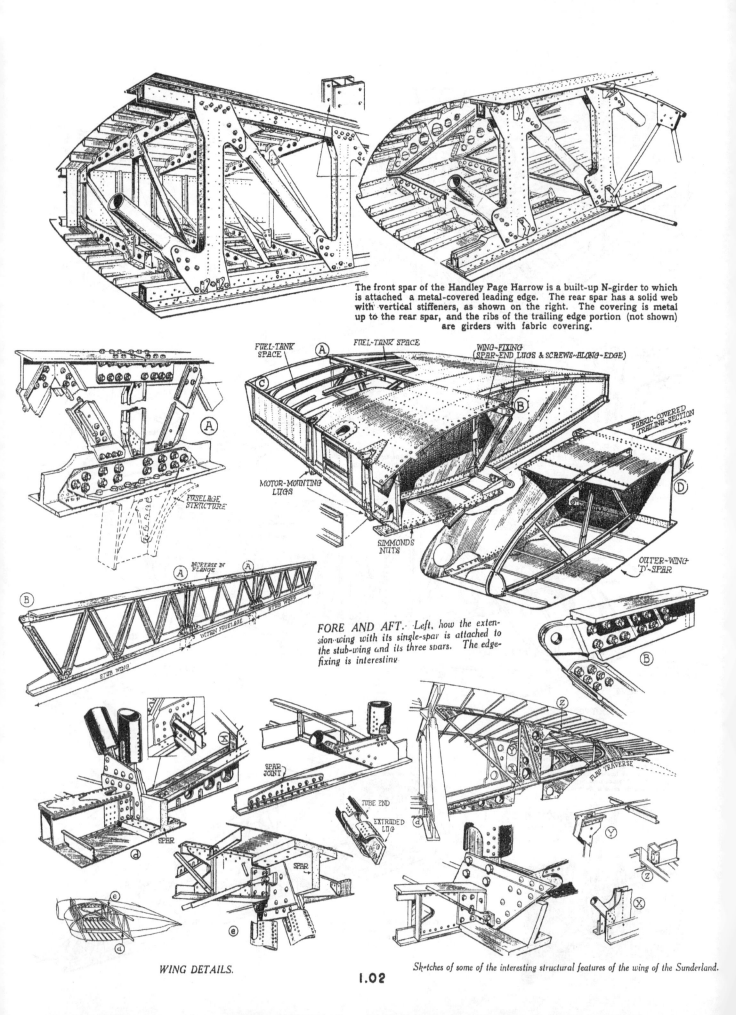

The front spar of the Handley Page Harrow is a built-up N-girder to which is attached a metal-covered leading edge. The rear spar has a solid web with vertical stiffeners, as shown on the right. The covering is metal up to the rear spar, and the ribs of the trailing edge portion (not shown) are girders with fabric covering.

FUEL-TANK SPACE

FUEL-TANK SPACE

WING~FIXING (SPAR-END LUGS & SCREWS~ALONG~EDGE)

FABRIC-COVERED TRAILING~SECTION

MOTOR-MOUNTING LUGS

SIMMONDS NUTS

OUTER~WING 'D'~SPAR

FUSELAGE STRUCTURE

INCREASE IN FLANGE

WITHIN FUSELAGE

STUB WING

FORE AND AFT.- *Left, how the extension-wing with its single-spar is attached to the stub-wing and its three spars. The edge-fixing is interesting.*

SPAR JOINT

SPAR

TUBE END

EXTRUDED LUG

FLAP TRAVERSE

SPAR

SPAR

WING DETAILS.

Sketches of some of the interesting structural features of the wing of the Sunderland.

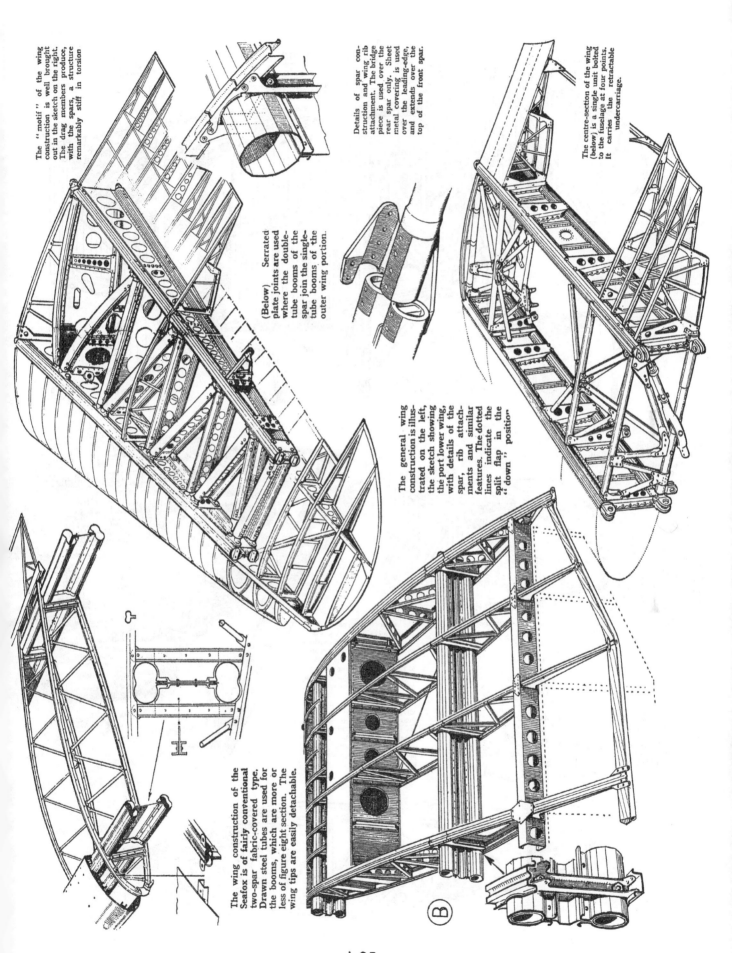

The "motif" of the wing construction is well brought out in the sketch on the right. The drag members produce, with the spars, a structure remarkably stiff in torsion

Details of spar construction and wing rib attachment. The bridge piece is used over the rear spar only. Sheet metal covering is used over the leading-edge, and extends over the top of the front spar.

(Below) Serrated plate joints are used where the double-tube booms of the spar join the single-tube booms of the outer wing portion.

The centre-section of the wing (below) is a single unit bolted to the fuselage at four points. It carries the retractable undercarriage.

The general wing construction is illustrated on the left, the sketch showing the port lower wing, with details of the spar, rib attachments and similar features. The dotted lines indicate the split flap in the "down" position

The wing construction of the Seafox is of fairly conventional two-spar fabric-covered type. Drawn steel tubes are used for the booms, which are more or less of figure eight section. The wing tips are easily detachable.

Ⓑ

1.03

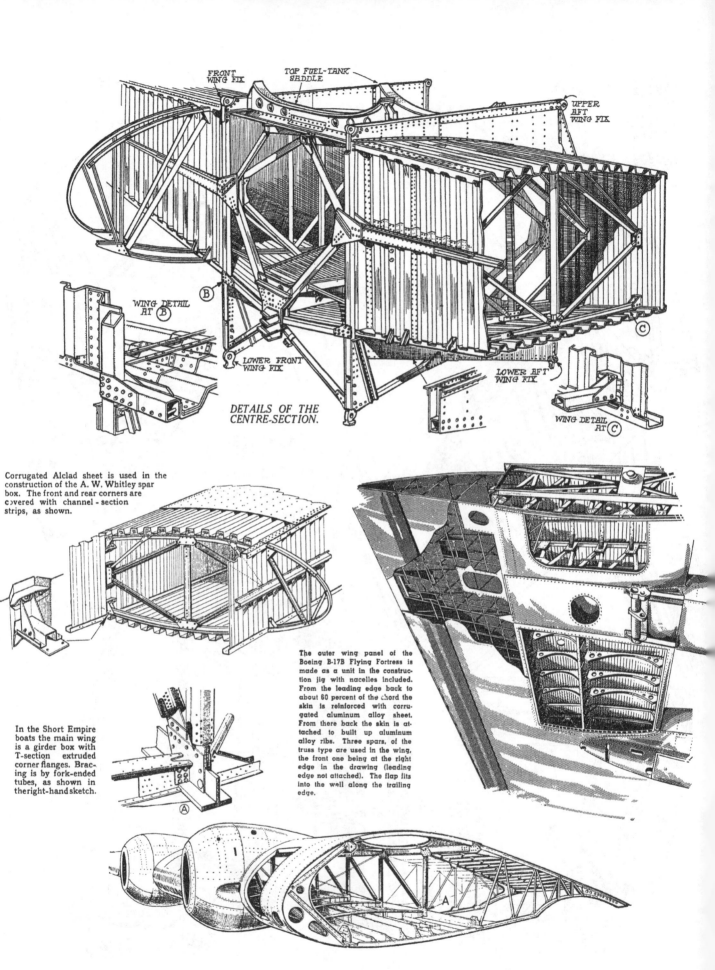

FRONT WING FIX

TOP FUEL-TANK SADDLE

UPPER AFT WING FIX

WING DETAIL AT Ⓑ

LOWER FRONT WING FIX

LOWER AFT WING FIX

WING DETAIL AT Ⓒ

DETAILS OF THE CENTRE-SECTION.

Corrugated Alclad sheet is used in the construction of the A. W. Whitley spar box. The front and rear corners are covered with channel - section strips, as shown.

In the Short Empire boats the main wing is a girder box with T-section extruded corner flanges. Bracing is by fork-ended tubes, as shown in the right-hand sketch.

Ⓐ

The outer wing panel of the Boeing B-17B Flying Fortress is made as a unit in the construction jig with nacelles included. From the leading edge back to about 60 percent of the chord the skin is reinforced with corrugated aluminum alloy sheet. From there back the skin is attached to built up aluminum alloy ribs. Three spars, of the truss type are used in the wing, the front one being at the right edge in the drawing (leading edge not attached). The flap fits into the well along the trailing edge.

A

1.04

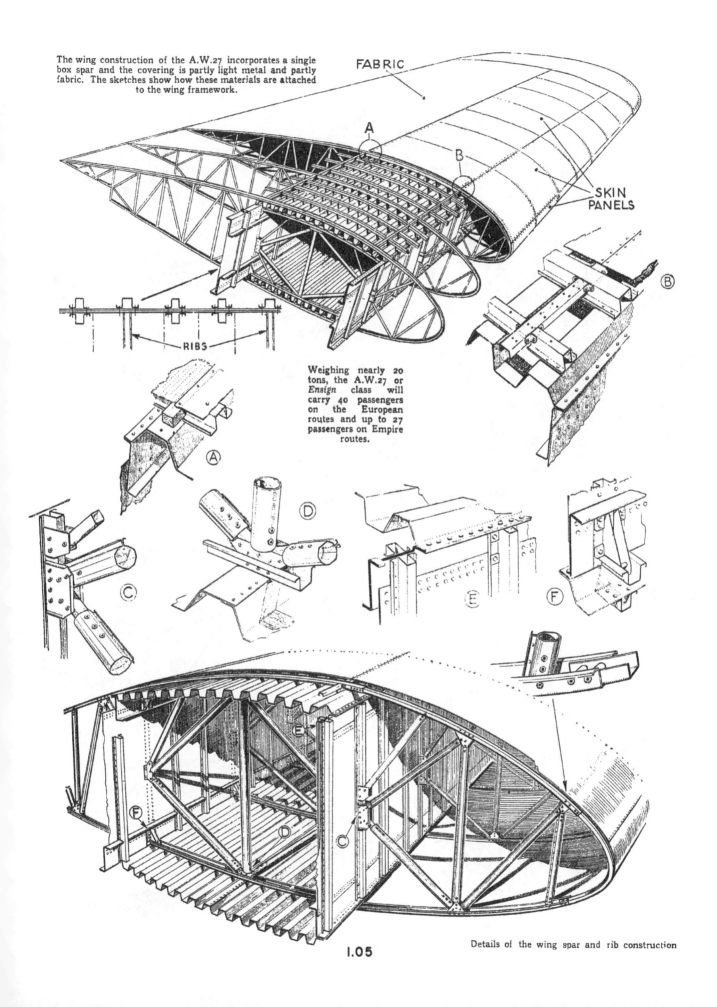

The wing construction of the A.W.27 incorporates a single box spar and the covering is partly light metal and partly fabric. The sketches show how these materials are attached to the wing framework.

FABRIC

SKIN PANELS

RIBS

Weighing nearly 20 tons, the A.W.27 or *Ensign* class will carry 40 passengers on the European routes and up to 27 passengers on Empire routes.

I.05

Details of the wing spar and rib construction

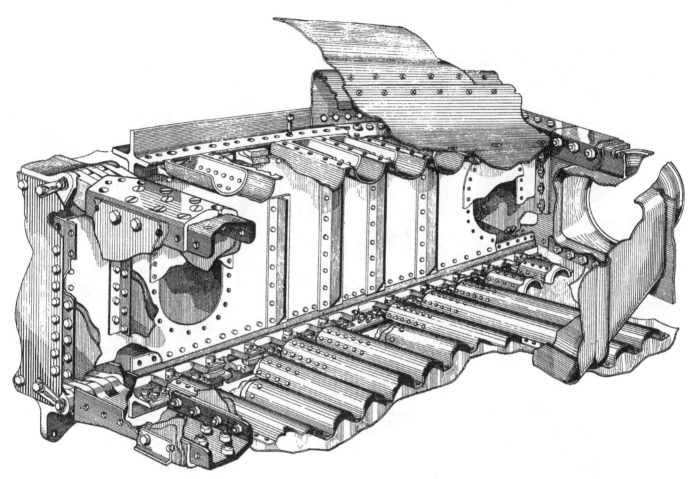

FIG. 4 WING-CENTER SECTION ATTACHMENT

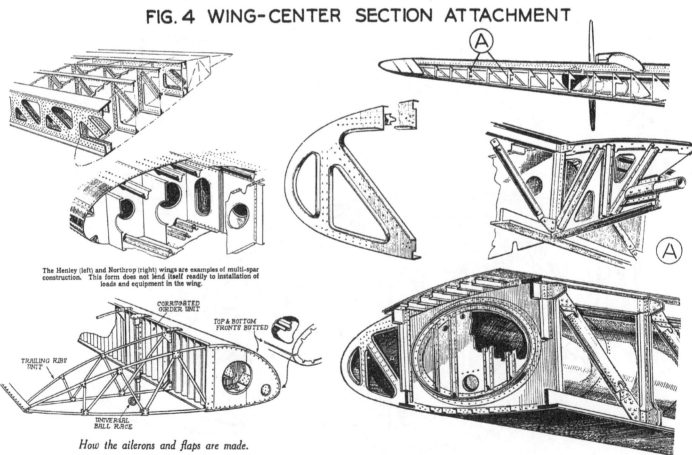

The Henley (left) and Northrop (right) wings are examples of multi-spar construction. This form does not lend itself readily to installation of loads and equipment in the wing.

CORRUGATED GIRDER UNIT

TOP & BOTTOM FRONTS BUTTED

TRAILING RIBS UNIT

UNIVERSAL BALL RACE

How the ailerons and flaps are made.

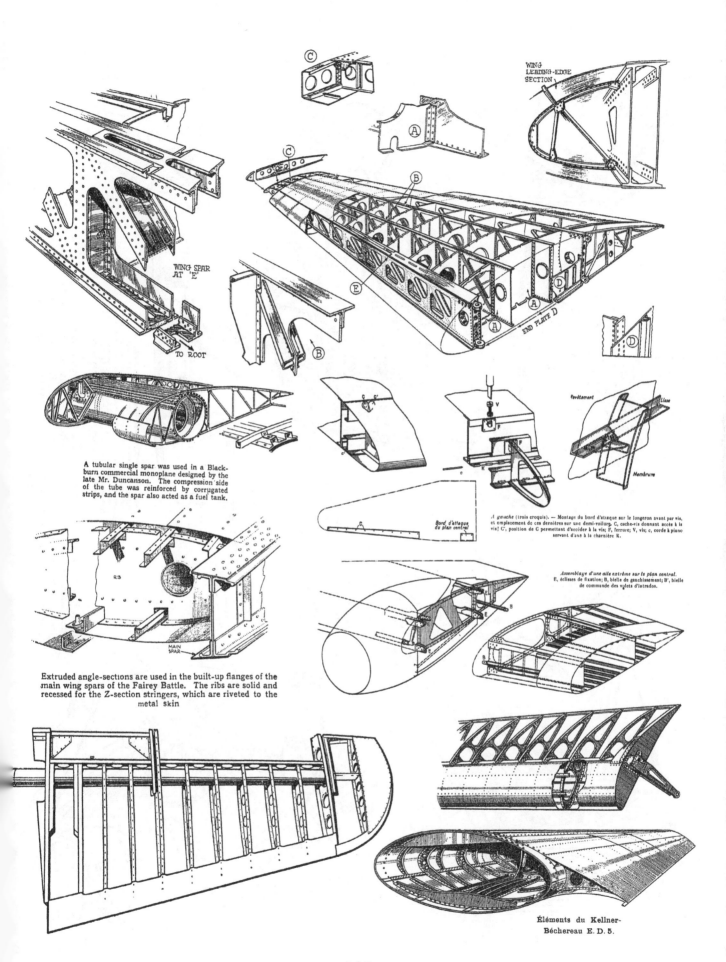

C

A

C

B

E

A

A

D

END PLATE D

D

WING SPAR AT 'E'

TO ROOT

WING LEADING-EDGE SECTION

A tubular single spar was used in a Blackburn commercial monoplane designed by the late Mr. Duncanson. The compression side of the tube was reinforced by corrugated strips, and the spar also acted as a fuel tank.

R3

MAIN SPAR

Extruded angle-sections are used in the built-up flanges of the main wing spars of the Fairey Battle. The ribs are solid and recessed for the Z-section stringers, which are riveted to the metal skin

Revêtement

Lisse

Membrure

Bord d'attaque du plan central

A gauche (trois croquis). — Montage du bord d'attaque sur le longeron avant par vis, et emplacement de ces dernières sur une demi-voilure. C, cache-vis donnant accès à la vis; C', position de C permettant d'accéder à la vis; F, ferrure; V, vis; c, corde à piano servant d'axe à la charnière K.

Assemblage d'une aile extrême sur le plan central. E, éclisses de fixation; B, bielle de gauchissement; B', bielle de commande des volets d'intrados.

Éléments du Kellner-Béchereau E. D. 5.

1.07

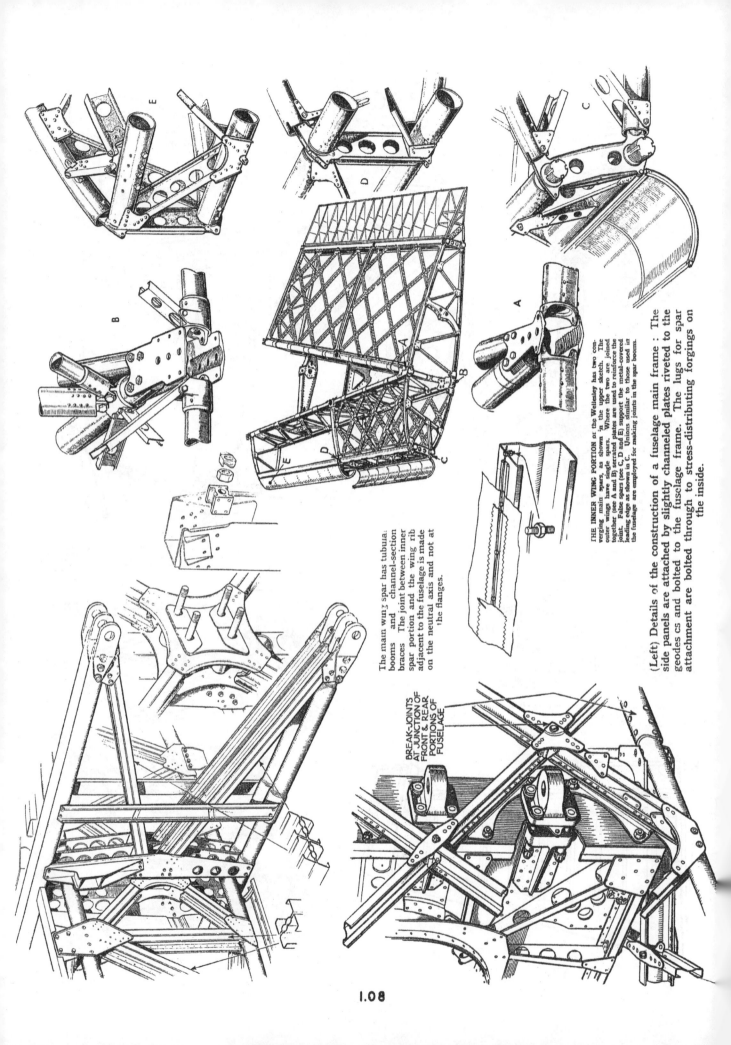

THE INNER WING PORTION or the Wellesley has two converging main spars, as shown in the upper sketch. The outer wings have single spars. Where the two are joined together (see A and B) serrated plates are used to reinforce the joint. False spars (see C, D and E) support the metal-covered leading edge as shown in C. Unions similar to those used in the fuselage are employed for making joints in the spar booms.

The main wing spar has tubular booms and channel-section braces. The joint between inner spar portion and the wing rib adjacent to the fuselage is made on the neutral axis and not at the flanges.

(Left) Details of the construction of a fuselage main frame : The side panels are attached by slightly channeled plates riveted to the geodetics and bolted to the fuselage frame. The lugs for spar attachment are bolted through to stress-distributing forgings on the inside.

BREAK-JOINTS AT JUNCTION OF FRONT & REAR PORTIONS OF FUSELAGE

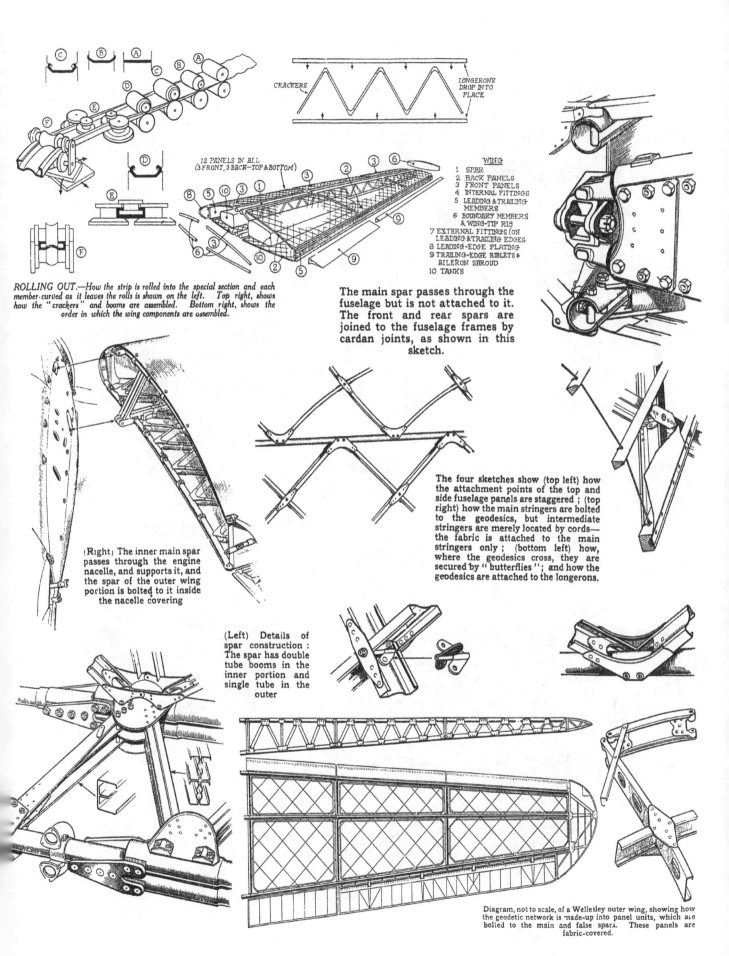

CRACKERS

LONGERONS DROP INTO PLACE

12 PANELS IN ALL
(3 FRONT, 3 BACK—TOP & BOTTOM)

WING

1 SPAR
2 BACK PANELS
3 FRONT PANELS
4 INTERNAL FITTINGS
5 LEADING & TRAILING MEMBERS
6 BOUNDARY MEMBERS & WING-TIP RIB
7 EXTERNAL FITTINGS (ON LEADING & TRAILING EDGES
8 LEADING-EDGE PLATING
9 TRAILING-EDGE RIBLETS & AILERON SHROUD
10 TANKS

ROLLING OUT.—How the strip is rolled into the special section and each member curved as it leaves the rolls is shown on the left. Top right, shows how the "crackers" and booms are assembled. Bottom right, shows the order in which the wing components are assembled.

The main spar passes through the fuselage but is not attached to it. The front and rear spars are joined to the fuselage frames by cardan joints, as shown in this sketch.

(Right) The inner main spar passes through the engine nacelle, and supports it, and the spar of the outer wing portion is bolted to it inside the nacelle covering

The four sketches show (top left) how the attachment points of the top and side fuselage panels are staggered ; (top right) how the main stringers are bolted to the geodesics, but intermediate stringers are merely located by cords—the fabric is attached to the main stringers only ; (bottom left) how, where the geodesics cross, they are secured by "butterflies"; and how the geodesics are attached to the longerons.

(Left) Details of spar construction : The spar has double tube booms in the inner portion and single tube in the outer

Diagram, not to scale, of a Wellesley outer wing, showing how the geodetic network is made-up into panel units, which are bolted to the main and false spars. These panels are fabric-covered.

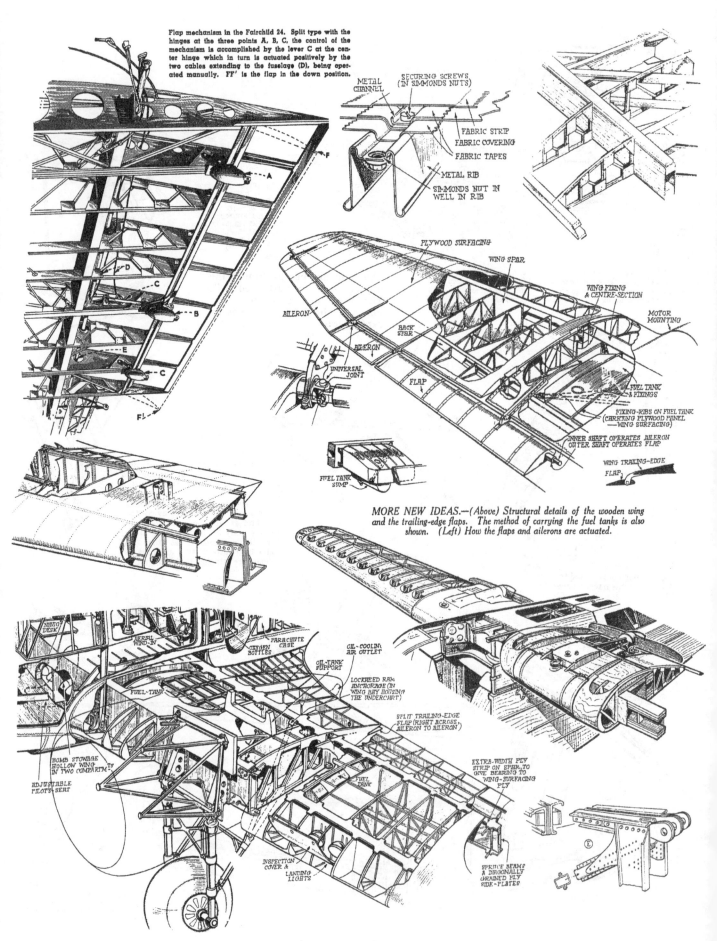

Flap mechanism in the Fairchild 24. Split type with the hinges at the three points A, B, C, the control of the mechanism is accomplished by the lever C at the center hinge which in turn is actuated positively by the two cables extending to the fuselage (D), being operated manually. FF' is the flap in the down position.

METAL CHANNEL

SECURING SCREWS (IN SIMMONDS NUTS)

FABRIC STRIP
FABRIC COVERING
FABRIC TAPES

METAL RIB

SIMMONDS NUT IN WELL IN RIB

PLYWOOD SURFACING

WING SPAR

WING FIXING & CENTRE-SECTION

MOTOR MOUNTING

AILERON

BACK SPAR

AILERON

UNIVERSAL JOINT

FLAP

FUEL TANK & FIXINGS

FIXING-RIBS ON FUEL TANK (CARRYING PLYWOOD PANEL —WING SURFACING)

INNER SHAFT OPERATES AILERON
OUTER SHAFT OPERATES FLAP

WING TRAILING-EDGE FLAP

FUEL TANK SUMP

MORE NEW IDEAS.—(*Above*) *Structural details of the wooden wing and the trailing-edge flaps. The method of carrying the fuel tanks is also shown. (Left) How the flaps and ailerons are actuated.*

NAVIG DESK
AERIAL WIND-IN
PARACHUTE CASE
OXYGEN BOTTLES
OIL-TANK SUPPORT
OIL-COOLING AIR OUTLET

FUEL TANK

LOCKHEED RAM ANCHORAGE (IN WING BAY HOUSING THE UNDERCART)

SPLIT TRAILING-EDGE FLAP (RIGHT ACROSS AILERON TO AILERON)

BOMB STOWAGE HOLLOW WING IN TWO COMPARTM'TS

ADJUSTABLE PILOT'S SEAT

FUEL TANK

EXTRA-WIDTH PLY STRIP ON SPAR, TO GIVE BEARING TO WING-SURFACING PLY

INSPECTION COVER & LANDING LIGHTS

SPRUCE BEAMS A DIAGONALLY GRAINED PLY SIDE-PLATES

E

FIN
3 POINT FIX

TAIL-PLANE
3-SPAR FIXING

EXTRA STIFFENING
(ONLY NEAR ROOT)

DEFLECTION STRIP
THIS WIDE &
RIGHT ALONG
(UNDERSIDE ONLY)

ELEVATOR HALVES
INTERCH.

Servo Tab

Trim Tab

Navigation Light
Trim Tab

CAMBERED FIN
GIVES SIDE PULL
TO PORT

RUDDER SERVO LEVER
(ACTUALLY ON
STARB'D FACE)

ELEVATOR TRIM

RETRACTING
TAIL-WHEEL

3248

FABRIC-COVERED
RUDDER

NAVIGATION
LIGHT

2-Spar
Two-Piece
Fin

2-spar
Tailplane

Fabric-covered
Rudder

Trim & Balance Tabs

Elevator
Actuating Links

Elevator
adjustable
on ground

Navigation
Light

RADIO

Rudder
Lower Bearing

Fabric-covered
Elevator

Castoring Tailwheel

Dowty
Retracting
Tail Unit

TRIM
TABS

BUILT-IN
MASS BALANCE

GIRDER
POSTS

NAV LIGHT

TRIM TABS

TRIM TAB

TRIM TAB
(EACH SIDE)

WHEEL HOUSING

DOWTY RETRACTING
LEG & ARM

FABRIC

SPARS & DIAGONAL-BRACINGS
ALL BULB-FLANGED

FORMERS
OMITTED TO
REVEAL DIAGONAL
BRACINGS

ELEVATOR-HINGE
BRACKETS

HYDRAULIC
RETRACTING
TAILWHEEL

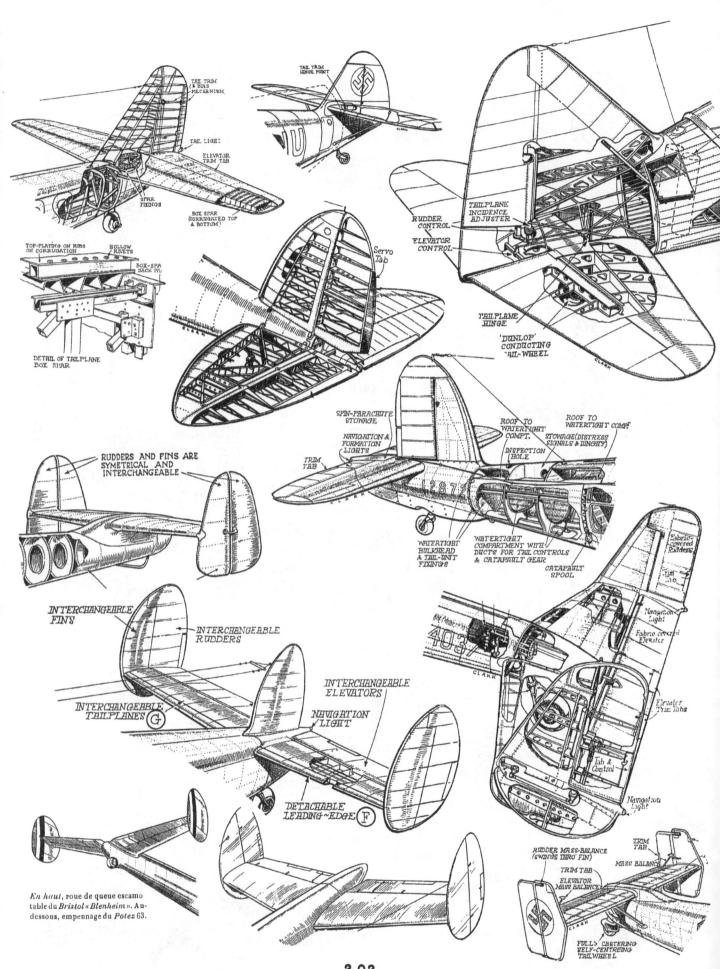

TAIL TRIM
(& BIAS)
MECHANISM

TAIL TRIM
HINGE POINT

TAIL LIGHT

ELEVATOR
TRIM TAB

SPAR
FIXINGS

BOX SPAR
(CORRUGATED TOP
& BOTTOM)

TOP-PLATING ON RIBS
ON CORRUGATION

HOLLOW
RIVETS

BOX-SPAR
BACK PL.

DETAIL OF TAILPLANE
BOX SPAR

Servo
Tab

RUDDER
CONTROL

ELEVATOR
CONTROL

TAILPLANE
INCIDENCE
ADJUSTER

TAILPLANE
HINGE

'DUNLOP'
CONDUCTING
TAIL-WHEEL

RUDDERS AND FINS ARE
SYMETRICAL AND
INTERCHANGEABLE

SPIN-PARACHUTE
STOWAGE

NAVIGATION &
FORMATION
LIGHTS

TRIM
TAB

ROOF TO
WATERTIGHT
COMPT.

ROOF TO
WATERTIGHT COMPT.

STOWAGE (DISTRESS
SIGNALS & DINGHY)

INSPECTION
HOLE

WATERTIGHT
BULKHEAD
& TAIL-UNIT
FIXINGS

WATERTIGHT
COMPARTMENT WITH
DUCTS FOR TAIL CONTROLS
& CATAPULT GEAR

CATAPULT
SPOOL

Fabric-
covered
Rudders

Trim
Tab

INTERCHANGEABLE
FINS

INTERCHANGEABLE
RUDDERS

INTERCHANGEABLE
ELEVATORS

NAVIGATION
LIGHT

INTERCHANGEABLE
TAILPLANES (G)

INTERCHANGEABLE
TAILPLANES (G)

DETACHABLE
LEADING~EDGE (F)

Navigation
Light

Fabric covered
Elevator

Elevator
Trim Tabs

Tab &
Control

Navigation
Light

En haut, roue de queue escamo
table du Bristol « Blenheim ». Au-
dessous, empennage du Potez 63.

RUDDER MASS-BALANCE
(SWINGS THRO' FIN)

TRIM TAB

MASS BALANCE

TRIM TAB

ELEVATOR
MASS BALANCE

FULLY CASTERING
SELF-CENTREING
TAILWHEEL

Trim Tab
3-Spar Tailplane
Trim Tab

DOWTY Tailwheel

The elevator and rudder hinge gaps of Lowe's Comper Swift were faired over with metal foil doped to the fabric.

HANDHOLE
NAV. LIGHT

L 4534

FLARE CHUTE
& FLAP COVER

DETAIL AT (A)

FIN-POST
STEPPED AT
FRONT OF
BOX SPAR

RUDDER-POST
STEPPED AT
BACK OF
BOX SPAR

STARBOARD
TRAILING UNIT (5)

STARBOARD
LEADING EDGE UNIT
(ATTACHED TO
BOX SPAR)
(3)

HANDHOLES
(AFTERWARDS
COVERED)

CORRUGATED
TOP, BOTTOM &
SIDES

FIXING TO
FUSELAGE

THE TAIL.—Details of the tail-plane and fins. The disembodied
diagram shows the scheme of production.

D

The construction of the tail follows the same general system as that used in the main wing, but the gauges are, of course, very much lighter. Note the "Z" sections in the corners of the spar box

2.03

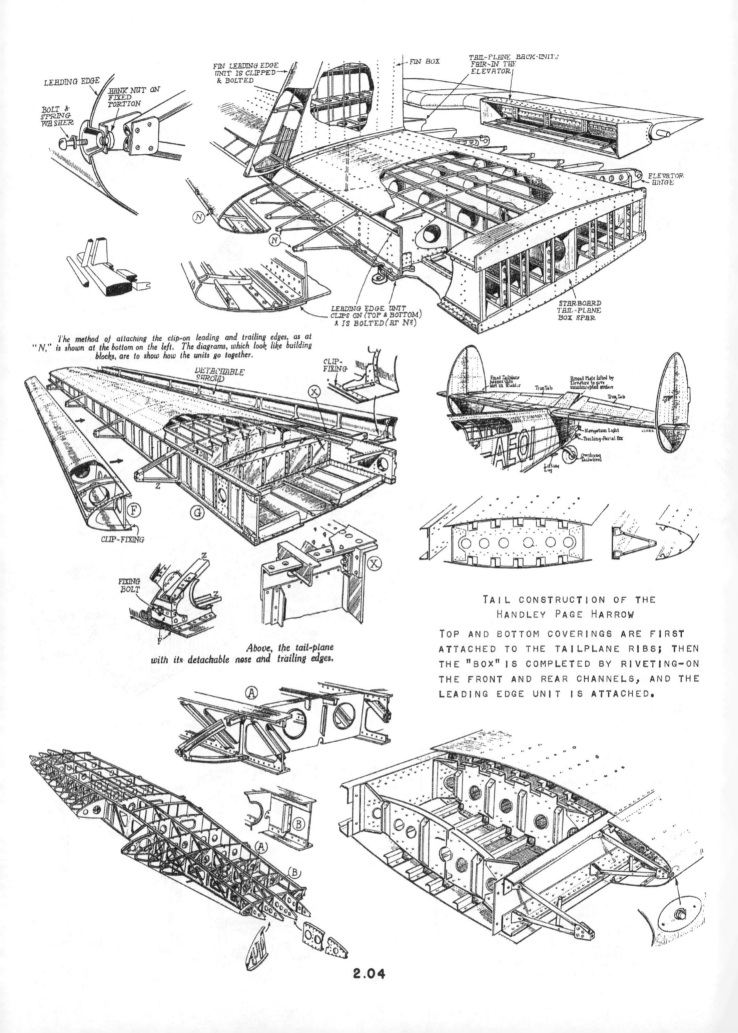

LEADING EDGE

BOLT &
SPRING
WASHER

HANK NUT ON
FIXED
PORTION

FIN LEADING EDGE
UNIT IS CLIPPED
& BOLTED

FIN BOX

TAIL-PLANE BACK-UNITS
FAIR-IN THE
ELEVATOR

ELEVATOR
HINGE

LEADING EDGE UNIT
CLIPS ON (TOP & BOTTOM)
& IS BOLTED (AT Nº)

STARBOARD
TAIL-PLANE
BOX SPAR

The method of attaching the clip-on leading and trailing edges, as at "N," is shown at the bottom on the left. The diagrams, which look like building blocks, are to show how the units go together.

DETACHABLE
SHROUD

CLIP-
FIXING

CLIP-FIXING

FIXING
BOLT

Above, the tail-plane with its detachable nose and trailing edges.

Fixed Tailplane
passes thro'
slot in Rudder

TrimTab

Hinged Plate lifted by
Elevator to give
uninterrupted surface

Trim Tab

Navigation Light

Trailing-Aerial Box

Lifting
Lug

Overhung
Tailwheel

A.E01

TAIL CONSTRUCTION OF THE
HANDLEY PAGE HARROW

TOP AND BOTTOM COVERINGS ARE FIRST
ATTACHED TO THE TAILPLANE RIBS; THEN
THE "BOX" IS COMPLETED BY RIVETING-ON
THE FRONT AND REAR CHANNELS, AND THE
LEADING EDGE UNIT IS ATTACHED.

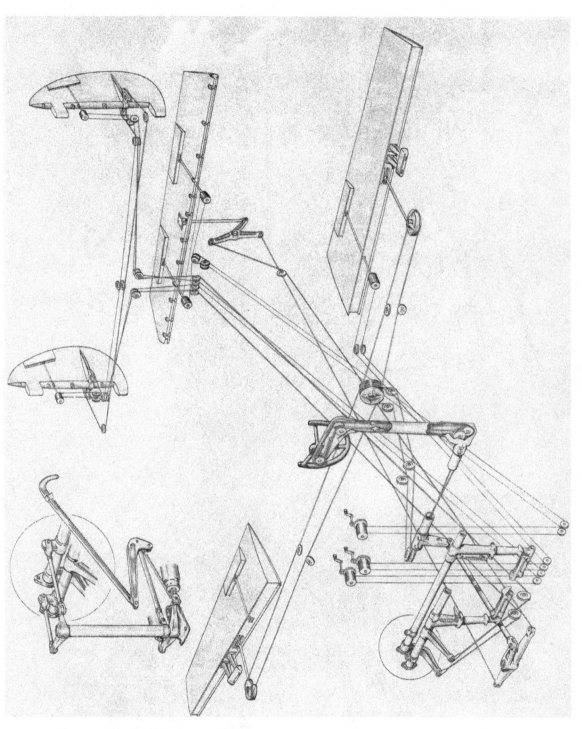

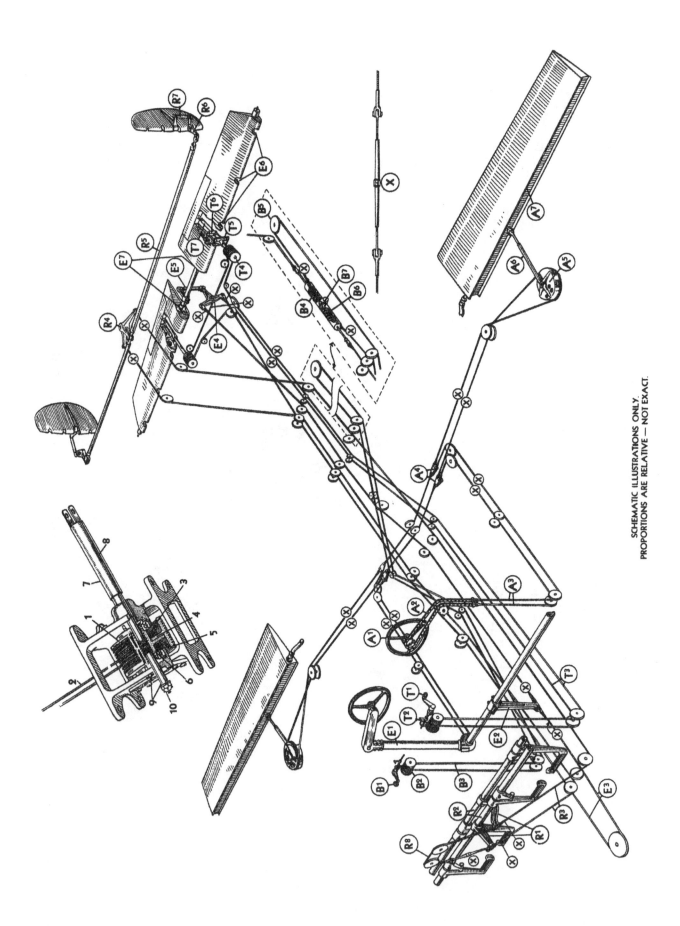

SCHEMATIC ILLUSTRATIONS ONLY.
PROPORTIONS ARE RELATIVE — NOT EXACT.

3.02

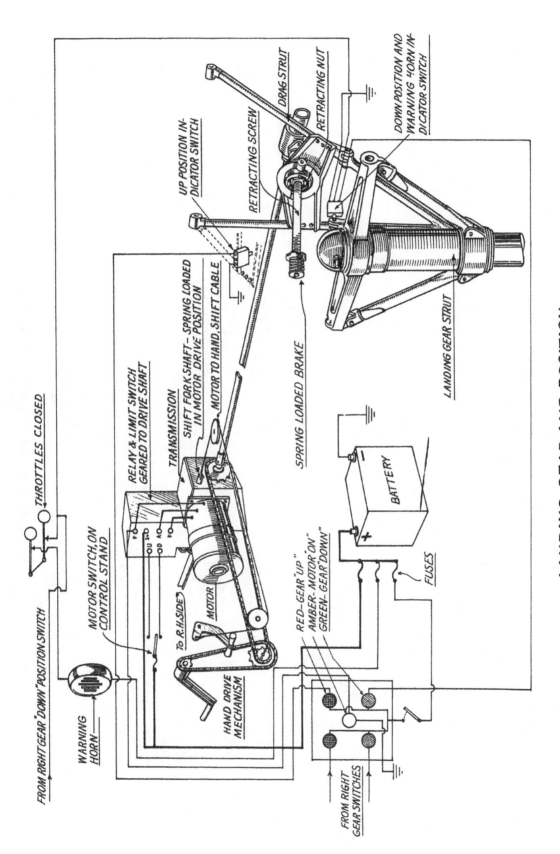

LANDING GEAR AND POSITION
SIGNAL MECHANISM—MODEL 10

THROTTLES CLOSED

FROM RIGHT GEAR "DOWN" POSITION SWITCH

MOTOR SWITCH, ON CONTROL STAND

WARNING HORN

RELAY & LIMIT SWITCH GEARED TO DRIVE SHAFT

TRANSMISSION

UP POSITION IN-DICATOR SWITCH

RETRACTING SCREW

DRAG STRUT

RETRACTING NUT

DOWN POSITION AND WARNING HORN IN-DICATOR SWITCH

SHIFT FORK SHAFT—SPRING LOADED IN MOTOR DRIVE POSITION

MOTOR TO HAND, SHIFT CABLE

SPRING LOADED BRAKE

LANDING GEAR STRUT

To R.H. SIDE

MOTOR

HAND DRIVE MECHANISM

RED-GEAR "UP"
AMBER- MOTOR "ON"
GREEN- GEAR "DOWN"

BATTERY

FUSES

FROM RIGHT GEAR SWITCHES

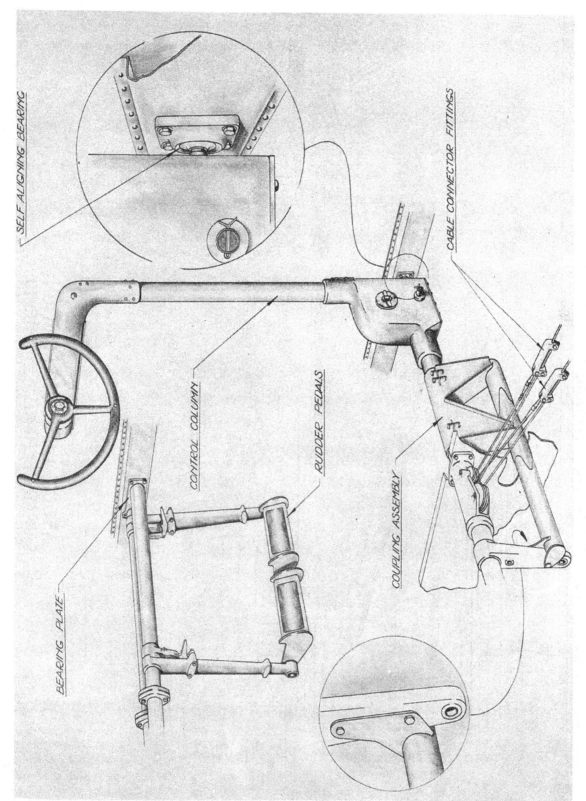

SELF ALIGNING BEARING

CABLE CONNECTOR FITTINGS

CONTROL COLUMN

RUDDER PEDALS

BEARING PLATE

COUPLING ASSEMBLY

CO-PILOT'S REMOVABLE (AUXILIARY) FLIGHT CONTROLS
BOMBER

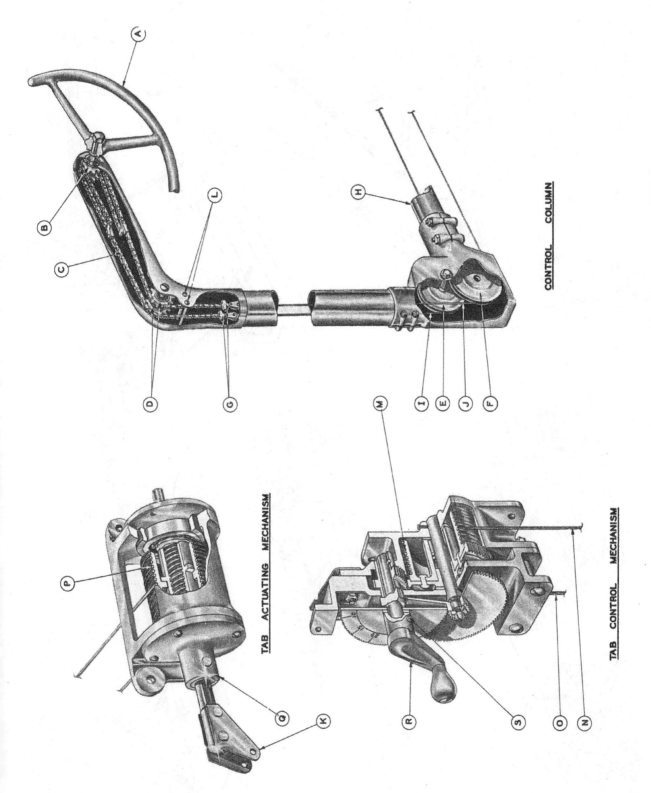

CONTROL COLUMN

TAB ACTUATING MECHANISM

TAB CONTROL MECHANISM

TAB AND CONTROL COLUMN MECHANISMS

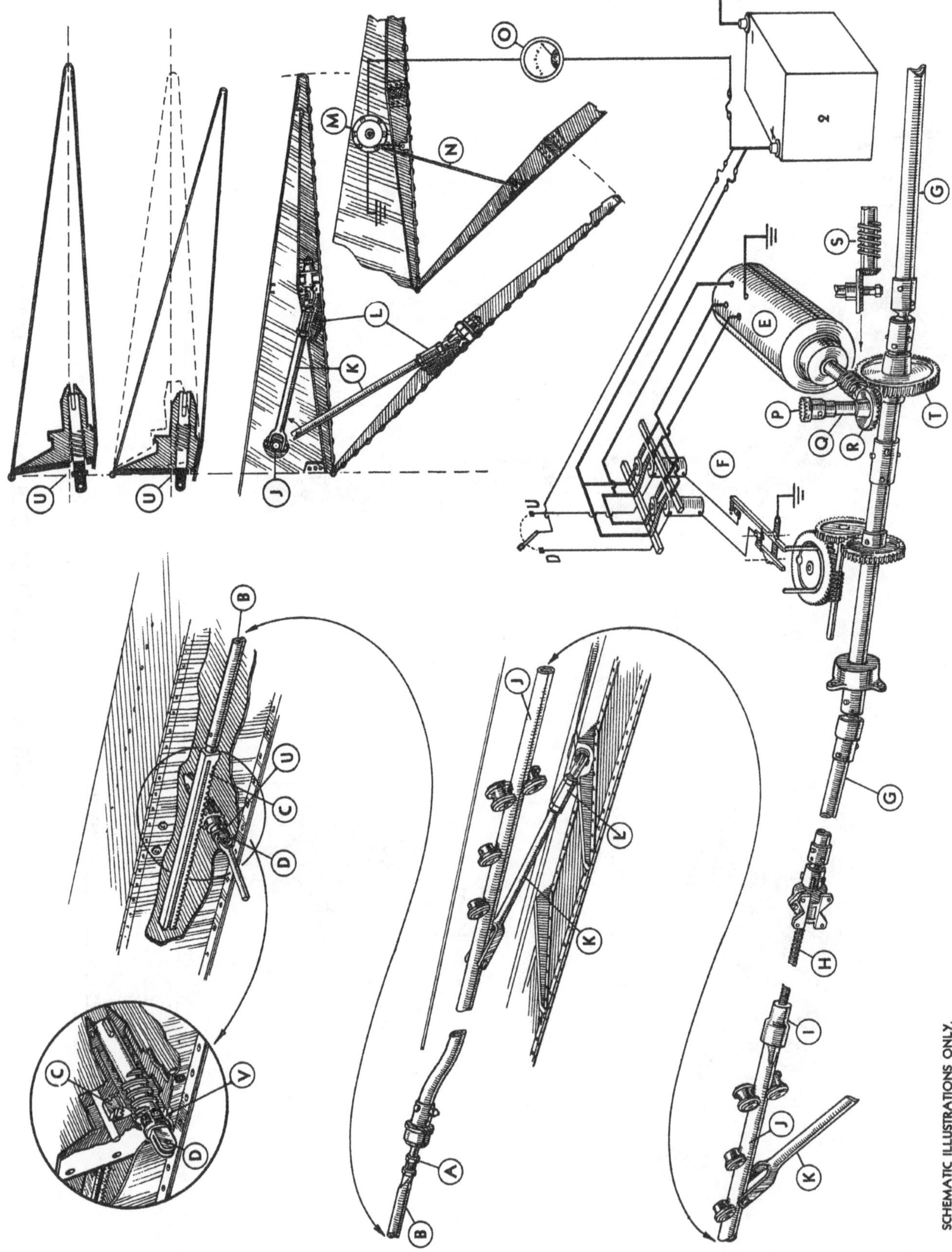

SCHEMATIC ILLUSTRATIONS ONLY.
PROPORTIONS ARE RELATIVE — NOT EXACT.

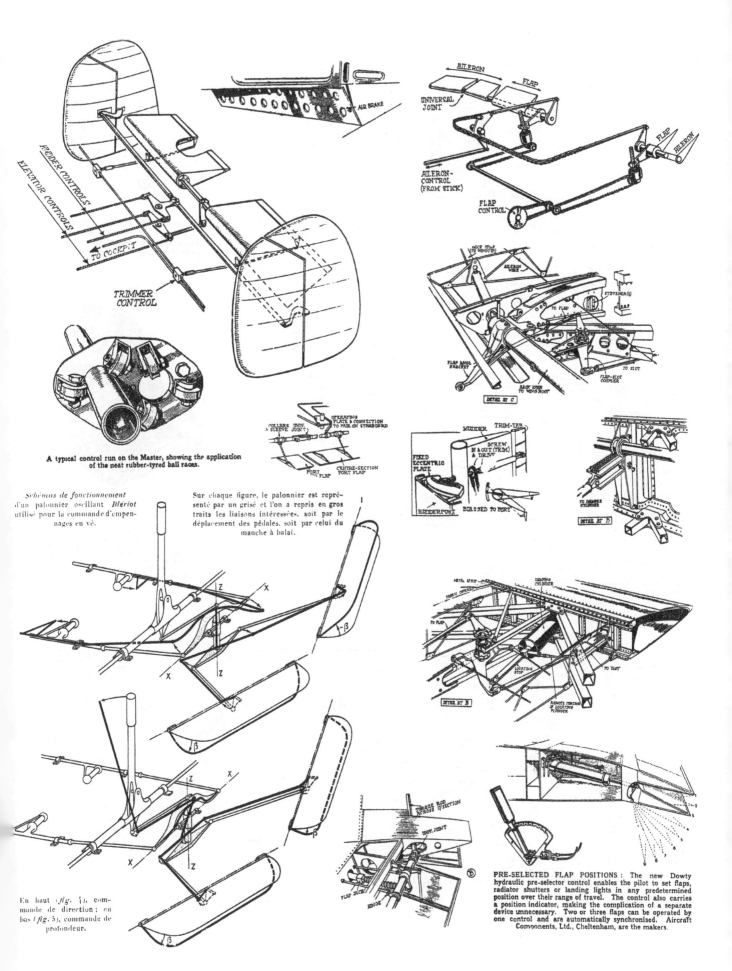

AILERON

FLAP

UNIVERSAL JOINT

FLAP

AILERON

AILERON CONTROL (FROM STICK)

FLAP CONTROL

RUDDER CONTROLS

ELEVATOR CONTROLS

TO COCKPIT

TRIMMER CONTROL

AIR BRAKE

A typical control run on the Master, showing the application of the neat rubber-tyred ball races.

OPERATING PLATE & CONNECTION TO PAIR ON STARBOARD

COLLARS UNIV. & SLEEVE JOINT

PORT FLAP

CENTRE-SECTION PORT FLAP

DETAIL AT C

RUDDER

TRIM-TAB

FIXED ECCENTRIC PLATE

SCREW IN & OUT (TRIM) & DRIVE

BIASSED TO PORT

RUDDERPOST

DETAIL AT D

Schémas de fonctionnement d'un palonnier oscillant Blériot utilisé pour la commande d'empennages en vé.

Sur chaque figure, le palonnier est représenté par un grisé et l'on a repris en gros traits les liaisons intéressées, soit par le déplacement des pédales, soit par celui du manche à balai.

DETAIL AT B

PRE-SELECTED FLAP POSITIONS : The new Dowty hydraulic pre-selector control enables the pilot to set flaps, radiator shutters or landing lights in any predetermined position over their range of travel. The control also carries a position indicator, making the complication of a separate device unnecessary. Two or three flaps can be operated by one control and are automatically synchronised. Aircraft Components, Ltd., Cheltenham, are the makers.

En haut (*fig.* 1), commande de direction ; en bas (*fig.* 5), commande de profondeur.

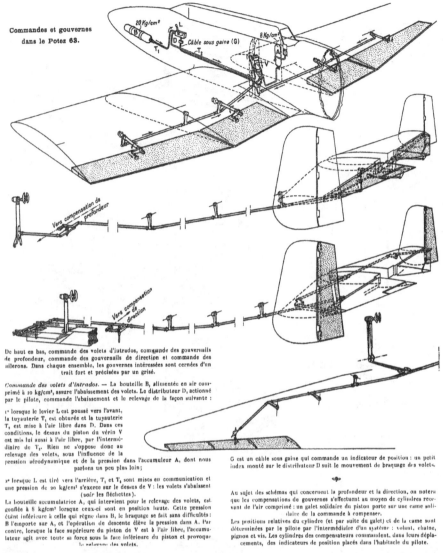

Commandes et gouvernes
dans le Potez 63.

20 Kg/cm² 8 Kg/cm²

Câble sous gaine (G)

Vers compensation de profondeur

Vers compensation de direction

De haut en bas, commande des volets d'intrados, commande des gouvernails de profondeur, commande des gouvernails de direction et commande des ailerons. Dans chaque ensemble, les gouvernes intéressées sont cernées d'un trait fort et précisées par un grisé.

Commande des volets d'intrados. — La bouteille B, alimentée en air comprimé à 20 kg/cm², assure l'abaissement des volets. Le distributeur D, actionné par le pilote, commande l'abaissement et le relevage de la façon suivante :

1° lorsque le levier L est poussé vers l'avant, la tuyauterie T₁ est obturée et la tuyauterie T₂ est mise à l'air libre dans D. Dans ces conditions, le dessus du piston du vérin V est mis lui aussi à l'air libre, par l'intermédiaire de T₂. Rien ne s'oppose donc au relevage des volets, sous l'influence de la pression aérodynamique et de la pression dans l'accumuleur A, dont nous parlons un peu plus loin;

2° lorsque L est tiré vers l'arrière, T₁ et T₂ sont mises en communication et une pression de 20 kg/cm² s'exerce sur le dessus de V : les volets s'abaissent (*voir les fléchettes*).

La bouteille accumulatrice A, qui intervient pour le relevage des volets, est gonflée à 8 kg/cm² lorsque ceux-ci sont en position haute. Cette pression étant inférieure à celle qui règne dans B, le braquage se fait sans difficultés : B l'emporte sur A, et l'opération de descente élève la pression dans A. Par contre, lorsque la face supérieure du piston de V est à l'air libre, l'accumulateur agit avec toute sa force sous la face inférieure du piston et provoque le relevage des volets.

G est un câble sous gaine qui commande un indicateur de position : un petit index monté sur le distributeur D suit le mouvement de braquage des volets.

❧

Au sujet des schémas qui concernent la profondeur et la direction, on notera que les compensations de gouvernes s'effectuent au moyen de cylindres recevant de l'air comprimé : un galet solidaire du piston porte sur une came solidaire de la commande à compenser.

Les positions relatives du cylindre (et par suite du galet) et de la came sont déterminées par le pilote par l'intermédiaire d'un système : volant, chaîne, pignon et vis. Les cylindres des compensateurs commandent, dans leurs déplacements, des indicateurs de position placés dans l'habitacle du pilote.

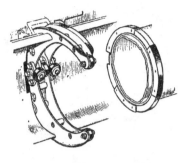

The elevator tube runs on rollers carried on "horseshoes" on the tailplane spar, instead of the more orthodox hinge arrangement.

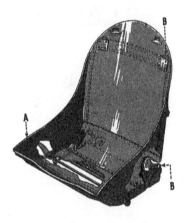

The pilot's seat designed and built by the Kellett Autogyro Corp., is of 24-ST Alclad construction spot welded. The seat can be adjusted vertically along the supports "B" and other adjustments by the handle "A." The angle of the back and bottom is 101 degrees. The seat has withstood a vertical downward load of 4000 lb. and one against the back of the seat of 1225 lb.

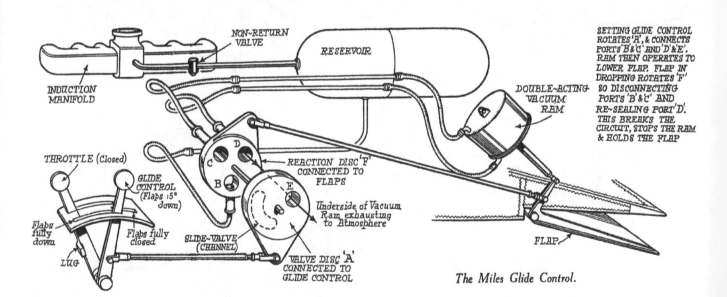

NON-RETURN VALVE

RESERVOIR

INDUCTION MANIFOLD

THROTTLE (Closed)

GLIDE CONTROL (Flaps 15° down)

Flaps fully down

Flaps fully closed

LUG

SLIDE-VALVE (CHANNEL)

REACTION DISC 'F' CONNECTED TO FLAPS

Underside of Vacuum Ram exhausting to Atmosphere

VALVE DISC 'A' CONNECTED TO GLIDE CONTROL

DOUBLE-ACTING VACUUM RAM

FLAP

SETTING GLIDE CONTROL ROTATES 'A', & CONNECTS PORTS 'B'&'C' AND 'D'&'E'. RAM THEN OPERATES TO LOWER FLAP. FLAP IN DROPPING ROTATES 'F' SO DISCONNECTING PORTS 'B'&'C' AND RE-SEALING PORT 'D'. THIS BREAKS THE CIRCUIT, STOPS THE RAM & HOLDS THE FLAP

The Miles Glide Control.

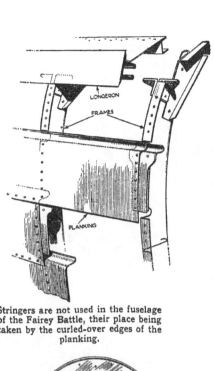

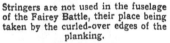

Stringers are not used in the fuselage of the Fairey Battle, their place being taken by the curled-over edges of the planking.

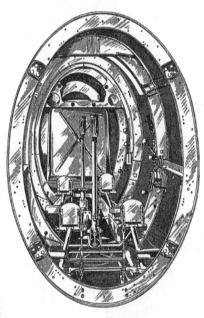

'Split' construction is a production feature. This sketch shows the main units into which the structure is divided. The middle and tail portions are split vertically into port and starboard halves (see sketches below).

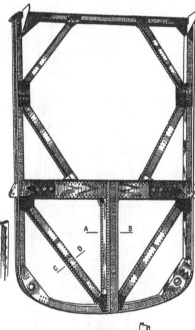

Assemblage des trois parties du fuselage.
Les deux croquis placés à gauche et à droite de la légende montrent la façon dont les couples qui terminent les diverses tranches du fuselage sont assemblés par boulons.

Éléments de structure des F. 223 et F. 2231.

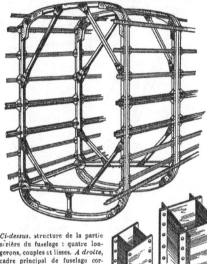

Ci-dessus, structure de la partie arrière du fuselage : quatre longerons, couples et lisses. *A droite*, cadre principal de fuselage correspondant à l'attache de l'aile ; les coupes AB et CD sont reprises par deux croquis de détail.

Croquis originaux de J. GAUDEFOY.

Coupes CD et AB.

The Ryan STM-2 trainer has caused a great deal of interest in its construction as well as its performance. A cross section (above) of the fuselage reveals the semi-monocoque, stressed skin type of construction used. Elliptical in section one steel and seven aluminum alloy bulkheads are used. Six pieces of 24ST sections form the covering. Complete dual controls with dual toe brakes are installed. A torque tube mounted on aluminum alloy bearings connects the two sticks for aileron control and a push-pull tube inside the torque tube provides the elevator connection.

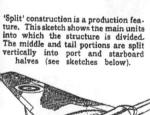

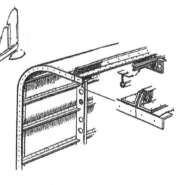

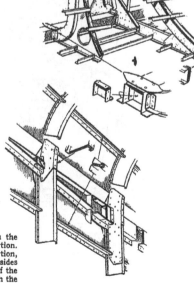

Fuselage details of the Hampden. On the left, the construction of the split tail portion. In the centre, details of the middle portion, showing how the decking locks the sides together. On the right, the structure of the wing-fuselage fairing, built integral with the fuselage.

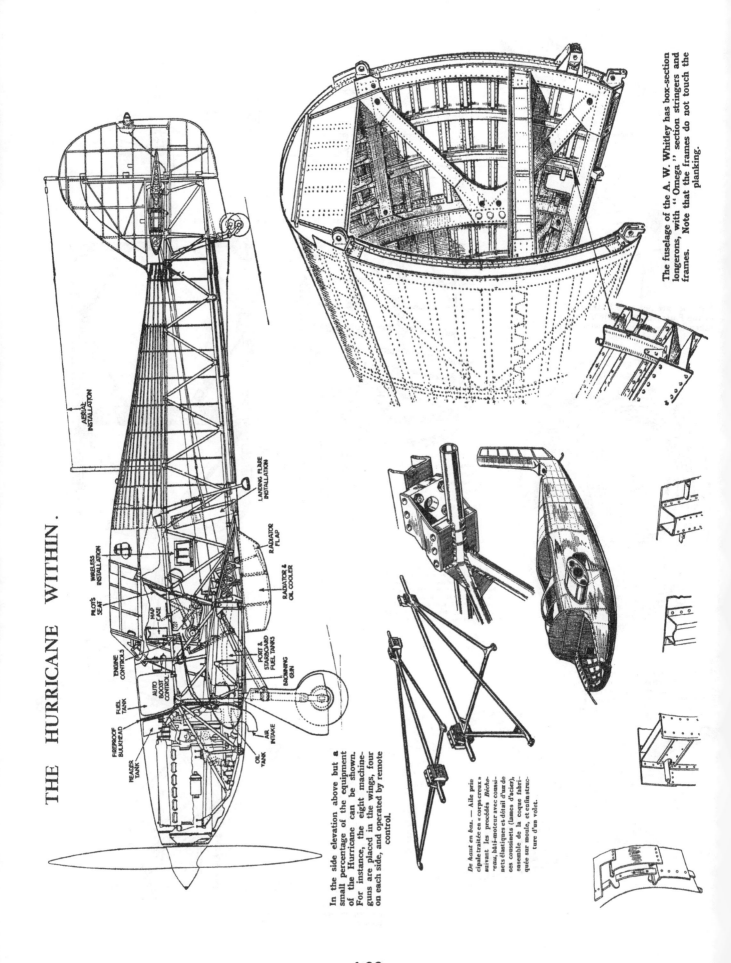

THE HURRICANE WITHIN.

AERIAL INSTALLATION

LANDING FLARE INSTALLATION

RADIATOR FLAP

WIRELESS INSTALLATION

RADIATOR & OIL COOLER

PILOT'S SEAT

MAP CASE

ENGINE CONTROLS

PORT & STARBOARD FUEL TANKS

BROWNING GUN

AUTO BOOST CONTROL

FUEL TANK

FIREPROOF BULKHEAD

HEADER TANK

OIL TANK

AIR INTAKE

In the side elevation above but a small percentage of the equipment of the Hurricane can be shown. For instance, the eight machine-guns are placed in the wings, four on each side, and operated by remote control.

De haut en bas. — Aile principale traitée en « corps creux » suivant les procédés *Béchereau*, bâti-moteur avec coussinets élastiques et détail d'un de ces coussinets (lames d'acier), ensemble de la coque fabriquée sur moule, et enfin structure d'un volet.

The fuselage of the A. W. Whitley has box-section longerons, with " Omega " section stringers and frames. Note that the frames do not touch the planking.

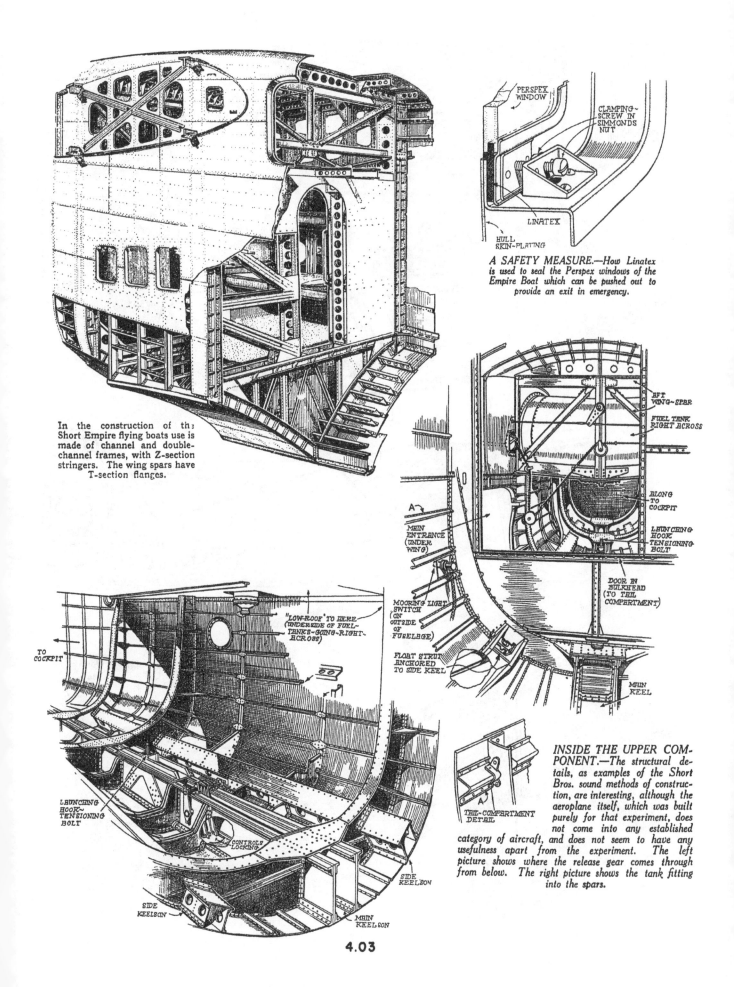

In the construction of the Short Empire flying boats use is made of channel and double-channel frames, with Z-section stringers. The wing spars have T-section flanges.

A SAFETY MEASURE.—How Linatex is used to seal the Perspex windows of the Empire Boat which can be pushed out to provide an exit in emergency.

PERSPEX WINDOW
CLAMPING-SCREW IN SIMMONDS NUT
LINATEX
HULL SKIN-PLATING

AFT WING-SPAR
FUEL TANK RIGHT ACROSS
BLONG TO COCKPIT
LAUNCHING HOOK TENSIONING BOLT
DOOR IN BULKHEAD (TO TAIL COMPARTMENT)
MAIN KEEL
MAIN ENTRANCE (UNDER WING)
MOORING LIGHT SWITCH (ON OUTSIDE OF FUSELAGE)
FLOAT STRUT ANCHORED TO SIDE KEEL
A

TO COCKPIT
"LOW-ROOF" TO HERE (UNDERSIDE OF FUEL-TANKS-GOING-RIGHT-ACROSS)
LAUNCHING HOOK-TENSIONING BOLT
CONTROLS LOCKING
SIDE KEELSON
SIDE KEELSON
MAIN KEELSON

TAIL-COMPARTMENT DETAIL

INSIDE THE UPPER COMPONENT.—The structural details, as examples of the Short Bros. sound methods of construction, are interesting, although the aeroplane itself, which was built purely for that experiment, does not come into any established category of aircraft, and does not seem to have any usefulness apart from the experiment. The left picture shows where the release gear comes through from below. The right picture shows the tank fitting into the spars.

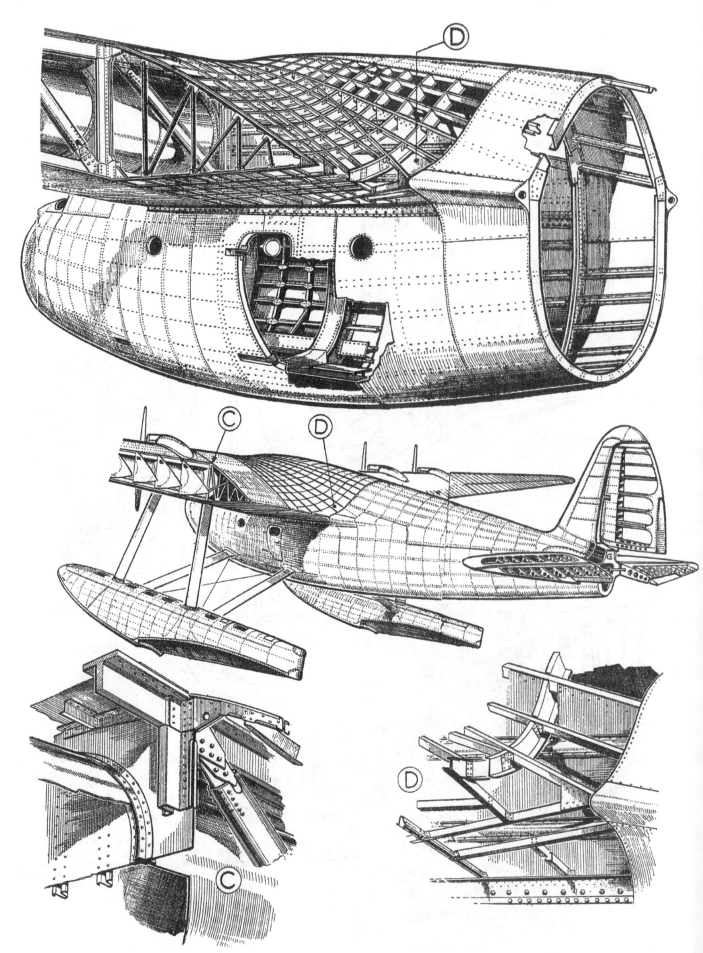

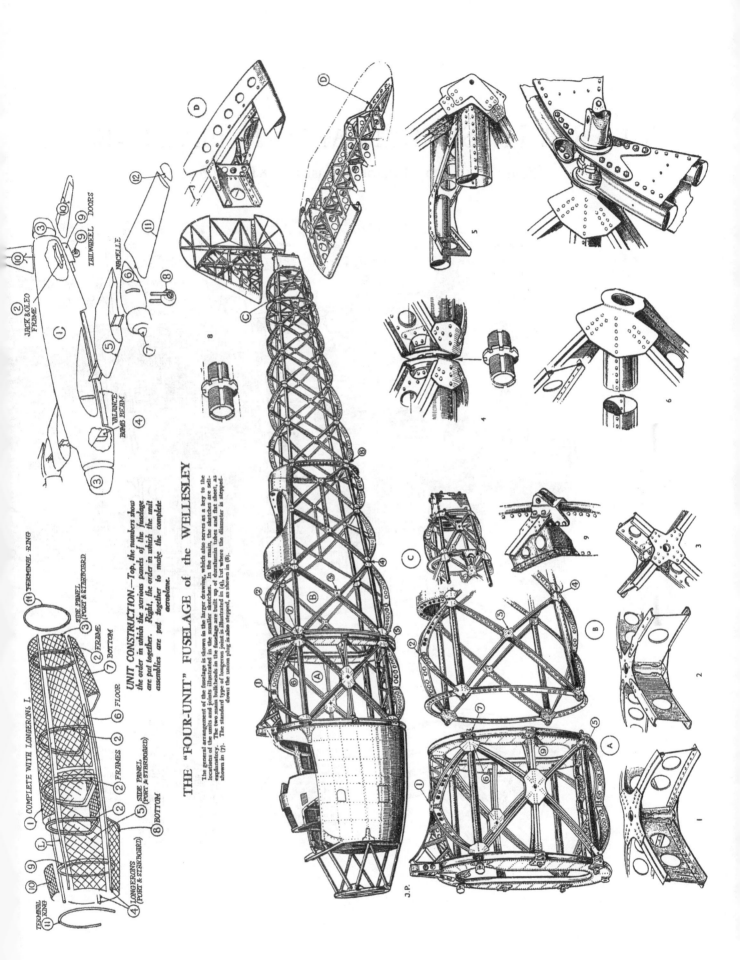

THE "FOUR-UNIT" FUSELAGE of the WELLESLEY

The general arrangement of the fuselage is shown in the larger drawing, which also serves as a key to the location of the units and joints illustrated in the smaller sketches. In the main, the sketches are self-explanatory. The two main bulkheads in the fuselage are built up of duralumin tubes and flat sheet, as shown in (7). The standard type of longeron joint is illustrated in (4), but where the diameter is stepped-down the union plug is also stepped, as shown in (8).

UNIT CONSTRUCTION.—Top, the numbers show the order in which the various panels of the fuselage are put together. Right, the order in which the unit assemblies are put together to make the complete aeroplane.

① COMPLETE WITH LONGERONS L
② FRAMES
⑤ SIDE PANEL (PORT & STARBOARD)
⑧ BOTTOM
③ SIDE PANEL (PORT & STARBOARD)
② FRAME
⑦ BOTTOM
⑥ FLOOR
④ LONGERONS (PORT & STARBOARD)
⑪ TERMINAL RING
⑩ TERMINAL RING

JACK & OLEO FRAME
TAIL-WHEEL DOORS
NACELLE
VALANCE
BOMB BEAM

J.P.

THE R.A.F. SUNDERLAND I FLYING-BOAT

(Four 1,010 h.p. Bristol Pegasus XXII Motors)

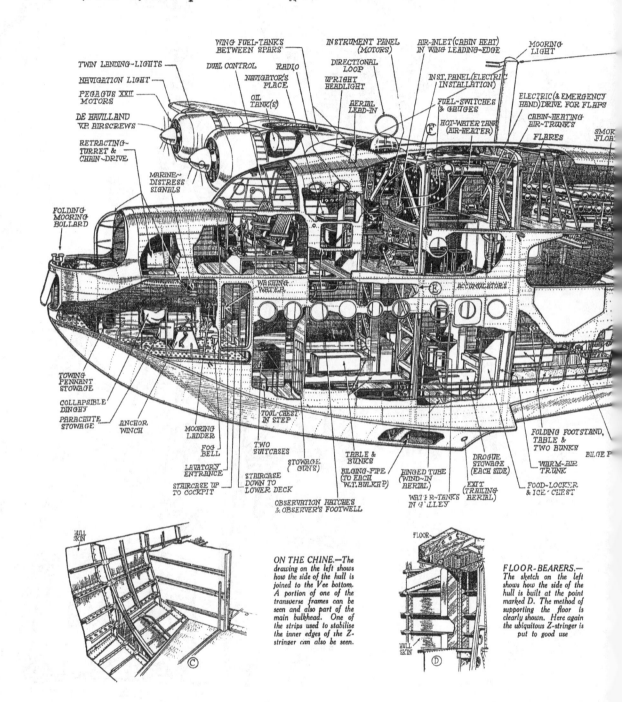

ON THE CHINE.—The drawing on the left shows how the side of the hull is joined to the Vee bottom. A portion of one of the transverse frames can be seen and also part of the main bulkhead. One of the strips used to stabilise the inner edges of the Z-stringer can also be seen.

FLOOR-BEARERS.— The sketch on the left shows how the side of the hull is built at the point marked D. The method of supporting the floor is clearly shown. Here again the ubiquitous Z-stringer is put to good use

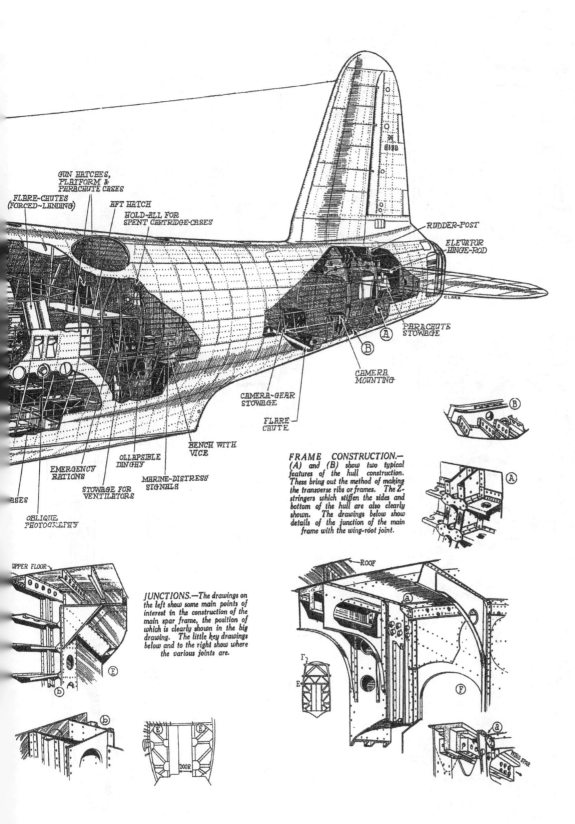

GUN HATCHES,
PLATFORM &
PARACHUTE CASES

FLARE-CHUTES
(FORCED-LANDING)

AFT HATCH

HOLD-ALL FOR
SPENT CARTRIDGE-CASES

RUDDER-POST

ELEVATOR
HINGE-ROD

CLARK

PARACHUTE
STOWAGE

CAMERA
MOUNTING

CAMERA-GEAR
STOWAGE

FLARE
CHUTE

BENCH WITH
VICE

COLLAPSIBLE
DINGHY

MARINE-DISTRESS
SIGNALS

EMERGENCY
RATIONS

STOWAGE FOR
VENTILATORS

CASES

OBLIQUE
PHOTOGRAPHY

UPPER FLOOR

ROOF

FRAME CONSTRUCTION.— (A) and (B) show two typical features of the hull construction. These bring out the method of making the transverse ribs or frames. The Z-stringers which stiffen the sides and bottom of the hull are also clearly shown. The drawings below show details of the junction of the main frame with the wing-root joint.

JUNCTIONS.—The drawings on the left show some main points of interest in the construction of the main spar frame, the position of which is clearly shown in the big drawing. The little key drawings below and to the right show where the various joints are.

DOOR

WING SPAR

4.07

4.08

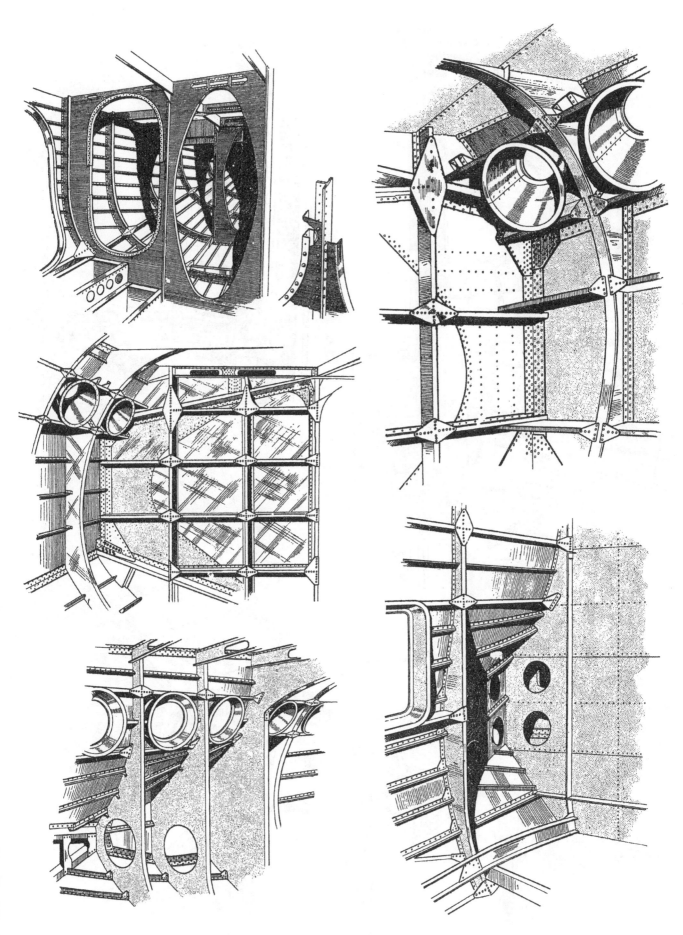

4.09

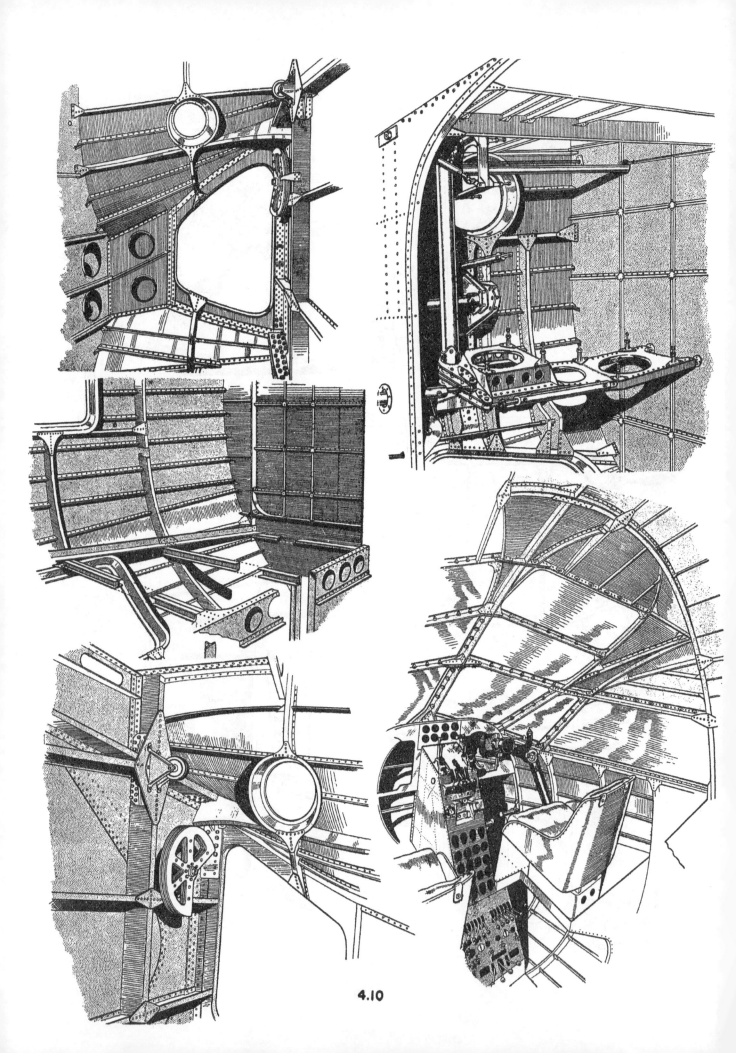

4.10

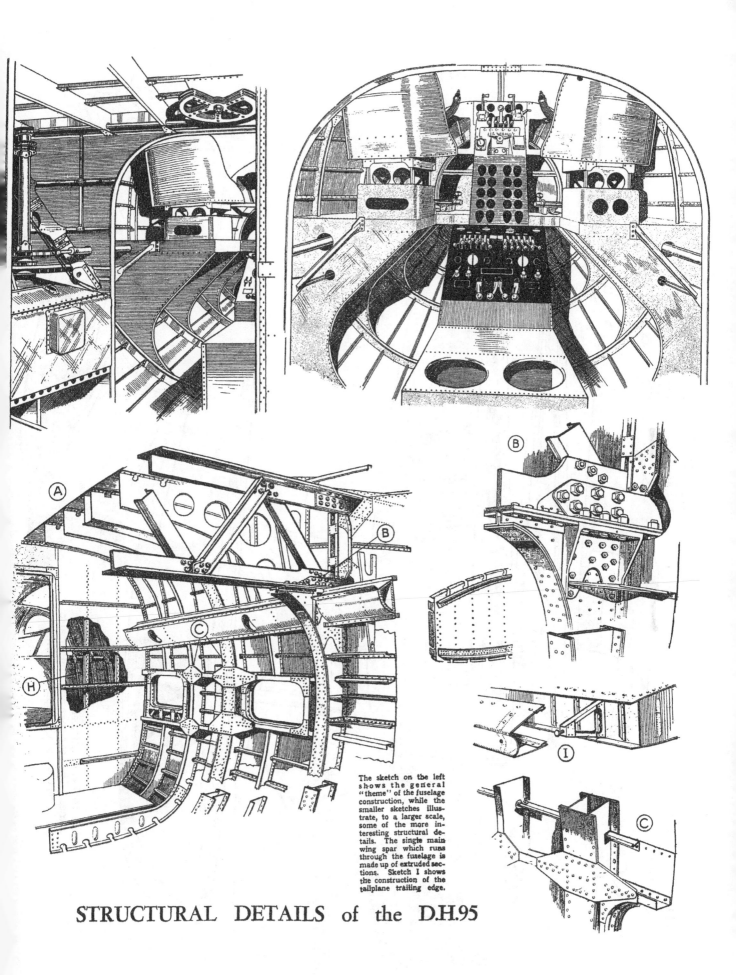

The sketch on the left shows the general "theme" of the fuselage construction, while the smaller sketches illustrate, to a larger scale, some of the more interesting structural details. The single main wing spar which runs through the fuselage is made up of extruded sections. Sketch I shows the construction of the tailplane trailing edge.

STRUCTURAL DETAILS of the D.H.95

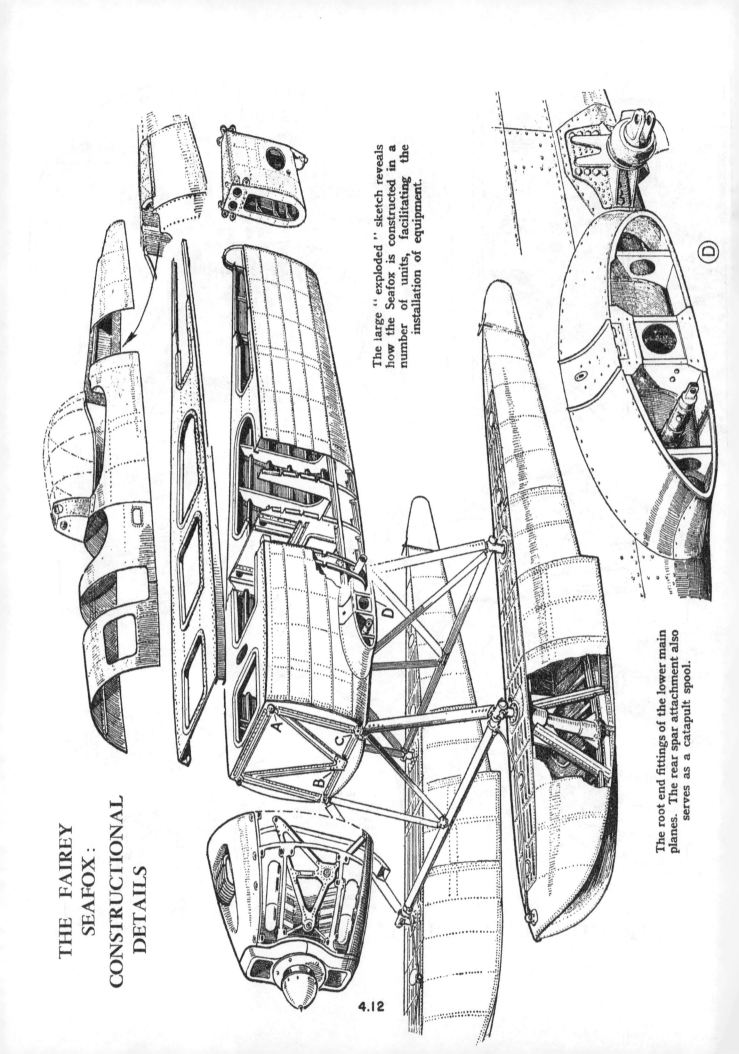

THE FAIREY
SEAFOX:
CONSTRUCTIONAL
DETAILS

The large " exploded " sketch reveals how the Seafox is constructed in a number of units, facilitating the installation of equipment.

The root end fittings of the lower main planes. The rear spar attachment also serves as a catapult spool.

4.12

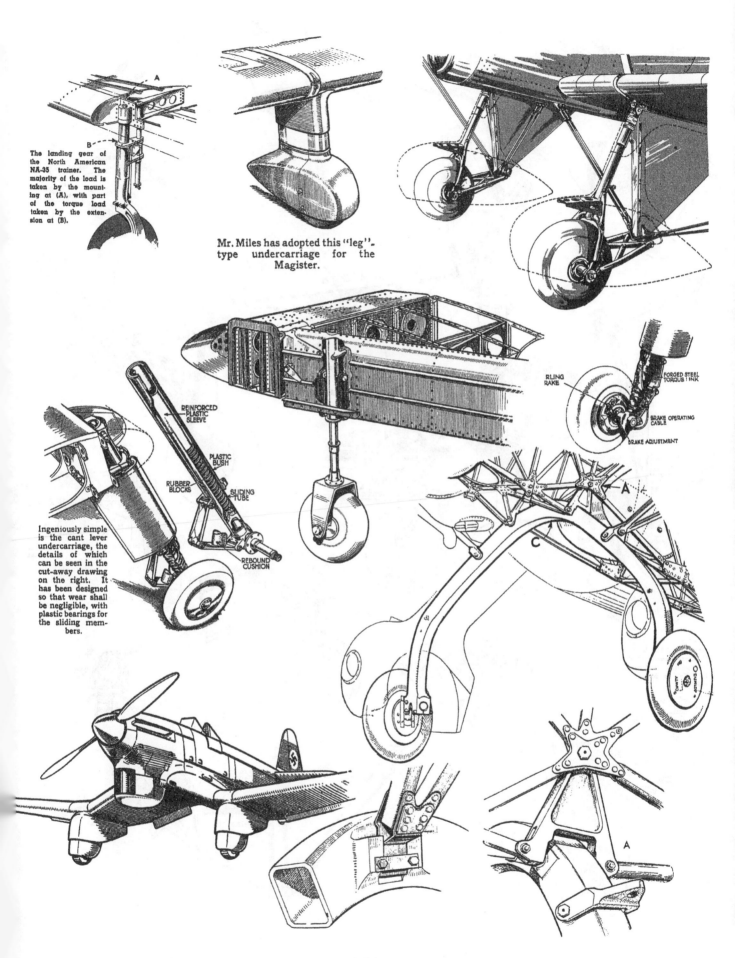

The landing gear of the North American NA-35 trainer. The majority of the load is taken by the mounting at (A), with part of the torque load taken by the extension at (B).

Mr. Miles has adopted this "leg"-type undercarriage for the Magister.

REINFORCED PLASTIC SLEEVE

PLASTIC BUSH

RUBBER BLOCKS

SLIDING TUBE

Ingeniously simple is the cant lever undercarriage, the details of which can be seen in the cut-away drawing on the right. It has been designed so that wear shall be negligible, with plastic bearings for the sliding members.

REBOUND CUSHION

RLING RAKE

FORGED STEEL TORQUE LINK

BRAKE OPERATING CABLE

BRAKE ADJUSTMENT

A

C

A

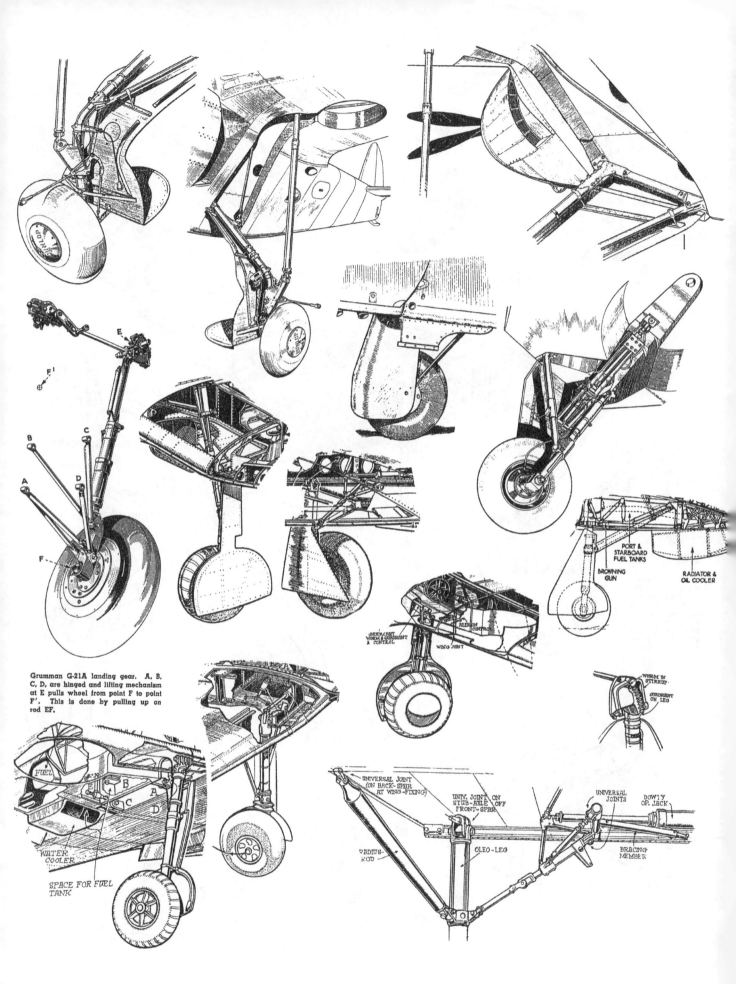

Grumman G-21A landing gear. A, B, C, D, are hinged and lifting mechanism at E pulls wheel from point F to point F'. This is done by pulling up on rod EF.

E

F'

B

C

A

D

F

PORT & STARBOARD FUEL TANKS

BROWNING GUN

RADIATOR & OIL COOLER

UNDERCART WORM & QUADRANT A CONTROL

WING JOINT

AILERON CONTROL

WORM IN STIRRUP

QUADRANT ON LEG

FUEL

B

C

A

D

WATER COOLER

SPACE FOR FUEL TANK

UNIVERSAL JOINT (ON BACK-SPAR AT WING-FIXING)

UNIV. JOINT ON STUB-AXLE OFF FRONT-SPAR

UNIVERSAL JOINTS

DOWTY OP. JACK

RADIUS ROD

OLEO-LEG

BRACING MEMBER

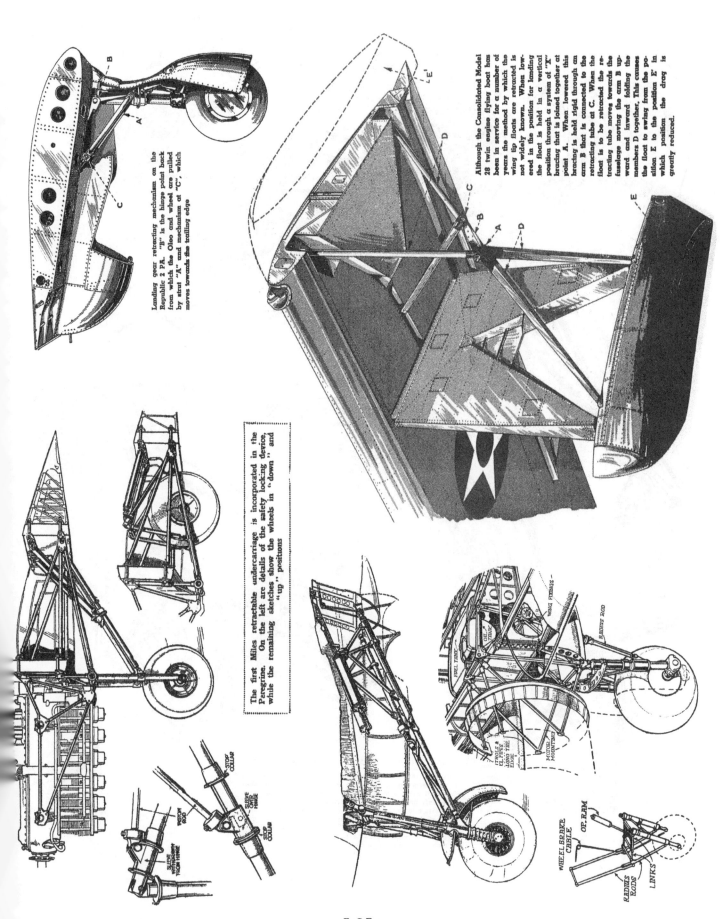

Landing gear retracting mechanism on the Republic 2 PA. "B" is the hinge point back from which the Oleo and wheel are pulled by strut "A" and mechanism at "C", which moves towards the trailing edge

Although the Consolidated Model 28 twin engine flying boat has been in service for a number of years the method by which the wing tip floats are retracted is not widely known. When lowered in the position for landing the float is held in a vertical position through a system of "T" bracing that is joined together at point A. When lowered this bracing is held rigid through an arm B that is connected to the retracting tube at C. When the float is to be retracted the retracting tube moves towards the fuselage moving the arm B upward and inward folding the members D together. This causes the float to swing from the position E to the position E' in which position the drag is greatly reduced.

The first Miles retractable undercarriage is incorporated in the Peregrine. On the left are details of the safety locking device, while the remaining sketches show the wheels in "down" and "up" positions

STOP COLLAR

SLEEVE WITH FORE HINGE

WORM ROD

STOP COLLAR

SLIDE WITHDRAWN FROM HINGE

OIL TANK

FUEL TANK

WING FIXING

RADIUS ROD

STRUTS & EL PIPES ALONG THE EDGE

MOTOR MOUNTING

WHEEL BRAKE CABLE

OP. RAM

RADIUS RODS

LINKS

5.03

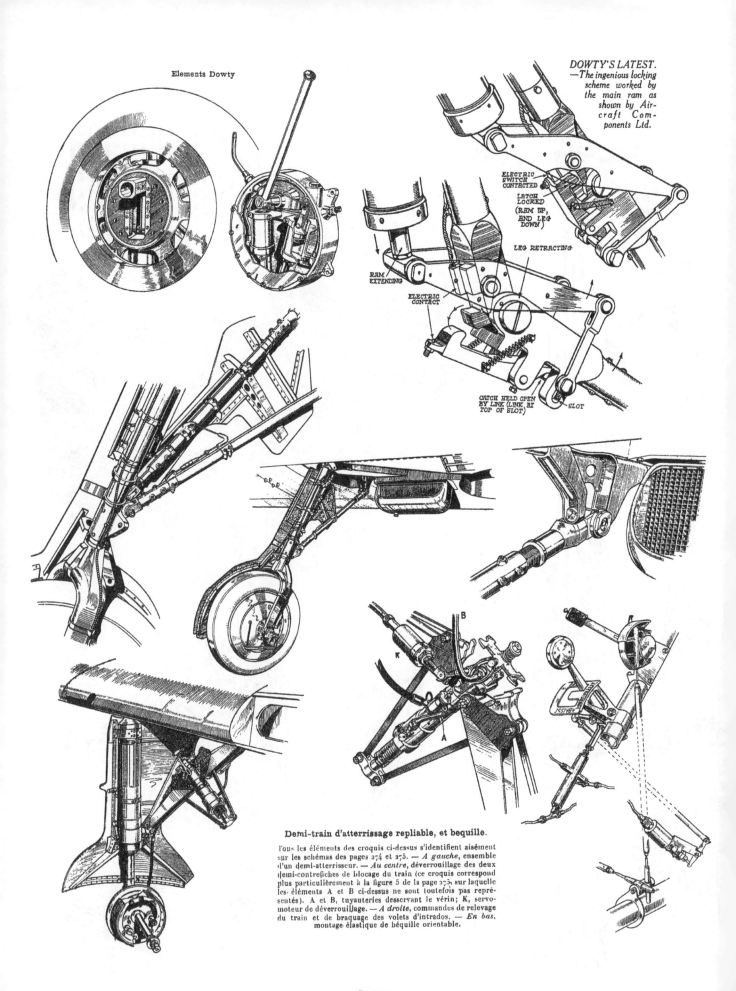

Elements Dowty

DOWTY'S LATEST.
—The ingenious locking scheme worked by the main ram as shown by Aircraft Components Ltd.

ELECTRIC SWITCH CONTACTED

LATCH LOCKED (RAM UP, AND LEG DOWN)

LEG RETRACTING

RAM EXTENDING

ELECTRIC CONTACT

CATCH HELD OPEN BY LINK (LINK AT TOP OF SLOT)

SLOT

B

K

A

Demi-train d'atterrissage repliable, et bequille.

Tous les éléments des croquis ci-dessus s'identifient aisément sur les schémas des pages 274 et 275. — *A gauche*, ensemble d'un demi-atterrisseur. — *Au centre*, déverrouillage des deux demi-contrefiches de blocage du train (ce croquis correspond plus particulièrement à la figure 5 de la page 275, sur laquelle les éléments A et B ci-dessus ne sont toutefois pas représentés). A et B, tuyauteries desservant le vérin; K, servomoteur de déverrouillage. — *A droite*, commandes de relevage du train et de braquage des volets d'intrados. — *En bas*, montage élastique de béquille orientable.

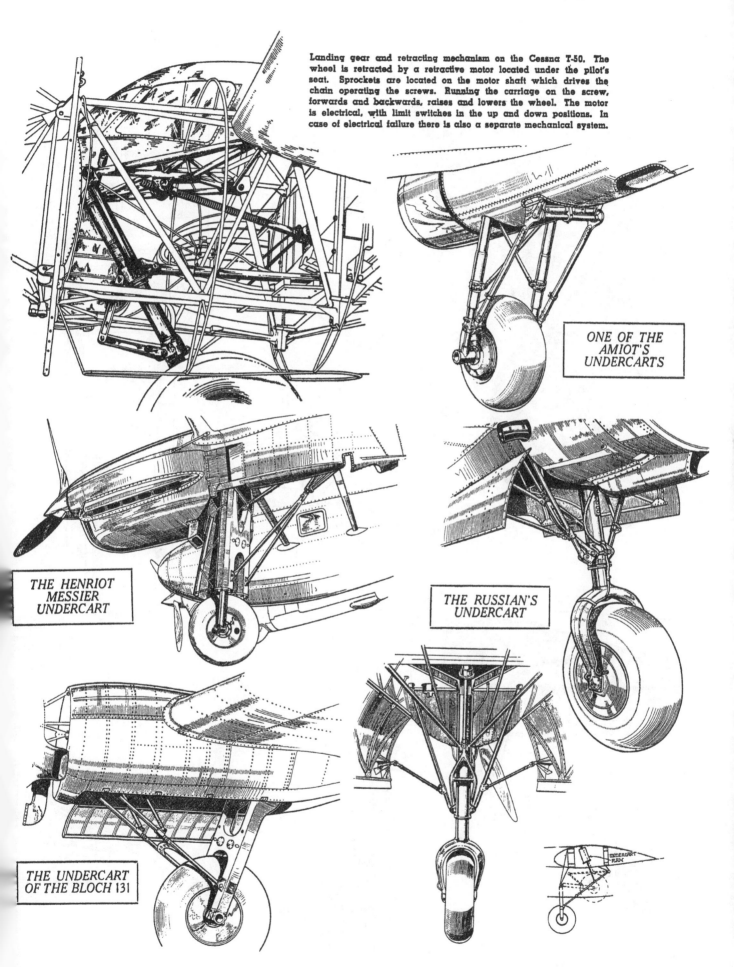

Landing gear and retracting mechanism on the Cessna T-50. The wheel is retracted by a retractive motor located under the pilot's seat. Sprockets are located on the motor shaft which drives the chain operating the screws. Running the carriage on the screw, forwards and backwards, raises and lowers the wheel. The motor is electrical, with limit switches in the up and down positions. In case of electrical failure there is also a separate mechanical system.

ONE OF THE AMIOT'S UNDERCARTS

THE HENRIOT MESSIER UNDERCART

THE RUSSIAN'S UNDERCART

THE UNDERCART OF THE BLOCH 131

UNDERCART RAM

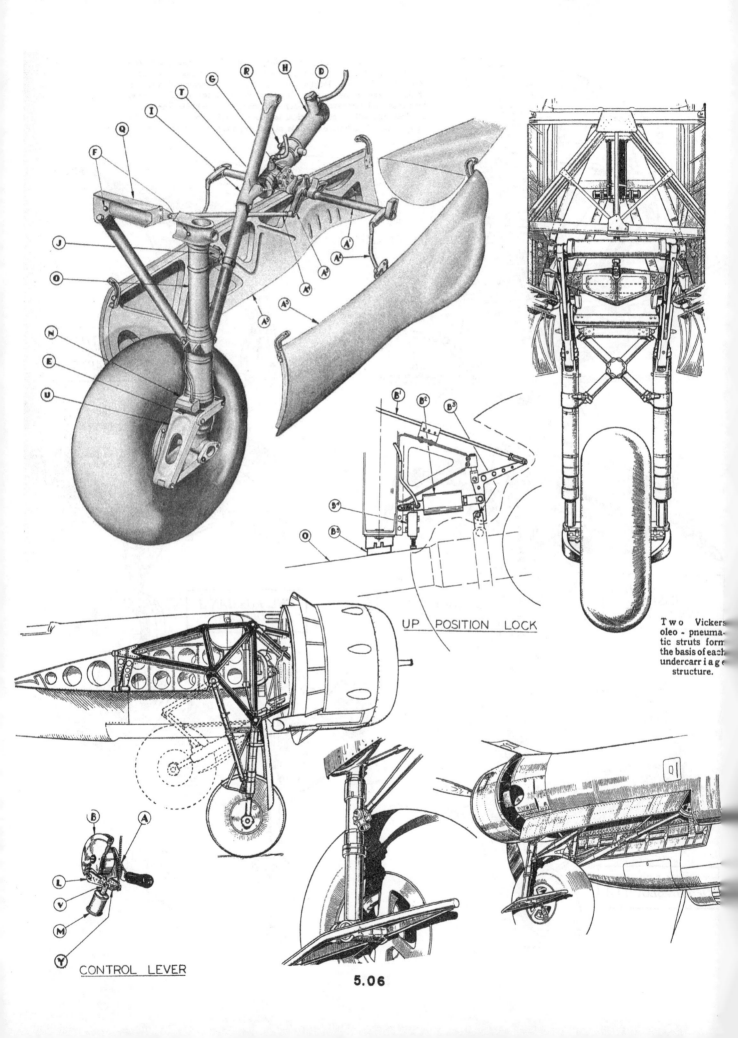

UP POSITION LOCK

Two Vickers
oleo - pneuma-
tic struts form
the basis of each
undercarriage
structure.

CONTROL LEVER

5.06

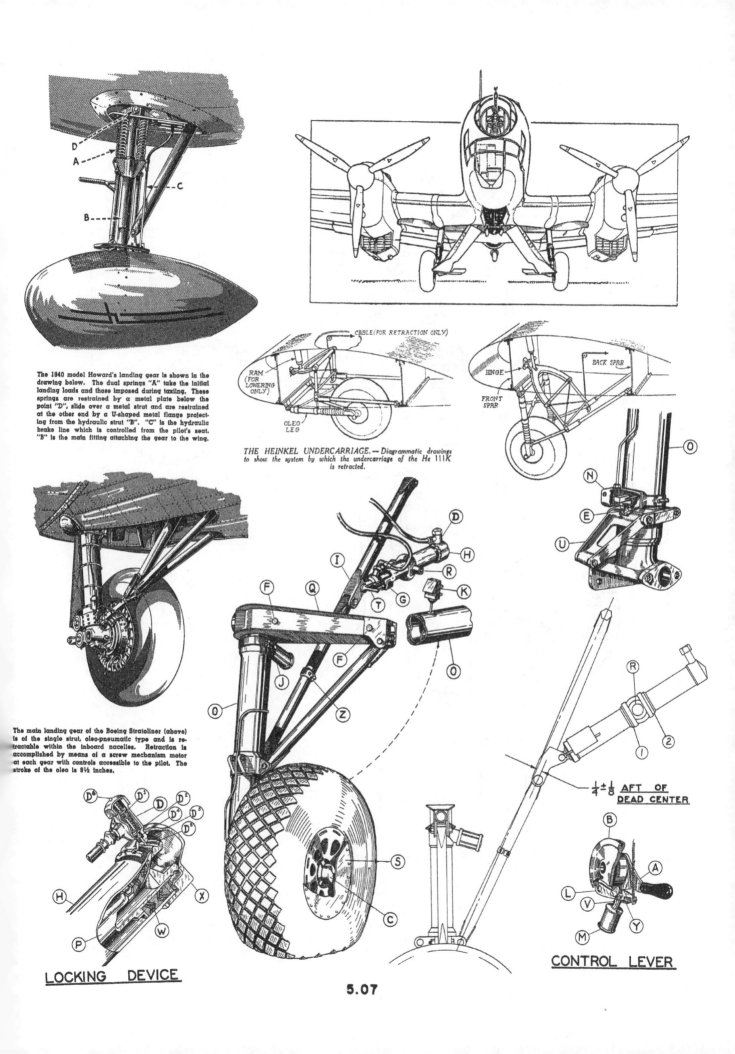

The 1940 model Howard's landing gear is shown in the drawing below. The dual springs "A" take the initial landing loads and those imposed during taxiing. These springs are restrained by a metal plate below the point "D", slide over a metal strut and are restrained at the other end by a U-shaped metal flange projecting from the hydraulic strut "B". "C" is the hydraulic brake line which is controlled from the pilot's seat. "B" is the main fitting attaching the gear to the wing.

THE HEINKEL UNDERCARRIAGE. — Diagrammatic drawings to show the system by which the undercarriage of the He 111K is retracted.

CABLE (FOR RETRACTION ONLY)

RAM (FOR LOWERING ONLY)

OLEO LEG

BACK SPAR

HINGE

FRONT SPAR

The main landing gear of the Boeing Stratoliner (above) is of the single strut, oleo-pneumatic type and is retractable within the inboard nacelles. Retraction is accomplished by means of a screw mechanism motor at each gear with controls accessible to the pilot. The stroke of the oleo is 9½ inches.

$\frac{1}{4} \pm \frac{1}{8}$ AFT OF DEAD CENTER

LOCKING DEVICE

CONTROL LEVER

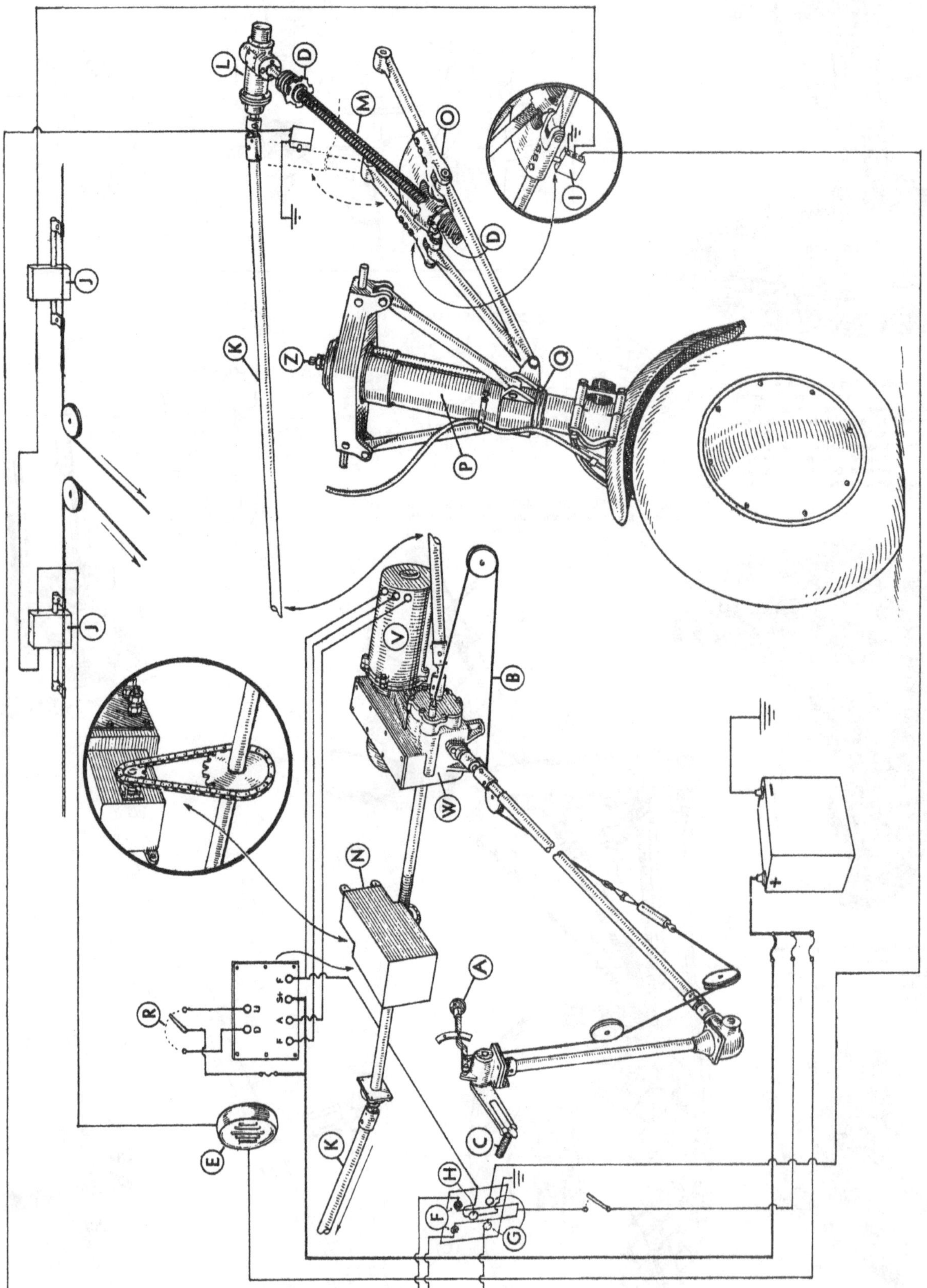

SCHEMATIC ILLUSTRATIONS ONLY.
PROPORTIONS ARE RELATIVE — NOT EXACT

5.08

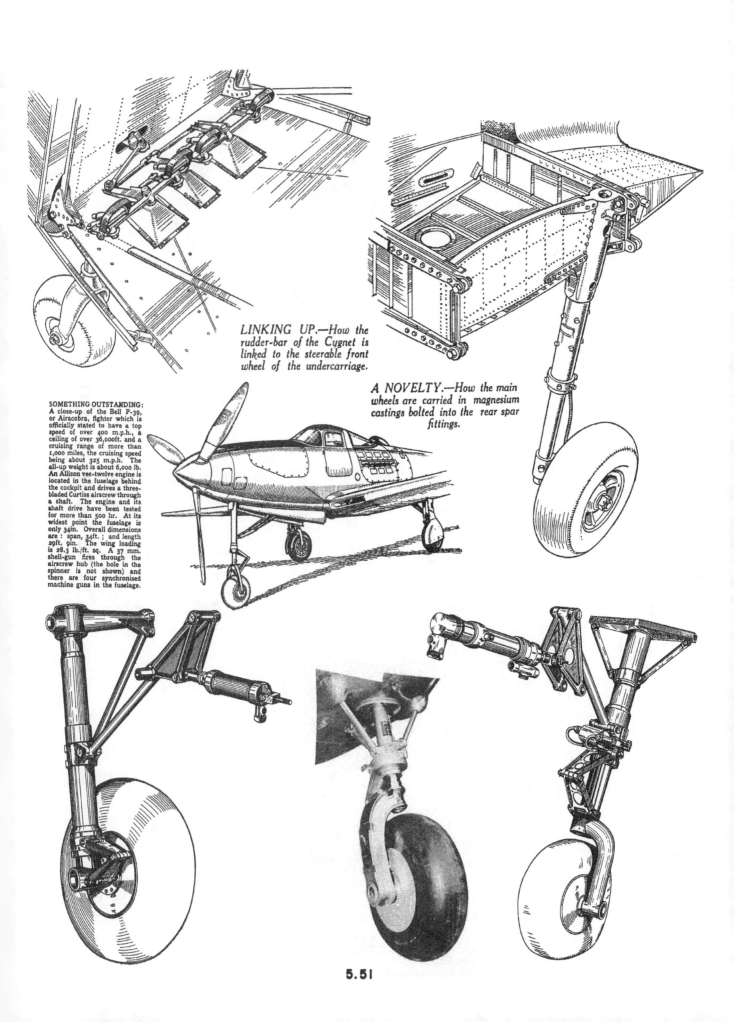

LINKING UP.—How the rudder-bar of the Cygnet is linked to the steerable front wheel of the undercarriage.

A NOVELTY.—How the main wheels are carried in magnesium castings bolted into the rear spar fittings.

SOMETHING OUTSTANDING: A close-up of the Bell P-39, or Airacobra, fighter which is officially stated to have a top speed of over 400 m.p.h., a ceiling of over 36,000ft. and a cruising range of more than 1,000 miles, the cruising speed being about 325 m.p.h. The all-up weight is about 6,000 lb. An Allison vee-twelve engine is located in the fuselage behind the cockpit and drives a three-bladed Curtiss airscrew through a shaft. The engine and its shaft drive have been tested for more than 500 hr. At its widest point the fuselage is only 34in. Overall dimensions are : span, 34ft. ; and length 29ft. 9in. The wing loading is 28.3 lb./ft. sq. A 37 mm. shell-gun fires through the airscrew hub (the hole in the spinner is not shown) and there are four synchronised machine guns in the fuselage.

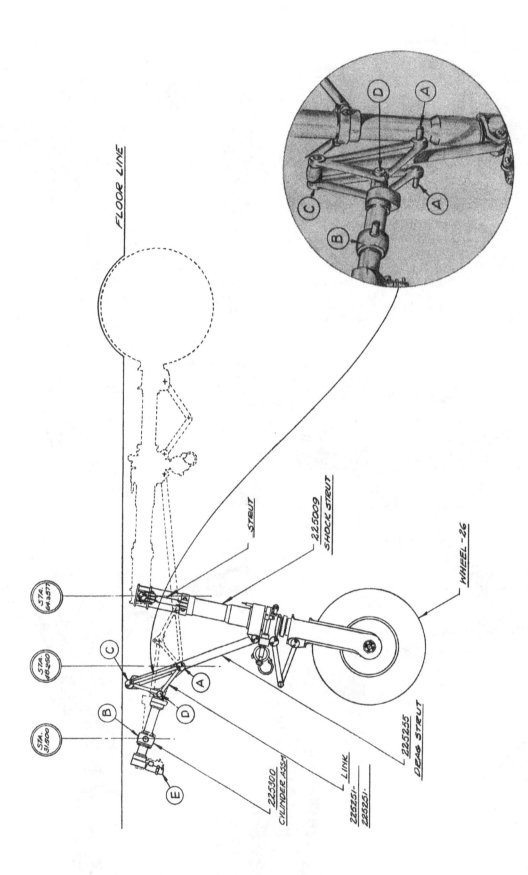

NOSE LANDING GEAR

5.52

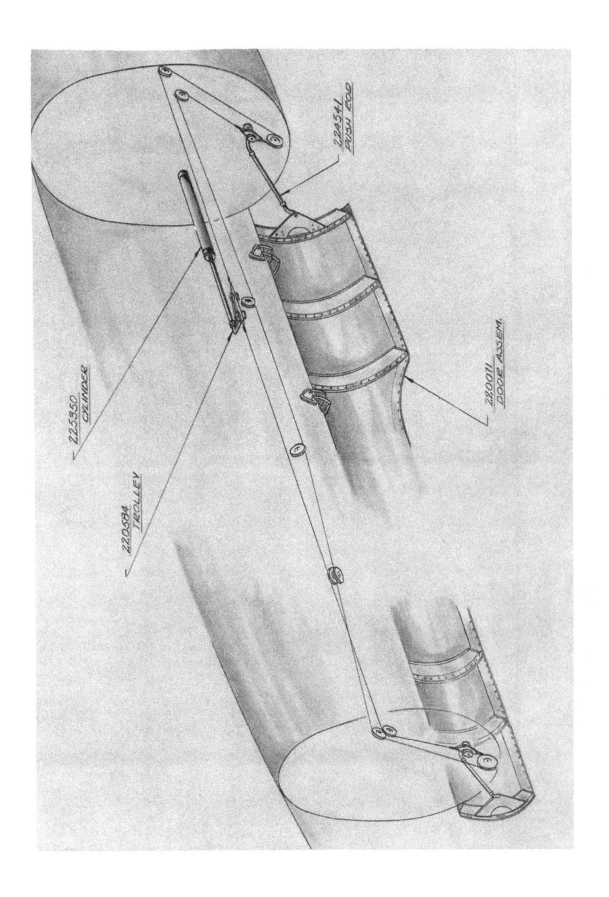

225350
CYLINDER

224541
PUSH ROD

22001L
DOOR ASSEM.

220584
TROLLEY

NOSE LANDING GEAR DOOR

5.53

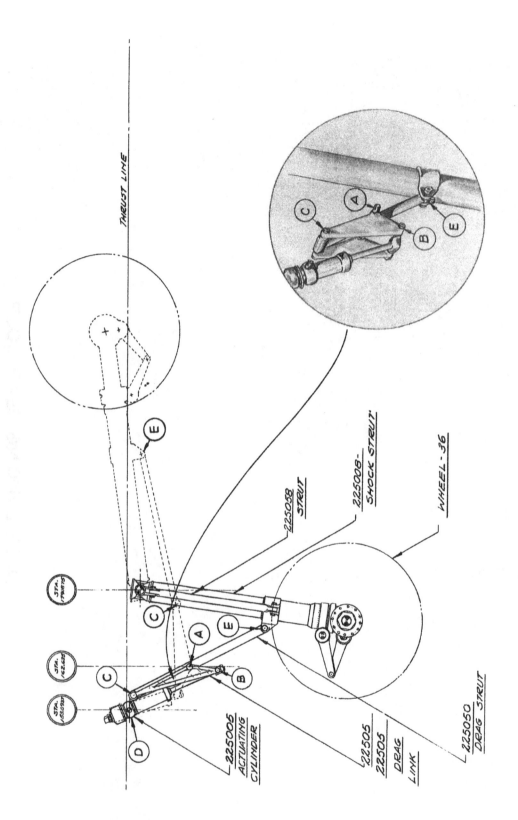

THRUST LINE

225058
STRUT

225008-
SHOCK STRUT

WHEEL - 36

225006
ACTUATING
CYLINDER

22505
22505
DRAG
LINK

225050
DRAG STRUT

STA. 177.875

STA. 142.625

STA. 102.531

MAIN LANDING GEAR

5.54

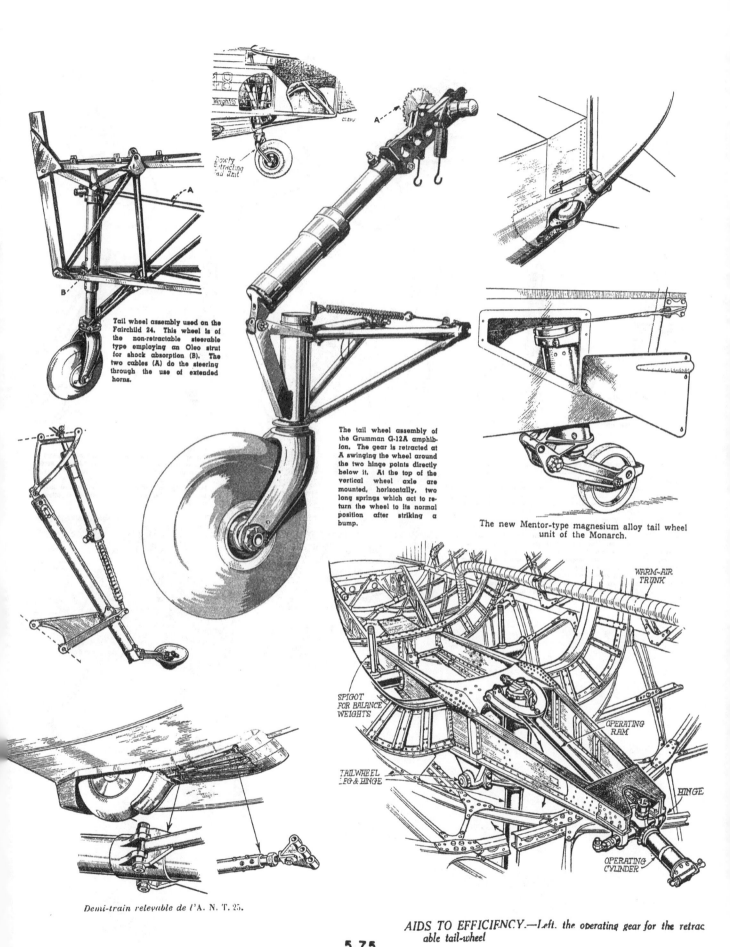

Tail wheel assembly used on the Fairchild 24. This wheel is of the non-retractable steerable type employing an Oleo strut for shock absorption (B). The two cables (A) do the steering through the use of extended horns.

Dowty Retracting Tail Unit

Weights

CLIP

A

The tail wheel assembly of the Grumman G-12A amphibion. The gear is retracted at A swinging the wheel around the two hinge points directly below it. At the top of the vertical wheel axle are mounted, horizontally, two long springs which act to return the wheel to its normal position after striking a bump.

The new Mentor-type magnesium alloy tail wheel unit of the Monarch.

WARM-AIR TRUNK

SPIGOT FOR BALANCE WEIGHTS

OPERATING RAM

TAILWHEEL LEG & HINGE

HINGE

OPERATING CYLINDER

Demi-train relevable de l'A. N. T. 25.

AIDS TO EFFICIENCY.—Left. the operating gear for the retractable tail-wheel

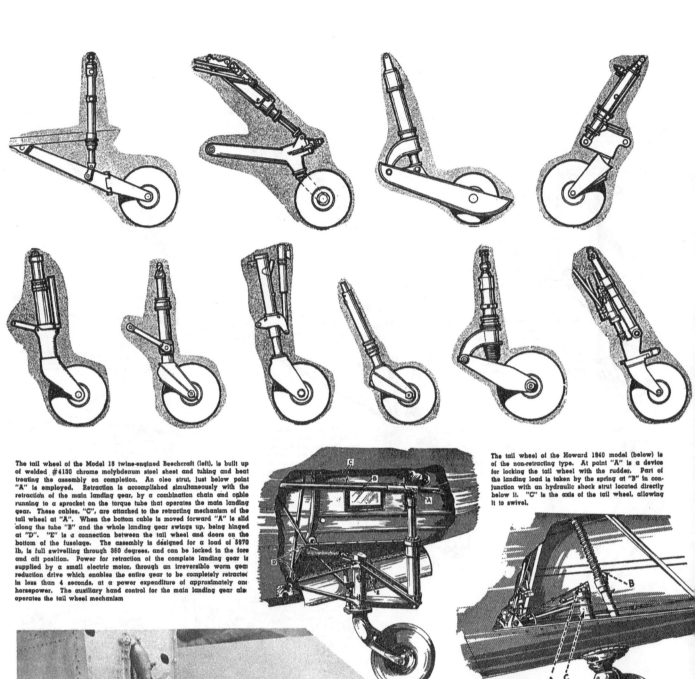

The tail wheel of the Model 18 twine-engined Beechcraft (left), is built up of welded #4130 chrome molybdenum steel sheet and tubing and heat treating the assembly on completion. An oleo strut, just below point "A" is employed. Retraction is accomplished simultaneously with the retraction of the main landing gear, by a combination chain and cable running to a sprocket on the torque tube that operates the main landing gear. These cables, "C", are attached to the retracting mechanism of the tail wheel at "A". When the bottom cable is moved forward "A" is slid along the tube "B" and the whole landing gear swings up, being hinged at "D". "E" is a connection between the tail wheel and doors on the bottom of the fuselage. The assembly is designed for a load of 5970 lb, is full swivelling through 360 degrees, and can be locked in the fore and aft position. Power for retraction of the complete landing gear is supplied by a small electric motor, through an irreversible worm gear reduction drive which enables the entire gear to be completely retracted in less than 4 seconds, at a power expenditure of approximately one horsepower. The auxiliary hand control for the main landing gear also operates the tail wheel mechanism

The tail wheel of the Howard 1840 model (below) is of the non-retracting type. At point "A" is a device for locking the tail wheel with the rudder. Part of the landing load is taken by the spring at "B" in conjunction with an hydraulic shock strut located directly below it. "C" is the axis of the tail wheel, allowing it to swivel.

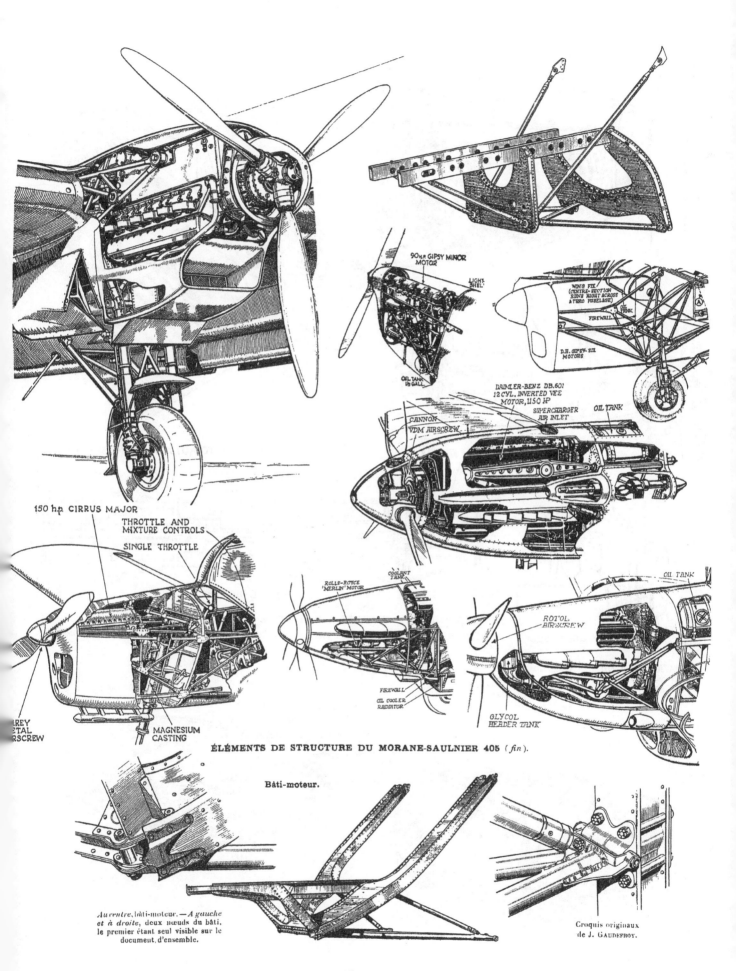

150 h.p. CIRRUS MAJOR

THROTTLE AND
MIXTURE CONTROLS

SINGLE THROTTLE

90 h.p. GIPSY MINOR
MOTOR

LIGHT
SHELL

OIL TANK
1½ GALL

WING FIX
(CENTRE-SECTION
RUNS RIGHT ACROSS
A'TERO FUSELAGE)

OIL
TANK

FIREWALL

D.H. GIPSY-SIX
MOTORS

DAIMLER-BENZ DB.601
12 CYL. INVERTED VEE
MOTOR, 1150 HP

SUPERCHARGER
AIR INLET

OIL TANK

CANNON

VDM AIRSCREW

COOLANT
TANK

ROLLS-ROYCE
'MERLIN' MOTOR

OIL TANK

ROT'OL
AIRSCREW

FIREWALL

OIL COOLER
RADIATOR

GLYCOL
HEADER TANK

REY
TAL
RSCREW

MAGNESIUM
CASTING

ÉLÉMENTS DE STRUCTURE DU MORANE-SAULNIER 405 (fin).

Bâti-moteur.

*Au centre, bâti-moteur. — A gauche
et à droite, deux nœuds du bâti,
le premier étant seul visible sur le
document, d'ensemble.*

Croquis originaux
de J. GAUDEFROY.

6.01

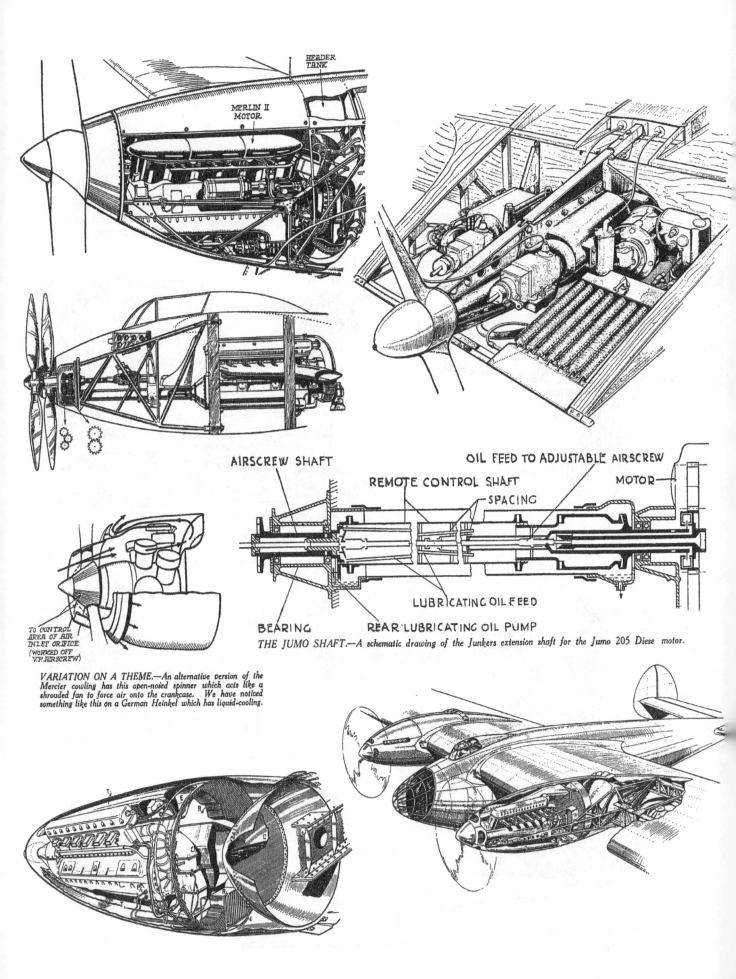

HEADER TANK

MERLIN II MOTOR

AIRSCREW SHAFT

OIL FEED TO ADJUSTABLE AIRSCREW

REMOTE CONTROL SHAFT

SPACING

MOTOR

BEARING

LUBRICATING OIL FEED

REAR LUBRICATING OIL PUMP

THE JUMO SHAFT.—A schematic drawing of the Junkers extension shaft for the Jumo 205 Diesel motor.

TO CONTROL AREA OF AIR INLET ORIFICE (WORKED OFF V.P. AIRSCREW)

VARIATION ON A THEME.—An alternative version of the Mercier cowling has this open-nosed spinner which acts like a shrouded fan to force air onto the crankcase. We have noticed something like this on a German Heinkel which has liquid-cooling.

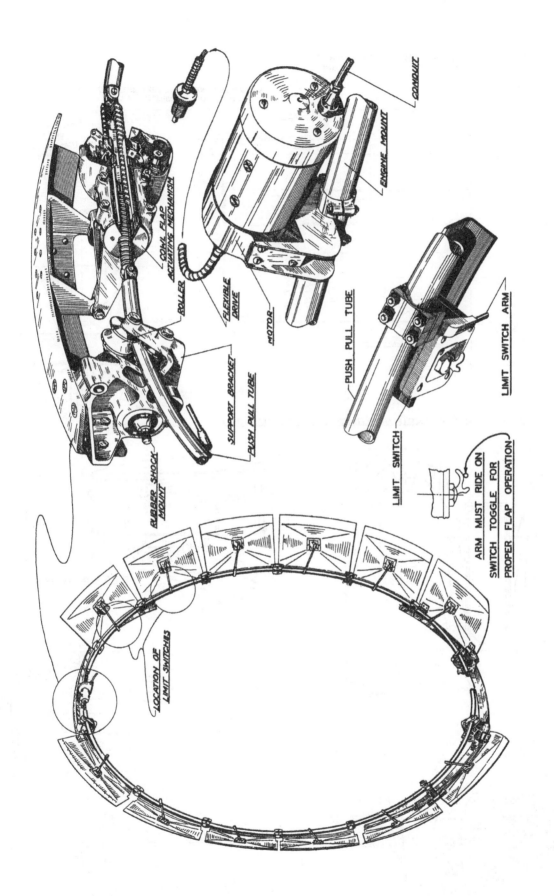

CONDUIT

ENGINE MOUNT

COWL FLAP ACTUATING MECHANISM

ROLLER

FLEXIBLE DRIVE

MOTOR

SUPPORT BRACKET

PUSH PULL TUBE

RUBBER SHOCK MOUNT

PUSH PULL TUBE

LIMIT SWITCH ARM

LIMIT SWITCH

ARM MUST RIDE ON SWITCH TOGGLE FOR PROPER FLAP OPERATION

LOCATION OF LIMIT SWITCHES

COWL FLAPS

FACTS AND FIGURES.-

Bottom, a new form of ducted cowling suggested by Mr. Fedden to reduce drag. It replaces the present circular cowl with controllable gills.

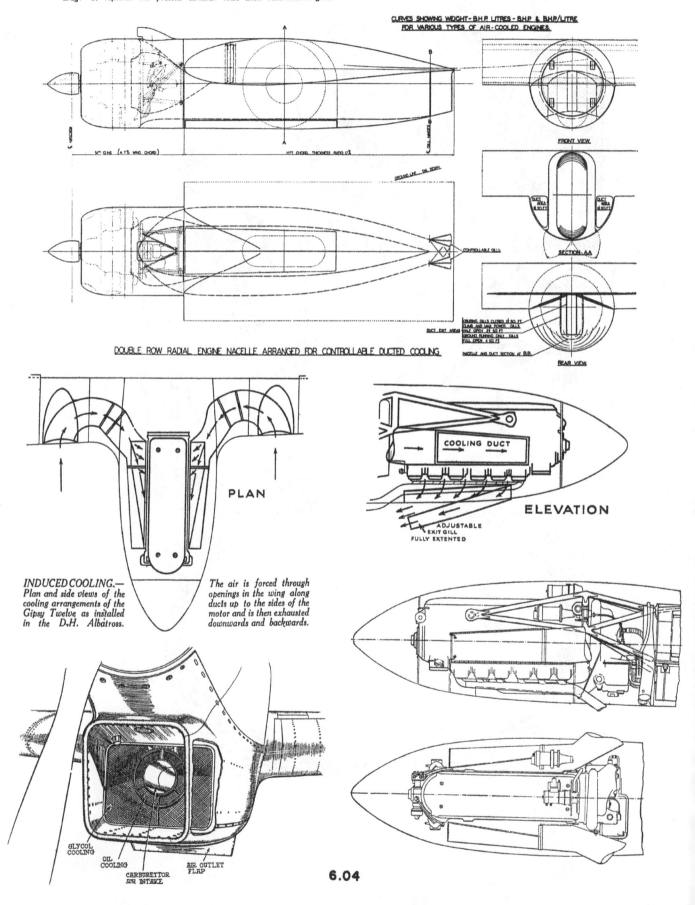

CURVES SHOWING WEIGHT-B.H.P. LITRES - B.H.P & B.H.P/LITRE
FOR VARIOUS TYPES OF AIR-COOLED ENGINES.

FRONT VIEW.

SECTION: AA.

REAR VIEW.

DOUBLE ROW RADIAL ENGINE NACELLE ARRANGED FOR CONTROLLABLE DUCTED COOLING

PLAN

COOLING DUCT

ELEVATION

ADJUSTABLE
EXIT GILL
FULLY EXTENTED

INDUCED COOLING.—
Plan and side views of the cooling arrangements of the Gipsy Twelve as installed in the D.H. Albatross.

The air is forced through openings in the wing along ducts up to the sides of the motor and is then exhausted downwards and backwards.

GLYCOL
COOLING

OIL
COOLING

CARBURETTOR
AIR INTAKE

AIR OUTLET
FLAP

6.04

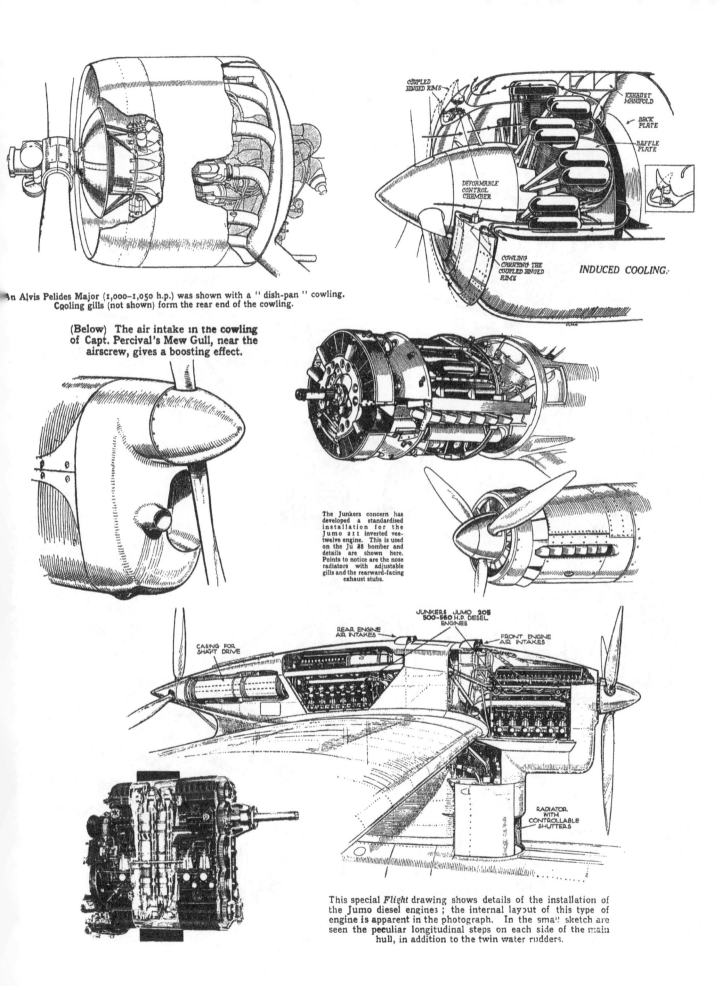

An Alvis Pelides Major (1,000–1,050 h.p.) was shown with a " dish-pan " cowling. Cooling gills (not shown) form the rear end of the cowling.

(Below) The air intake in the cowling of Capt. Percival's Mew Gull, near the airscrew, gives a boosting effect.

COUPLED HINGED RIMS

EXHAUST MANIFOLD

BACK PLATE

BAFFLE PLATE

DEFORMABLE CONTROL CHAMBER

COWLING CARRYING THE COUPLED HINGED RIMS

INDUCED COOLING.

The Junkers concern has developed a standardised installation for the Jumo 211 inverted vee-twelve engine. This is used on the Ju 88 bomber and details are shown here. Points to notice are the nose radiators with adjustable gills and the rearward-facing exhaust stubs.

CASING FOR SHAFT DRIVE

REAR ENGINE AIR INTAKES

JUNKERS JUMO 205 500–560 H.P. DIESEL ENGINES

FRONT ENGINE AIR INTAKES

RADIATOR WITH CONTROLLABLE SHUTTERS

This special *Flight* drawing shows details of the installation of the Jumo diesel engines; the internal layout of this type of engine is apparent in the photograph. In the small sketch are seen the peculiar longitudinal steps on each side of the main hull, in addition to the twin water rudders.

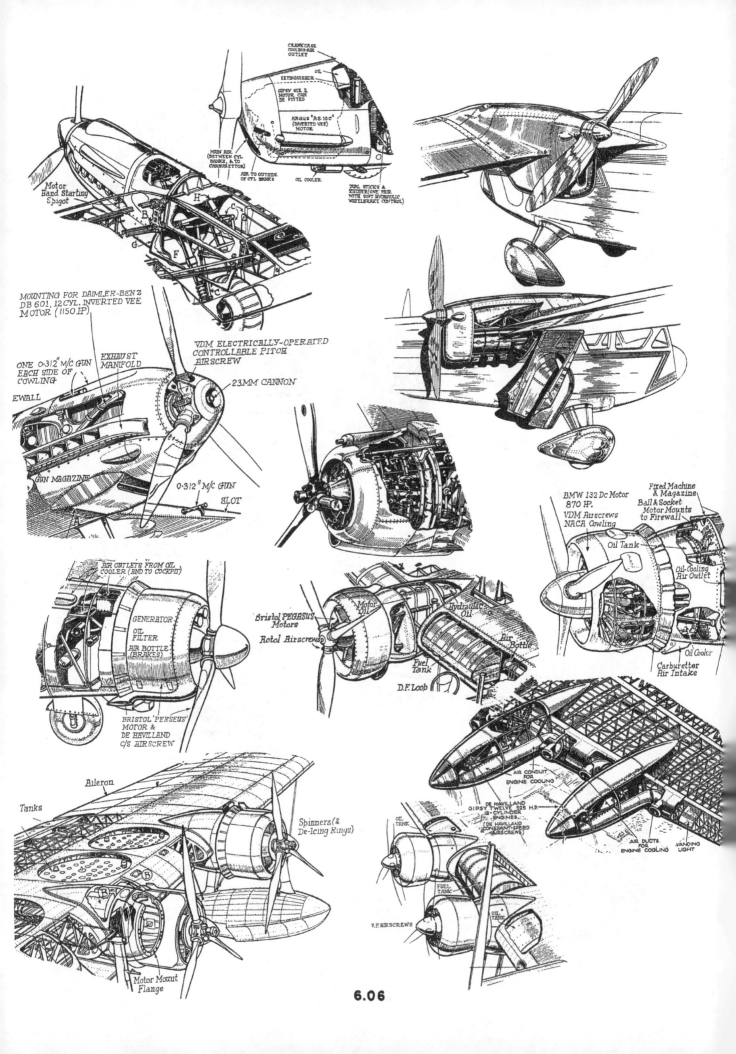

Motor Hand Starting Spigot

CRANKCASE COOLING-AIR OUTLET

OIL

EXTINGUISHER

GIPSY SIX II MOTOR CAN BE FITTED

ARGUS "AS·10 C" (INVERTED VEE) MOTOR

MAIN AIR (BETWEEN CYL. BANKS, & TO CARBURETTOR)

AIR TO OUTSIDE OF CYL. BANKS

OIL COOLER.

DUAL STICKS & RUDDER (ONE PAIR WITH SOFT HYDRAULIC WHEELBRAKE CONTROL)

MOUNTING FOR DAIMLER-BENZ DB 601, 12 CYL. INVERTED VEE MOTOR (1150 H.P.)

VDM ELECTRICALLY-OPERATED CONTROLLABLE PITCH AIRSCREW

ONE 0·312" M/C GUN EACH SIDE OF COWLING

EXHAUST MANIFOLD

EWALL

23MM CANNON

GUN MAGAZINE

0·312" M/C GUN

SLOT

AIR OUTLETS FROM OIL COOLER (AND TO COCKPIT)

GENERATOR

OIL FILTER

AIR BOTTLE (BRAKES)

BRISTOL 'PERSEUS' MOTOR & DE HAVILLAND C/S AIRSCREW

Bristol PEGASUS Motors

Rotol Airscrews

Motor Oil

Hydraulic Oil

Air Bottle

Fuel Tank

D.F. Loop

BMW 132 Dc Motor 870 H.P.

VDM Airscrews NACA Cowling

Fixed Machine & Magazine Ball & Socket Motor Mounts to Firewall

Oil Tank

Oil-Cooling Air Outlet

Oil Cooler

Carburetter Air Intake

Aileron

Tanks

Spinners (& De-Icing Rings)

Motor Mount Flange

AIR CONDUIT FOR ENGINE COOLING

DE HAVILLAND GIPSY TWELVE 525 H.P. 12-CYLINDER ENGINES. (DE HAVILLAND CONSTANT-SPEED AIRSCREW)

AIR DUCTS FOR ENGINE COOLING

LANDING LIGHT

OIL TANK

FUEL TANK

V.P. AIRSCREWS

OIL TANK

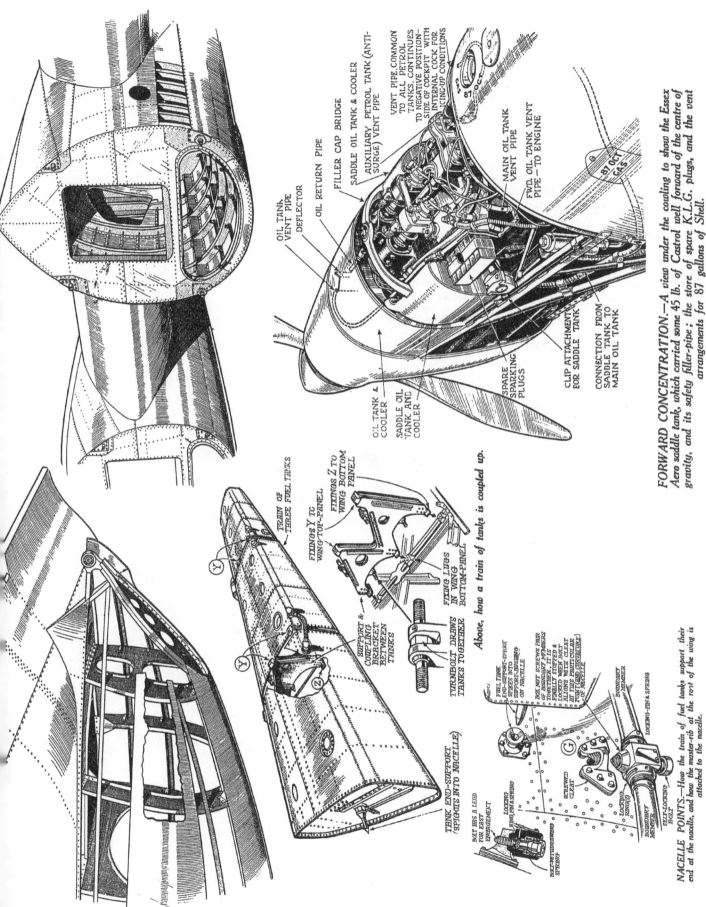

OIL TANK
VENT PIPE
DEFLECTOR

OIL RETURN PIPE

FILLER CAP BRIDGE

SADDLE OIL TANK & COOLER

AUXILIARY PETROL TANK (ANTI-SURGE) VENT PIPE

VENT PIPE, COMMON TO ALL PETROL TANKS, CONTINUES TO NEGATIVE POSITION—SIDE OF COCKPIT WITH INTERNAL COCK FOR 'CING-UP CONDITIONS

MAIN OIL TANK VENT PIPE

FWD. OIL TANK VENT PIPE—TO ENGINE

87 OCT GAS

OIL TANK & COOLER

SADDLE OIL TANK AND COOLER

SPARE SPARKING PLUGS

CLIP ATTACHMENT FOR SADDLE TANK

CONNECTION FROM SADDLE TANK TO MAIN OIL TANK

FORWARD CONCENTRATION.—A view under the cowling to show the Essex Aero saddle tank, which carried some 45 lb. of Castrol well forward of the centre of gravity, and its safety filler-pipe; the store of spare K.L.G. plugs, and the vent arrangements for 87 gallons of Shell.

TRAIN OF THREE FUEL TANKS

FIXINGS Y TO WING-TOP-PANEL

FIXINGS Z TO WING BOTTOM PANEL

FIXING LUGS IN WING BOTTOM-PANEL

SUPPORT & COUPLING BRACKET BETWEEN TANKS

TURNBOLT DRAWS TANKS TOGETHER

Above, how a train of tanks is coupled up.

TANK END-SUPPORT (SPIGOTS INTO NACELLE)

THE TANK END-SUPPORT-SPIGOT SPIGOTS INTO SUPPORT-BUSHING ON NACELLE

BOX NUT SCREWS PAIR OF BOUNDARY MEMBERS TOGETHER. IT IS FIRMLY STUFFED & LOCKED WITH CLEAT ALIGNS WITH CLEAT AT THIS PARTICULAR POINT (AND CURVATURE OF NACELLE

BOLT HAS A LEAD FOR EASY ENGAGEMENT

LOCKING-RING-PIN & SPRING

BOLT-WITHDRAWING SPRING

SCREWED CLEAT

LOCKING RING(S)

SELF-LOCKING BOLT

BOUNDARY MEMBER

BOUNDARY MEMBER

LOCKING-PIN & SPRING

NACELLE POINTS.—How the train of fuel tanks support their end at the nacelle, and how the master-rib at the root of the wing is attached to the nacelle.

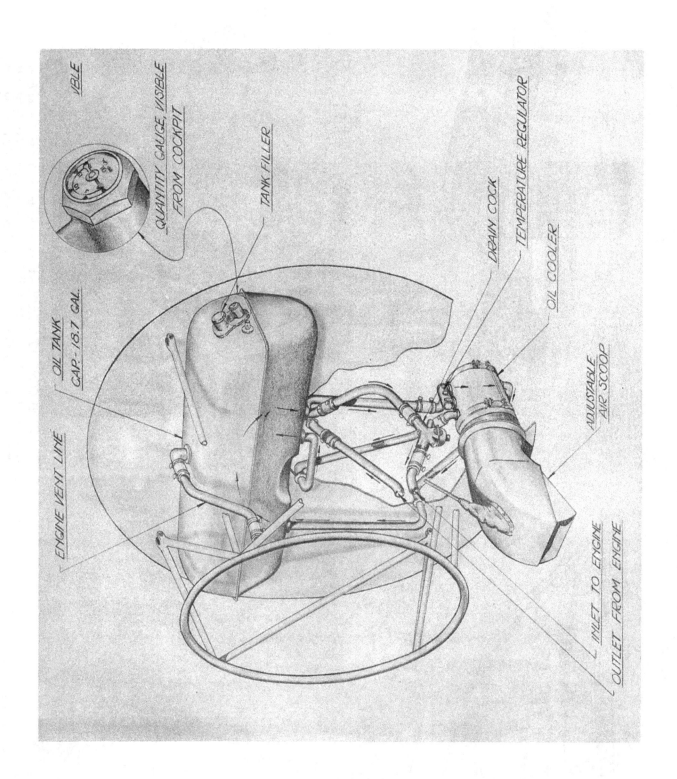

QUANTITY GAUGE, VISIBLE
FROM COCKPIT

VIBLE

TANK FILLER

OIL TANK
CAP - 16.7 GAL.

ENGINE VENT LINE

DRAIN COCK

TEMPERATURE REGULATOR

OIL COOLER

ADJUSTABLE
AIR SCOOP

INLET TO ENGINE

OUTLET FROM ENGINE

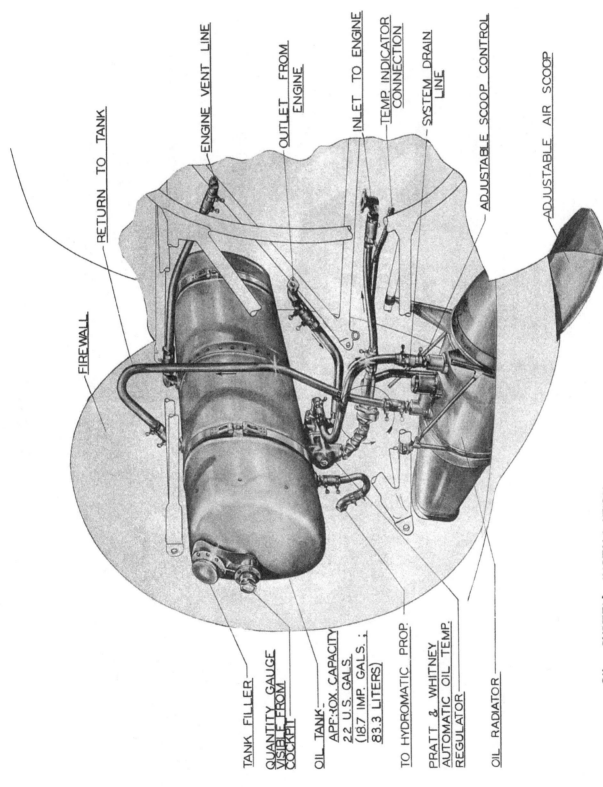

RETURN TO TANK

ENGINE VENT LINE

OUTLET FROM ENGINE

INLET TO ENGINE

TEMP. INDICATOR CONNECTION

SYSTEM DRAIN LINE

ADJUSTABLE SCOOP CONTROL

ADJUSTABLE AIR SCOOP

FIREWALL

TANK FILLER

QUANTITY GAUGE VISIBLE FROM COCKPIT

OIL TANK-
APPROX. CAPACITY
22 U.S. GALS.
(18.7 IMP. GALS. ;
83.3 LITERS)

TO HYDROMATIC PROP.

PRATT & WHITNEY AUTOMATIC OIL TEMP. REGULATOR

OIL RADIATOR

OIL SYSTEM INSTALLATION

6.09

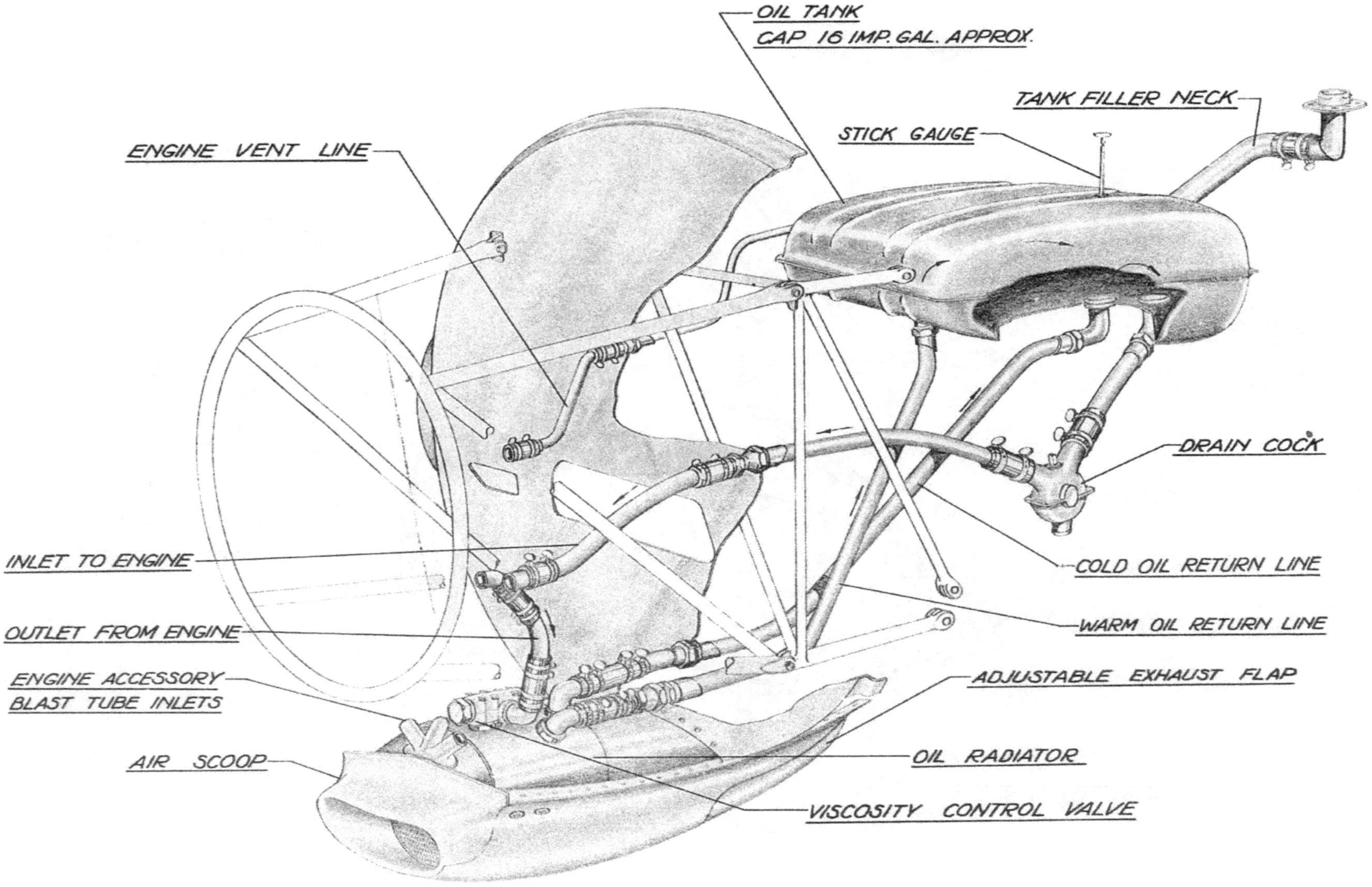

OIL TANK
CAP. 16 IMP. GAL. APPROX.

TANK FILLER NECK

STICK GAUGE

DRAIN COCK

COLD OIL RETURN LINE

WARM OIL RETURN LINE

ADJUSTABLE EXHAUST FLAP

OIL RADIATOR

VISCOSITY CONTROL VALVE

ENGINE VENT LINE

INLET TO ENGINE

OUTLET FROM ENGINE

ENGINE ACCESSORY
BLAST TUBE INLETS

AIR SCOOP

OIL SYSTEM INSTALLATION

6.10

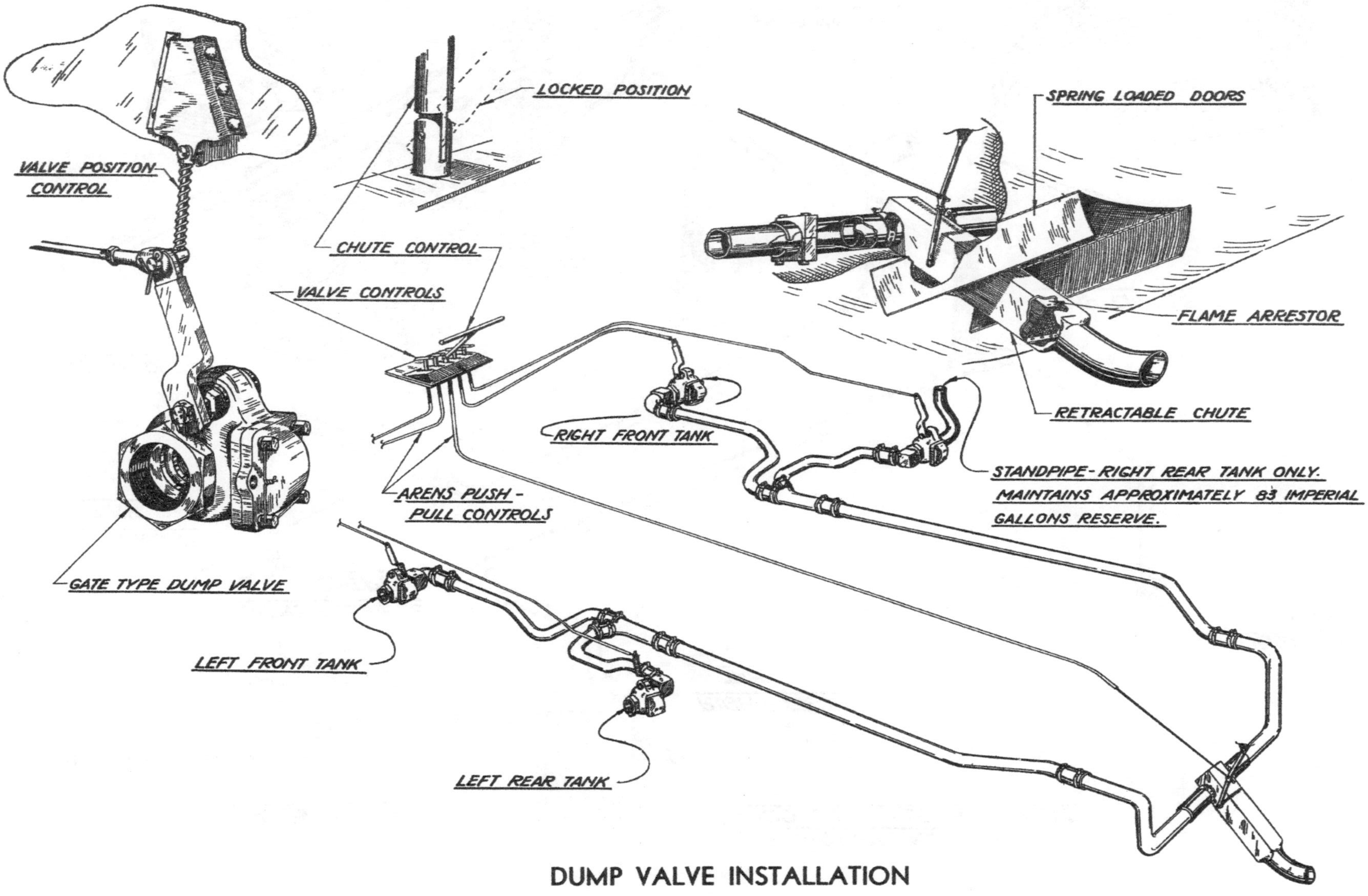

SPRING LOADED DOORS

FLAME ARRESTOR

RETRACTABLE CHUTE

STANDPIPE - RIGHT REAR TANK ONLY.
MAINTAINS APPROXIMATELY 8⅓ IMPERIAL
GALLONS RESERVE.

RIGHT FRONT TANK

LOCKED POSITION

CHUTE CONTROL

VALVE CONTROLS

ARENS PUSH -
PULL CONTROLS

LEFT REAR TANK

VALVE POSITION
CONTROL

LEFT FRONT TANK

GATE TYPE DUMP VALVE

DUMP VALVE INSTALLATION

6.11

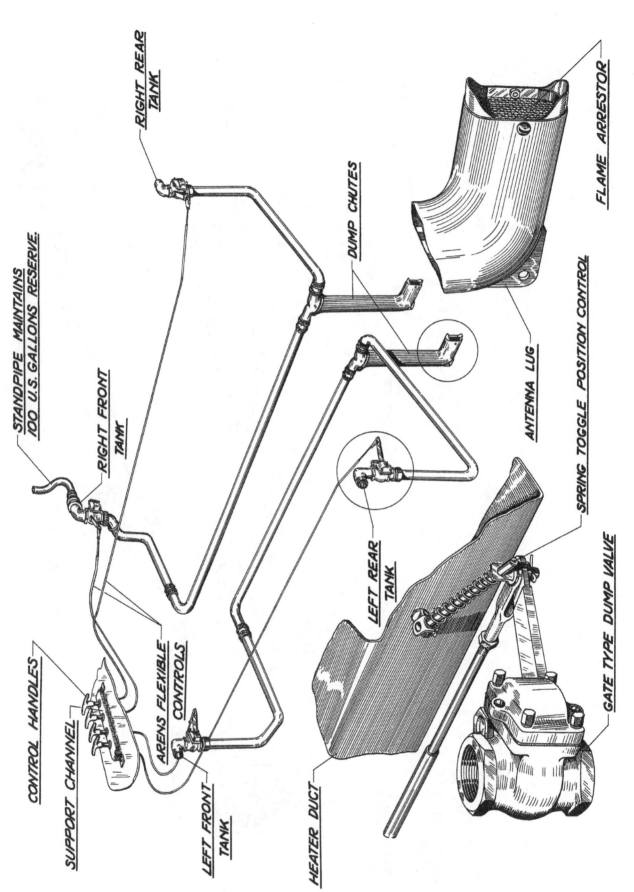

RIGHT REAR TANK

FLAME ARRESTOR

DUMP CHUTES

STANDPIPE MAINTAINS 100 U.S. GALLONS RESERVE

RIGHT FRONT TANK

ANTENNA LUG

SPRING TOGGLE POSITION CONTROL

LEFT REAR TANK

CONTROL HANDLES

SUPPORT CHANNEL

ARENS FLEXIBLE CONTROLS

LEFT FRONT TANK

HEATER DUCT

GATE TYPE DUMP VALVE

DUMP VALVE INSTALLATION

THE INSIDE STORY

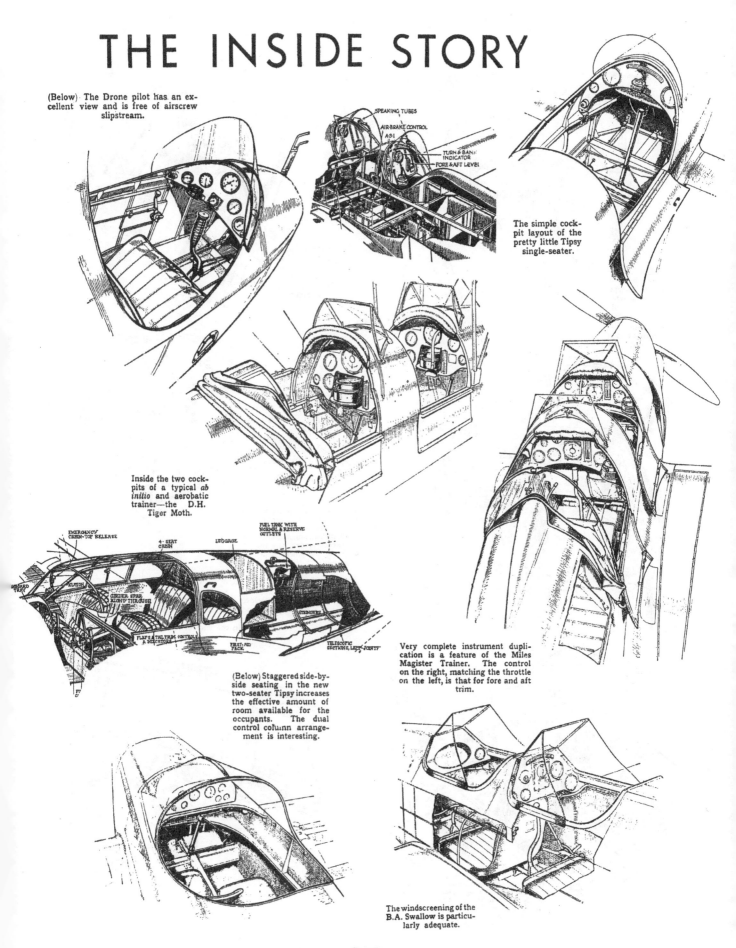

(Below) The Drone pilot has an excellent view and is free of airscrew slipstream.

SPEAKING TUBES
AIR-BRAKE CONTROL A.S.I
TURN & BANK INDICATOR
FORE & AFT LEVEL

The simple cockpit layout of the pretty little Tipsy single-seater.

Inside the two cockpits of a typical *ab initio* and aerobatic trainer—the D.H. Tiger Moth.

EMERGENCY CABIN-TOP RELEASE
4-SEAT CABIN
LUGGAGE
FUEL TANK WITH NORMAL & RESERVE OUTLETS

BOARD TRAY
ELEVON
CENTRE SPAR SIGHT THROUGH
STRINGERS
FLAPS & TAIL TRIM CONTROLS & INDICATORS
FIRST-AID PACK
TELESCOPIC SECTIONS, LEFT JOINT

(Below) Staggered side-by-side seating in the new two-seater Tipsy increases the effective amount of room available for the occupants. The dual control column arrangement is interesting.

Very complete instrument duplication is a feature of the Miles Magister Trainer. The control on the right, matching the throttle on the left, is that for fore and aft trim.

The windscreening of the B.A. Swallow is particularly adequate.

7.01

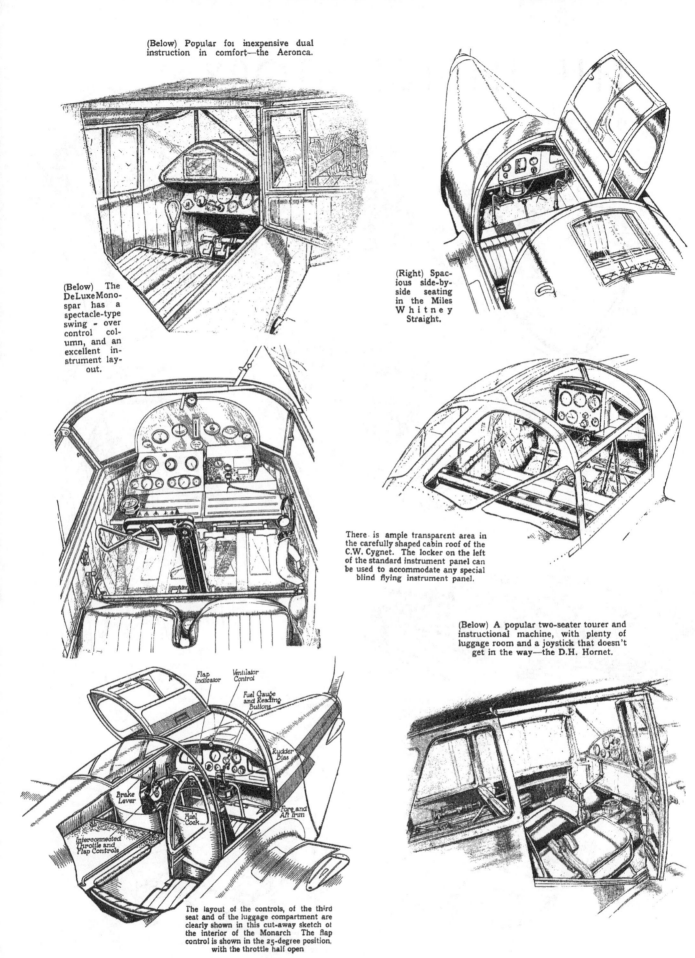

(Below) Popular for inexpensive dual instruction in comfort—the Aeronca.

(Below) The DeLuxe Monospar has a spectacle-type swing - over control column, and an excellent instrument layout.

(Right) Spacious side-by-side seating in the Miles Whitney Straight.

There is ample transparent area in the carefully shaped cabin roof of the C.W. Cygnet. The locker on the left of the standard instrument panel can be used to accommodate any special blind flying instrument panel.

(Below) A popular two-seater tourer and instructional machine, with plenty of luggage room and a joystick that doesn't get in the way—the D.H. Hornet.

Flap indicator
Ventilator Control
Fuel Gauge and Reading Buttons
Rudder Bias
Brake Lever
Fore and Aft Trim
Fuel Cock
Interconnected Throttle and Flap Controls

The layout of the controls, of the third seat and of the luggage compartment are clearly shown in this cut-away sketch of the interior of the Monarch The flap control is shown in the 25-degree position, with the throttle half open

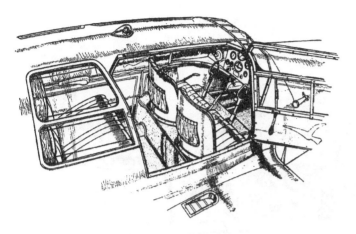

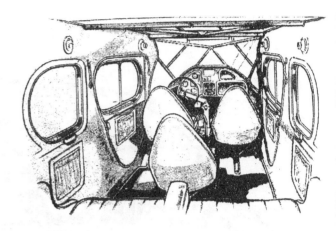

(Left) There is a genuine saloon car effect about the interior of the Percival Vega Gull.

(Right) Easy ingress and egress and an excellent view for the passengers are features of the Heston Phœnix.

(Below) Height and light : The B.A. Eagle.

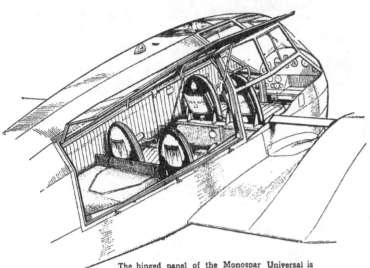

The hinged panel of the Monospar Universal is designed for ambulance and freighter work. A fifth seat may be "manufactured" from the luggage tray at the rear of the cabin.

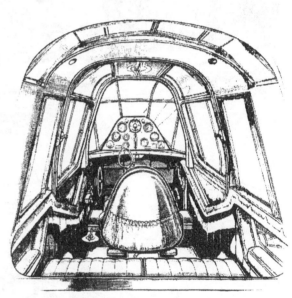

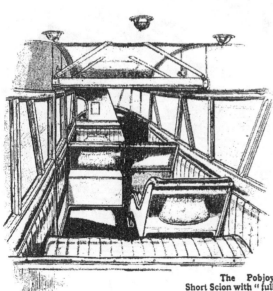

The Pobjoy Short Scion with "full house" seating arrangements.

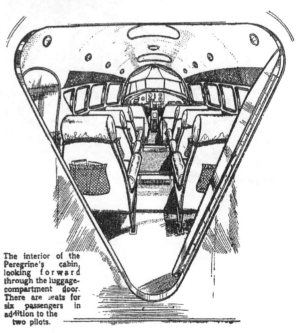

The interior of the Peregrine's cabin, looking forward through the luggage-compartment door. There are seats for six passengers in addition to the two pilots.

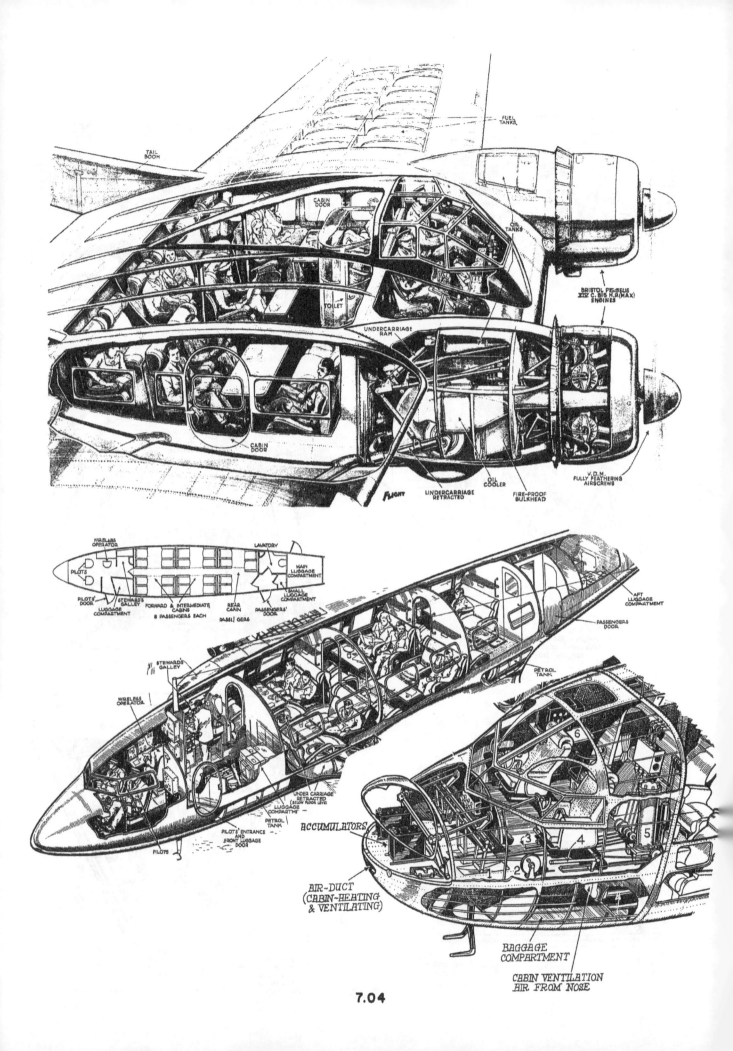

TAIL BOOM

CABIN DOOR

FUEL TANKS

OIL TANKS

BRISTOL PERSEUS XIV C. 815 H.P.(MAX) ENGINES

TOILET

UNDERCARRIAGE RAM

CABIN DOOR

UNDERCARRIAGE RETRACTED

OIL COOLER

FIRE-PROOF BULKHEAD

V.D.M. FULLY FEATHERING AIRSCREWS

FLIGHT

WIRELESS OPERATOR

LAVATORY

MAIN LUGGAGE COMPARTMENT

PILOTS

PILOTS' DOOR

STEWARD'S GALLEY

LUGGAGE COMPARTMENT

FORWARD & INTERMEDIATE CABINS 8 PASSENGERS EACH

REAR CABIN

PASSENGERS

PASSENGERS' DOOR

SMALL LUGGAGE COMPARTMENT

STEWARDS' GALLEY

WIRELESS OPERATOR

AFT LUGGAGE COMPARTMENT

PASSENGERS DOOR

PETROL TANK

UNDER CARRIAGE RETRACTED (BELOW FLOOR LEVEL

LUGGAGE COMPARTME

PETROL TANK

PILOTS' ENTRANCE AND FRONT LUGGAGE DOOR

PILOTS

ACCUMULATORS

AIR-DUCT (CABIN-HEATING & VENTILATING)

BAGGAGE COMPARTMENT

CABIN VENTILATION AIR FROM NOSE

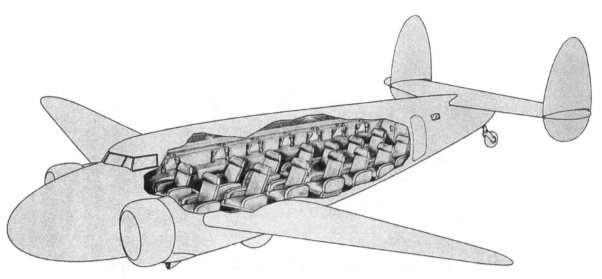

INTERIOR ARRANGEMENT—BASIC—01—TRANSPORT

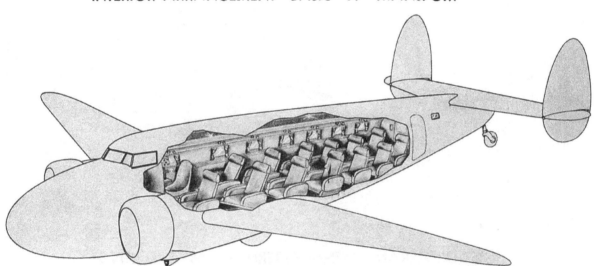

INTERIOR ARRANGEMENT—ALTERNATE—02—TRANSPORT

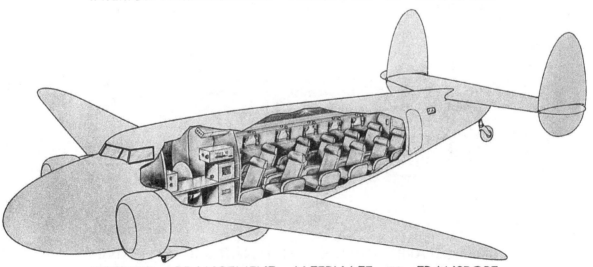

INTERIOR ARRANGEMENT—ALTERNATE—03—TRANSPORT

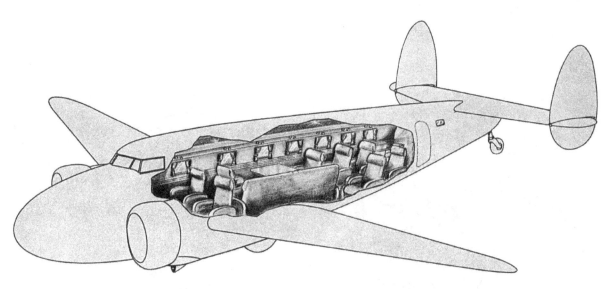

INTERIOR ARRANGEMENT—ALTERNATE—04—EXECUTIVE

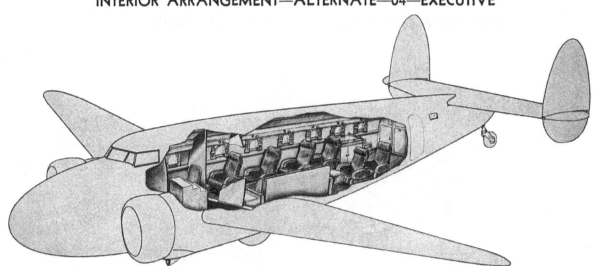

INTERIOR ARRANGEMENT—ALTERNATE—05—EXECUTIVE

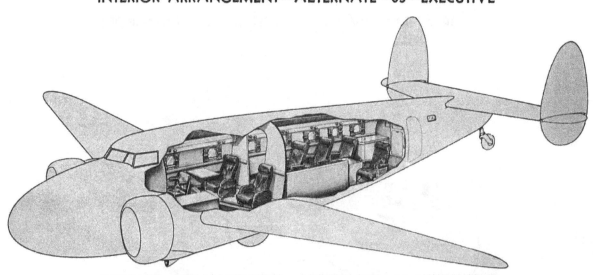

INTERIOR ARRANGEMENT—ALTERNATE—06—EXECUTIVE

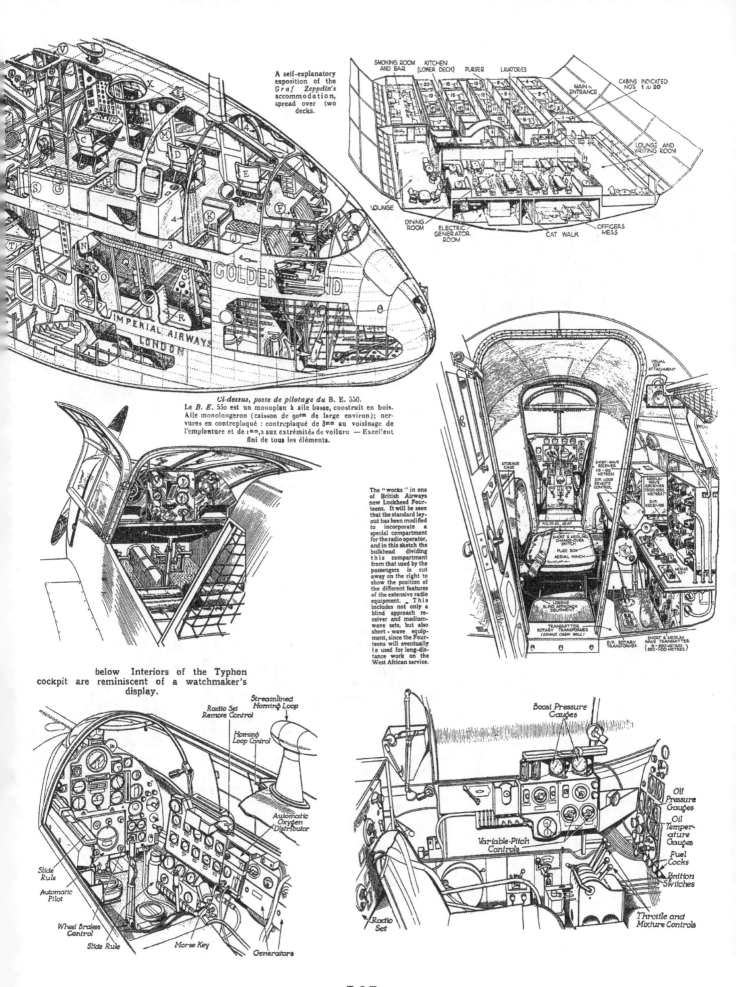

A self-explanatory exposition of the *Graf Zeppelin's* accommodation, spread over two decks.

SMOKING ROOM AND BAR · KITCHEN (LOWER DECK) · PURSER · LAVATORIES

MAIN ENTRANCE

CABINS INDICATED N0'S 1 to 20

LOUNGE AND WRITING ROOM

LOUNGE

DINING ROOM · ELECTRIC GENERATOR ROOM · CAT WALK · OFFICERS MESS

Ci-dessus, poste de pilotage du B. E. 550.
Le *B. E.* 550 est un monoplan à aile basse, construit en bois.
Aile monolongeron (caisson de 90^{cm} de large environ); nervures en contreplaqué : contreplaqué de 3^{mm} au voisinage de l'emplanture et de 1^{mm},2 aux extrémités de voilure — Excellent fini de tous les éléments.

The "works" in one of British Airways new Lockheed Fourteens. It will be seen that the standard layout has been modified to incorporate a special compartment for the radio operator, and in this sketch the bulkhead dividing this compartment from that used by the passengers is cut away on the right to show the position of the different features of the extensive radio equipment. This includes not only a blind approach receiver and medium-wave sets, but also short-wave equipment, since the Fourteens will eventually be used for long-distance work on the West African service.

VISUAL D/F ATTACHMENT

STORAGE CASE · SHORT-WAVE RECEIVER (15 - 150 METRES) · D/F LOOP REMOTE CONTROL · MEDIUM WAVE RECEIVER (300-650 METRES) · D/F RECEIVER

FOLDING SEAT · SHORT & MEDIUM CHANGE-OVER SWITCH · FUSE BOX · AERIAL WINCH

LORENZ BLIND APPROACH EQUIPMENT

TRANSMITTER ROTARY TRANSFORMER (BEHIND CABIN WALL) · D/F ROTARY TRANSFORMER · SHORT & MEDIUM WAVE TRANSMITTER (15 - 200 METRES, 850 - 1100 METRES)

below Interiors of the Typhon cockpit are reminiscent of a watchmaker's display.

Radio Set Remote Control · Streamlined Homing Loop · Homing Loop Control · Automatic Oxygen Distributor

Slide Rule · Automatic Pilot · Wheel Brakes Control · Slide Rule · Morse Key · Generators

Boost Pressure Gauges

Oil Pressure Gauges · Oil Temperature Gauges · Fuel Cocks · Ignition Switches · Throttle and Mixture Controls

Variable-Pitch Controls

Radio Set

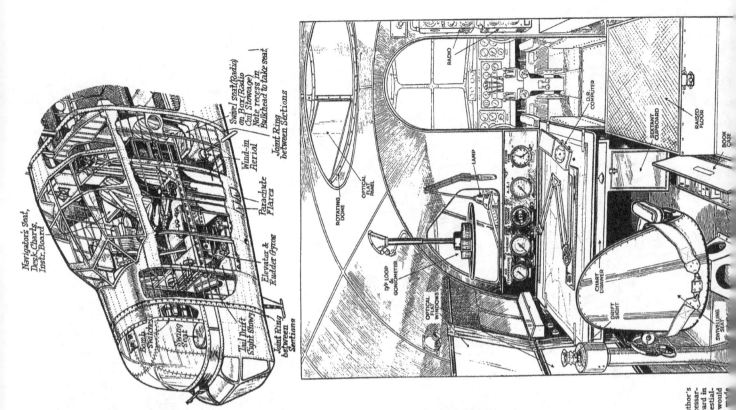

Navigator's Seat,
Desk, Charts,
Instr. Board

Swivel seat (Radio)
on Box (Radio
Coil Stowage)
Note recess in
Bulkhead to take seat

Wind-in
Aerial

Joint Ring
between Sections

Parachute
Flares

Elevator &
Rudder Gyros

Bomb
Switches

Swing
Seat

Tail Drift
Sight Show

Joint Ring
between
Sections

RADIO

D.R.
COMPUTER

INSTRUMENT
CUPBOARD

RAISED
FLOOR

BOOK
CASE

ROTATING
DOME

OPTICAL
FLAT
PANEL

LAMP

CHART
DRAWER

DRIFT
SIGHT

SWIVELLING
SEAT

D/F LOOP
GONIOMETER

OPTICAL
FLAT
WINDOWS

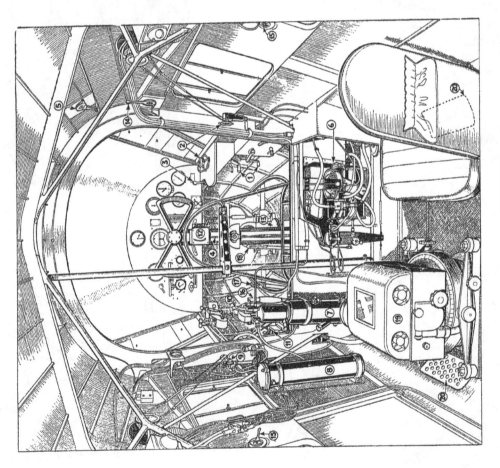

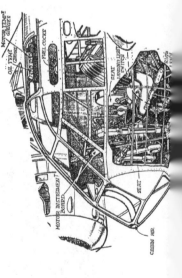

MOTOR TEMP
GUAGES

OIL TEMP
Gauge

FUEL COCKS

SEAT ADJUSTING
SWITCH

MOTOR INSTRUMENT
BOARD

SEAT.

CABIN AIR.

*Details of the Control
and Instrument Lay-
out : Some Remarks
on the Flying Char-
acteristics*

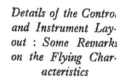

The control-cabin of the prototype D.H. 95. In production machines the controls and instruments in the roof will be mounted on a single panel, but otherwise the layout shown is substantially that which will apply to later machines. The depth of the windscreen is noteworthy ; coupled with a short nose, this gives the crew an exceptionally good field of view.

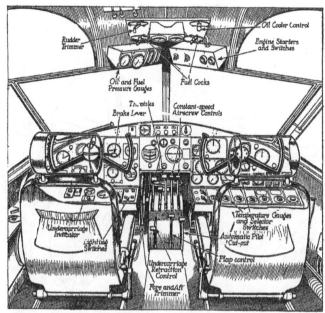

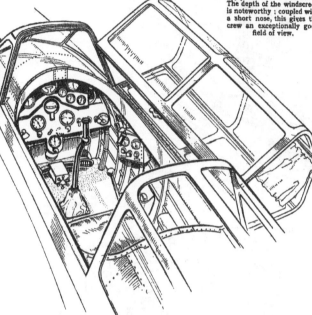

Pilot's and navigator's cockpits. Note, in the latter, the fuel tanks, drift window, windows in the fuselage sides, radio and flying instruments.

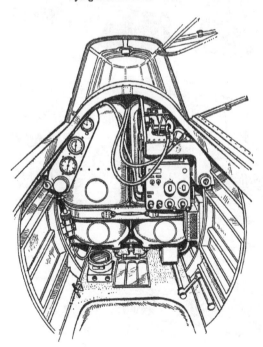

THE
COMET'S
COCKPIT

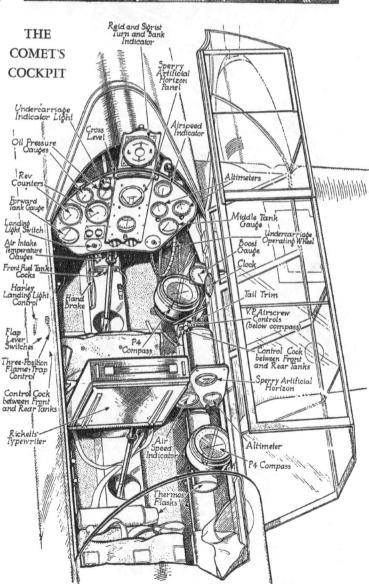

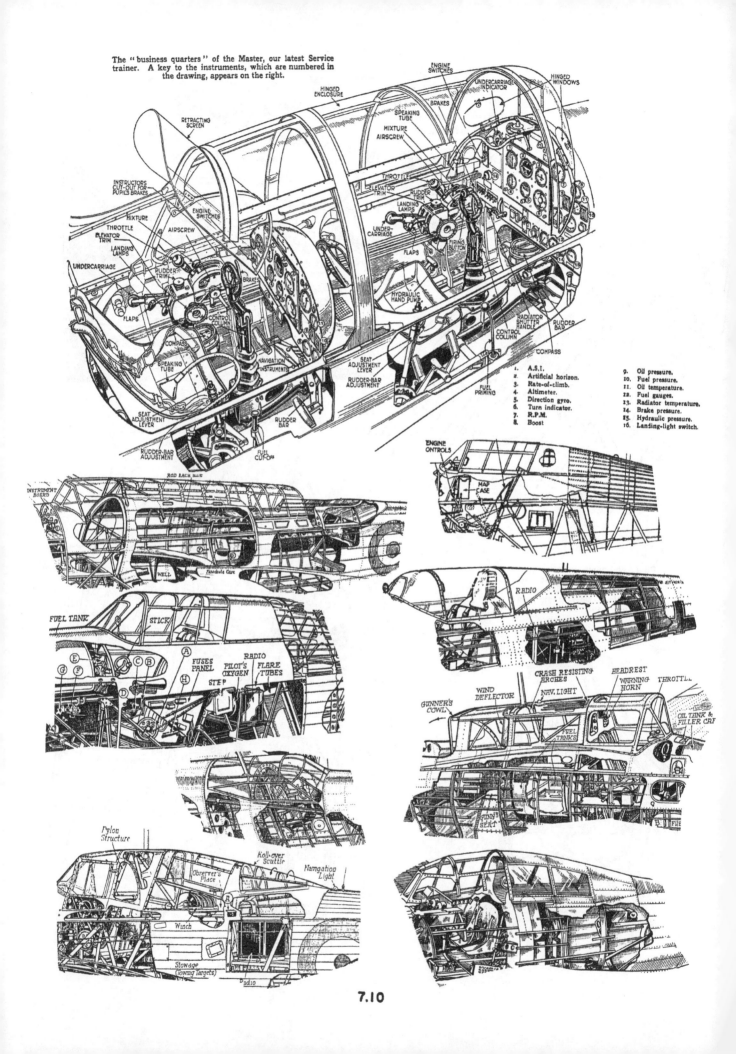

The "business quarters" of the Master, our latest Service trainer. A key to the instruments, which are numbered in the drawing, appears on the right.

1. A.S.I.
2. Artificial horizon.
3. Rate-of-climb.
4. Altimeter.
5. Direction gyro.
6. Turn indicator.
7. R.P.M.
8. Boost
9. Oil pressure.
10. Fuel pressure.
11. Oil temperature.
12. Fuel gauges.
13. Radiator temperature.
14. Brake pressure.
15. Hydraulic pressure.
16. Landing-light switch.

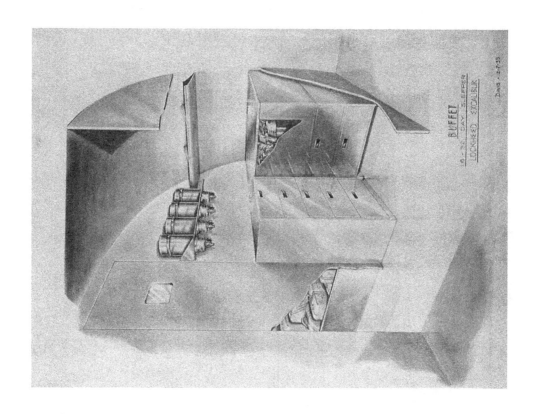

BUFFET
16 · 52 · DAY SLEEPER
LOCKHEED EXCALIBUR

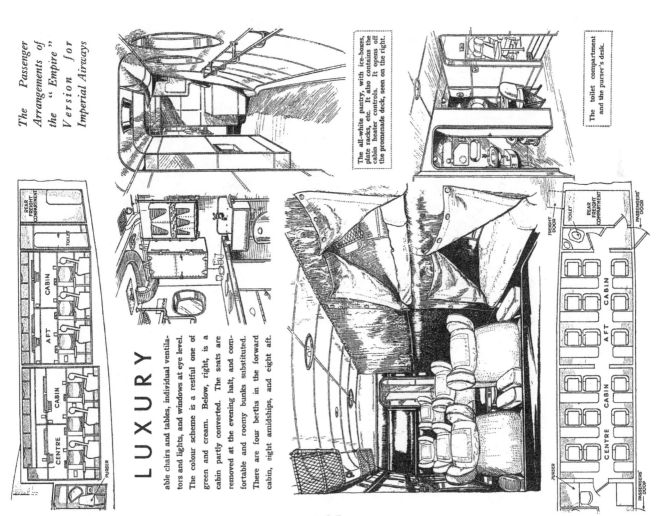

The Passenger Arrangements of the "Empire" Version for Imperial Airways

LUXURY

able chairs and tables, individual ventilators and lights, and windows at eye level. The colour scheme is a restful one of green and cream. Below, right, is a cabin partly converted. The seats are removed at the evening halt, and comfortable and roomy bunks substituted. There are four berths in the forward cabin, eight amidships, and eight aft.

The all-white pantry, with ice-boxes, plate racks, etc. It also contains the cabin heater controls. It opens off the promenade deck, seen on the right.

The toilet compartment and the purser's desk.

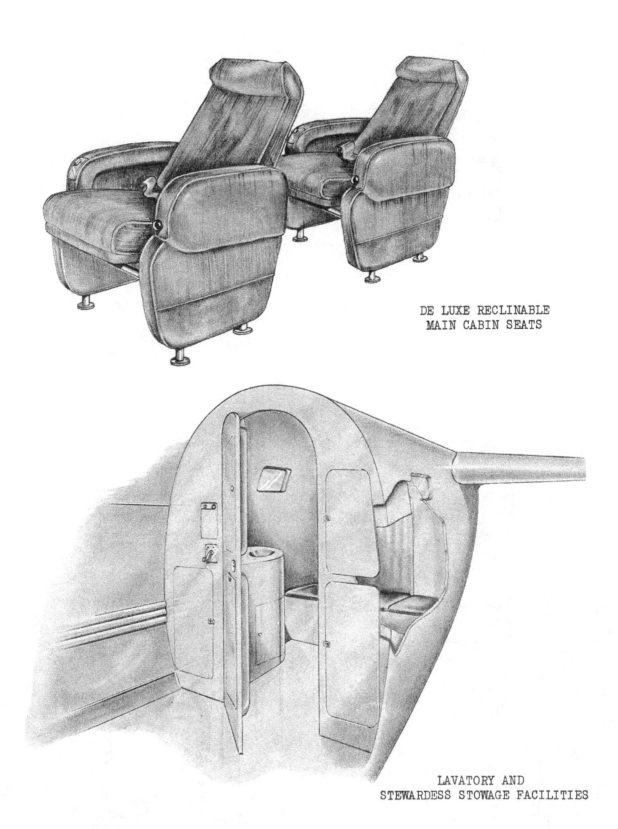

DE LUXE RECLINABLE
MAIN CABIN SEATS

LAVATORY AND
STEWARDESS STOWAGE FACILITIES

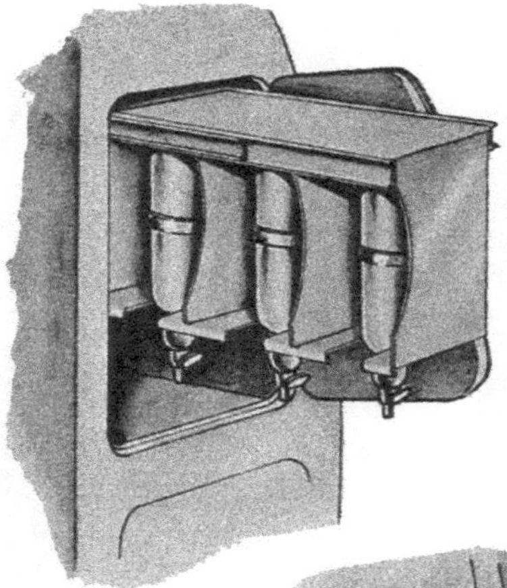

THERMOS STOWAGE
FOR
THREE 2 QT. VACUUM
(LIQUID) BOTTLES

U.A.L. TYPE LUNCH
BOX STOWAGE

STOWAGE PROVISION FOR SERVING TRAYS,
FOOD JUGS, SILVERWARE, CIGARETTES AND
DRY ICE FOR PERISHABLE FOOD SUNDRIES.

STEWARDESS STOWAGE FACILITIES

7.27

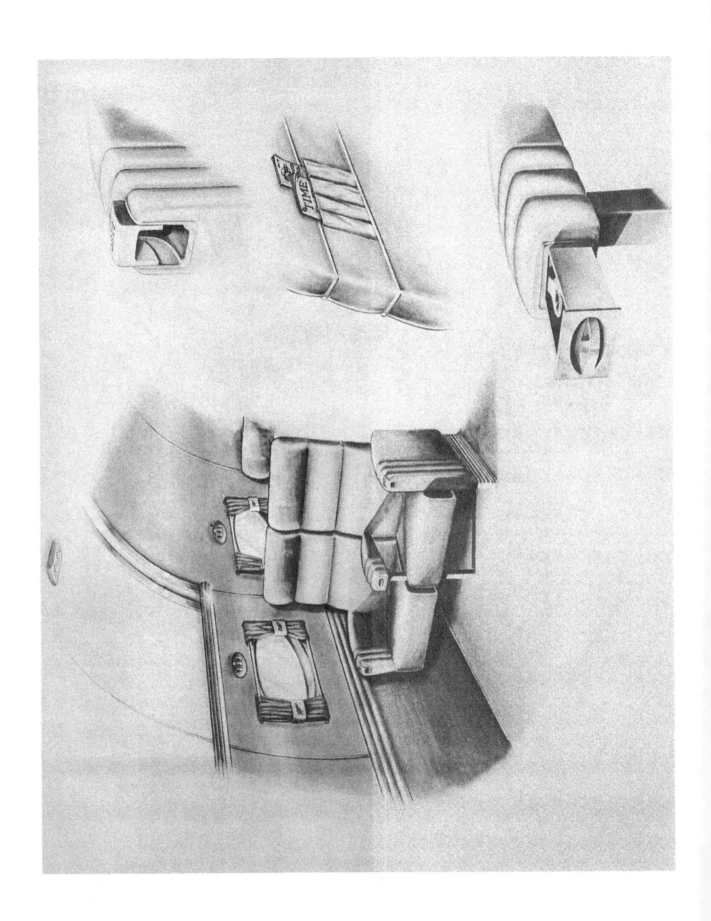

7.28

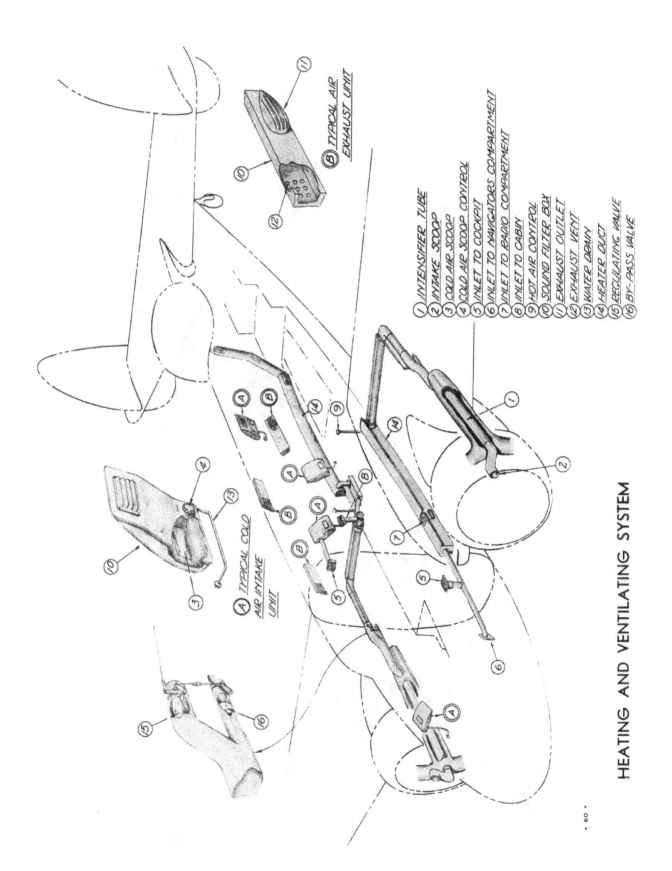

B — TYPICAL AIR EXHAUST UNIT

A — TYPICAL COLD AIR INTAKE UNIT

1. INTENSIFIER TUBE
2. INTAKE SCOOP
3. COLD AIR SCOOP
4. COLD AIR SCOOP CONTROL
5. INLET TO COCKPIT
6. INLET TO NAVIGATORS COMPARTMENT
7. INLET TO RADIO COMPARTMENT
8. INLET TO CABIN
9. HOT AIR CONTROL
10. SOUND FILTER BOX
11. EXHAUST VENT
12. EXHAUST OUTLET
13. WATER DRAIN
14. HEATER DUCT
15. REGULATING VALVE
16. BY-PASS VALVE

HEATING AND VENTILATING SYSTEM

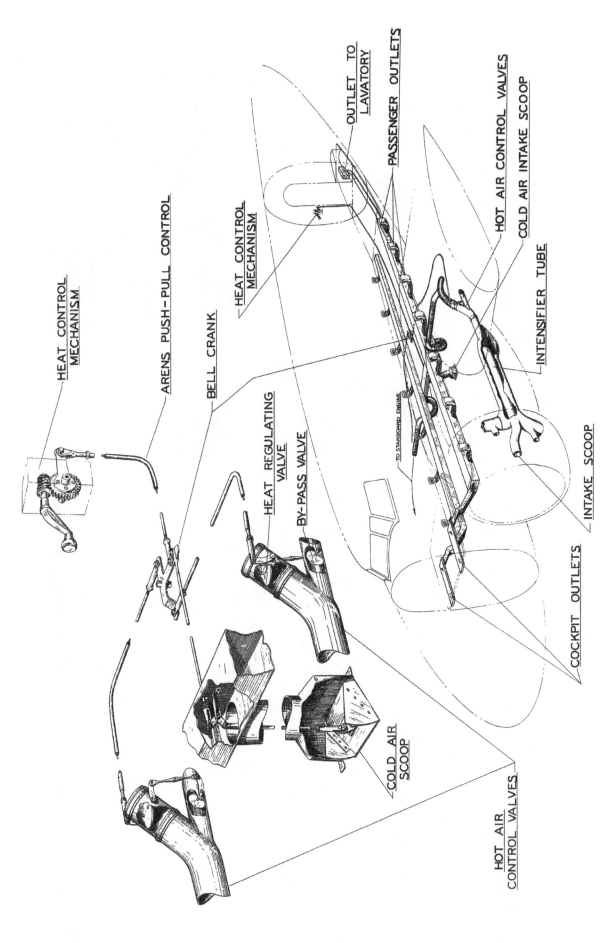

HEAT CONTROL MECHANISM

ARENS PUSH-PULL CONTROL

BELL CRANK

HEAT CONTROL MECHANISM

HEAT REGULATING VALVE

BY-PASS VALVE

OUTLET TO LAVATORY

PASSENGER OUTLETS

HOT AIR CONTROL VALVES

COLD AIR INTAKE SCOOP

INTENSIFIER TUBE

TO STARBOARD ENGINE

INTAKE SCOOP

COCKPIT OUTLETS

COLD AIR SCOOP

HOT AIR CONTROL VALVES

HEATING SYSTEM

7.52

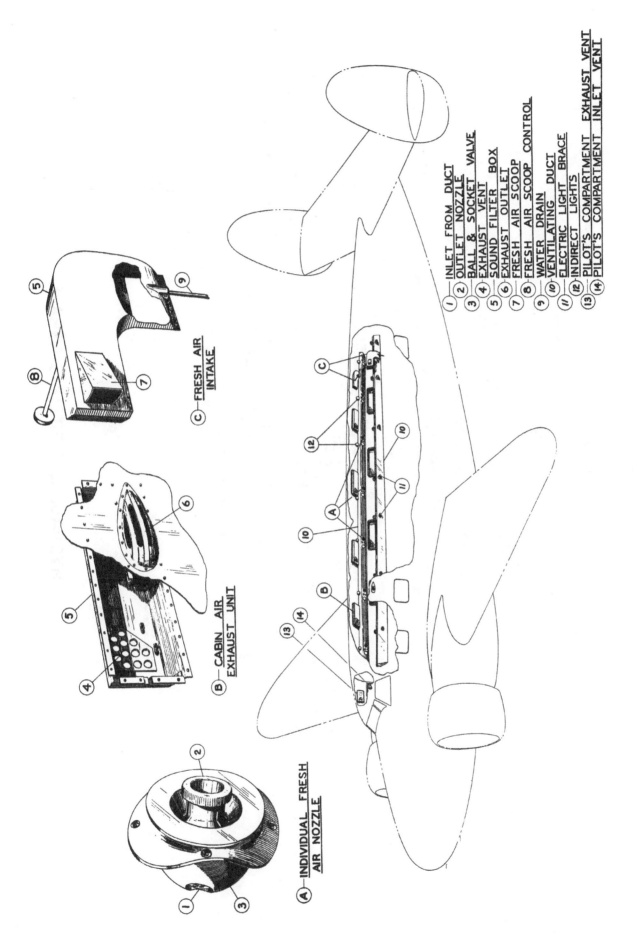

1. INLET FROM DUCT
2. OUTLET NOZZLE
3. BALL & SOCKET VALVE
4. EXHAUST VENT
5. SOUND FILTER BOX
6. EXHAUST OUTLET
7. FRESH AIR SCOOP
8. FRESH AIR SCOOP CONTROL
9. WATER DRAIN
10. VENTILATING DUCT
11. ELECTRIC LIGHT BRACE
12. INDIRECT LIGHTS
13. PILOT'S COMPARTMENT EXHAUST VENT
14. PILOT'S COMPARTMENT INLET VENT

A — INDIVIDUAL FRESH AIR NOZZLE

B — CABIN AIR EXHAUST UNIT

C — FRESH AIR INTAKE

VENTILATING SYSTEM

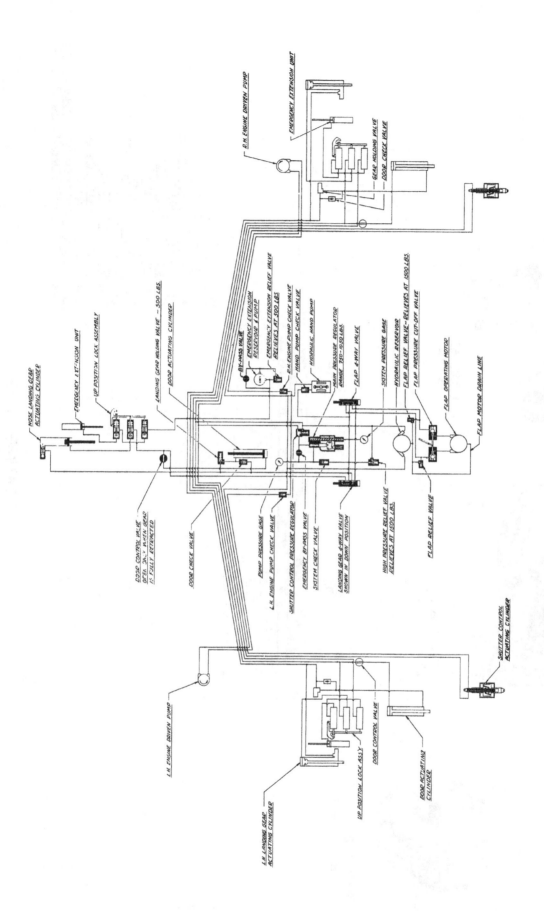

HYDRAULIC SYSTEM DIAGRAM

R.H. ENGINE DRIVEN PUMP

EMERGENCY EXTENSION UNIT

GEAR HOLDING VALVE

DOOR CHECK VALVE

NOSE LANDING GEAR ACTUATING CYLINDER

EMERGENCY EXTENSION UNIT

UP POSITION LOCK ASSEMBLY

LANDING GEAR HOLDING VALVE — 500 LBS.

DOOR ACTUATING CYLINDER

BY-PASS VALVE

EMERGENCY EXTENSION RESERVOIR & PUMP

EMERGENCY EXTENSION RELIEF VALVE RELIEVES AT 500 LBS.

R.H. ENGINE PUMP CHECK VALVE

HAND PUMP CHECK VALVE

HYDRAULIC HAND PUMP

MAIN PRESSURE REGULATOR RANGE 750-1050 LBS.

FLAP 4-WAY VALVE

SYSTEM PRESSURE GAGE

HYDRAULIC RESERVOIR

FLAP RELIEF VALVE—RELIEVES AT 1500 LBS.

FLAP PRESSURE CUT-OFF VALVE

FLAP OPERATING MOTOR

FLAP MOTOR DRAIN LINE

DOOR CONTROL VALVE OPEN ON-Y WHEN GEAR IS FULLY EXTENDED

DOOR CHECK VALVE

PUMP PRESSURE GAGE

L.H. ENGINE PUMP CHECK VALVE

SHUTTER CONTROL PRESSURE REGULATOR

EMERGENCY BY-PASS VALVE

SYSTEM CHECK VALVE

LANDING GEAR 4-WAY VALVE SHOWN IN DOWN POSITION

HIGH PRESSURE RELIEF VALVE RELIEVES AT 1500 LBS.

FLAP RELIEF VALVE

SHUTTER CONTROL ACTUATING CYLINDER

L.H. ENGINE DRIVEN PUMP

L.H. LANDING GEAR ACTUATING CYLINDER

UP POSITION LOCK ASS'Y

DOOR CONTROL VALVE

DOOR ACTUATION CYLINDER

7.54

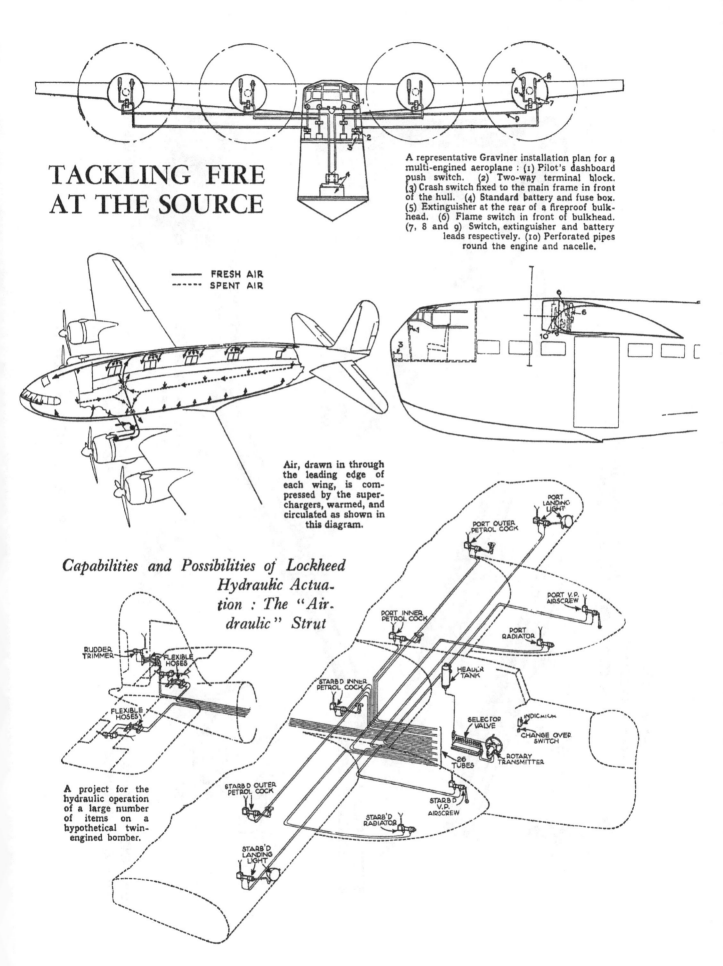

TACKLING FIRE AT THE SOURCE

A representative Graviner installation plan for a multi-engined aeroplane : (1) Pilot's dashboard push switch. (2) Two-way terminal block. (3) Crash switch fixed to the main frame in front of the hull. (4) Standard battery and fuse box. (5) Extinguisher at the rear of a fireproof bulk-head. (6) Flame switch in front of bulkhead. (7, 8 and 9) Switch, extinguisher and battery leads respectively. (10) Perforated pipes round the engine and nacelle.

—— FRESH AIR
----- SPENT AIR

Air, drawn in through the leading edge of each wing, is com-pressed by the super-chargers, warmed, and circulated as shown in this diagram.

Capabilities and Possibilities of Lockheed Hydraulic Actua-tion : The "Air-draulic" Strut

RUDDER TRIMMER
FLEXIBLE HOSES
FLEXIBLE HOSES

A project for the hydraulic operation of a large number of items on a hypothetical twin-engined bomber.

PORT LANDING LIGHT
PORT OUTER PETROL COCK
PORT V.P. AIRSCREW
PORT INNER PETROL COCK
PORT RADIATOR
STARB'D INNER PETROL COCK
HEADER TANK
SELECTOR VALVE
INDICATOR
CHANGE OVER SWITCH
ROTARY TRANSMITTER
26 TUBES
STARB'D OUTER PETROL COCK
STARB'D V.P. AIRSCREW
STARB'D RADIATOR
STARB'D LANDING LIGHT

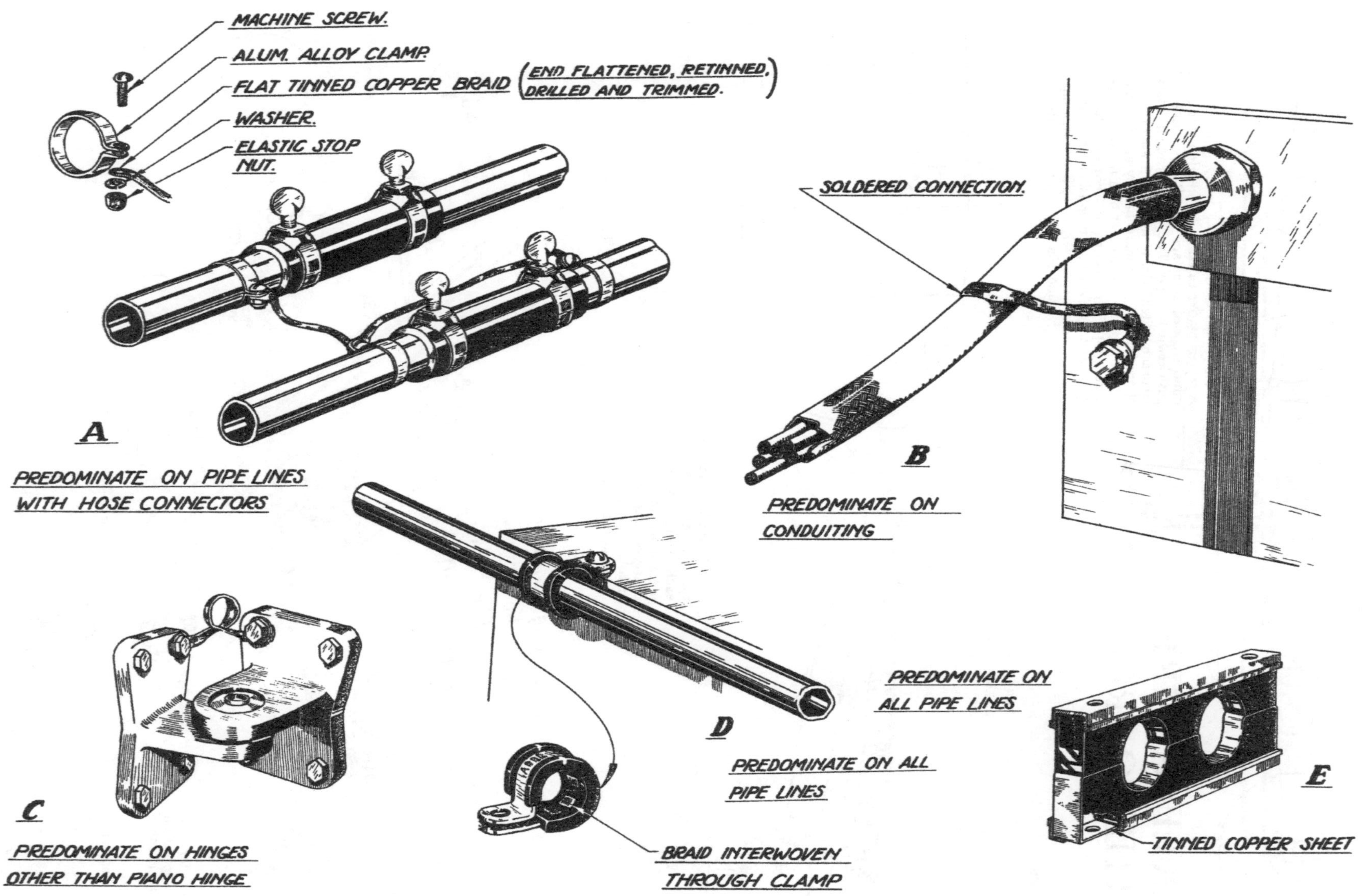

SOLDERED CONNECTION.

B

PREDOMINATE ON
CONDUITING

E

TINNED COPPER SHEET

PREDOMINATE ON
ALL PIPE LINES

PREDOMINATE ON ALL
PIPE LINES

D

BRAID INTERWOVEN
THROUGH CLAMP

MACHINE SCREW.

ALUM. ALLOY CLAMP.

FLAT TINNED COPPER BRAID (END FLATTENED, RETINNED,
DRILLED AND TRIMMED.)

WASHER.

ELASTIC STOP
NUT.

A

PREDOMINATE ON PIPE LINES
WITH HOSE CONNECTORS

C

PREDOMINATE ON HINGES
OTHER THAN PIANO HINGE

TYPICAL BONDING METHODS

7.76

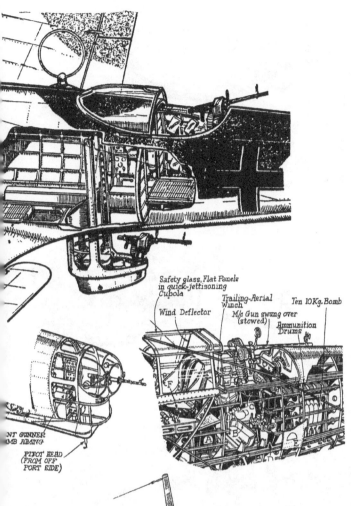

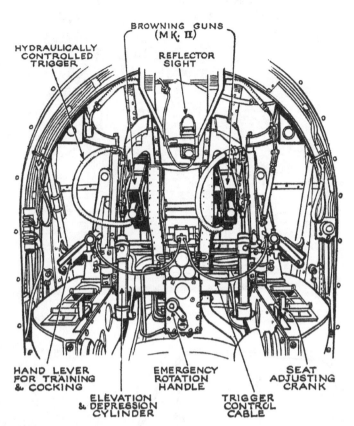

BROWNING GUNS
(M K. II)

HYDRAULICALLY
CONTROLLED
TRIGGER

REFLECTOR
SIGHT

HAND LEVER
FOR TRAINING
& COCKING

ELEVATION
& DEPRESSION
CYLINDER

EMERGENCY
ROTATION
HANDLE

TRIGGER
CONTROL
CABLE

SEAT
ADJUSTING
CRANK

The interior of the Wellington nose turret with some of the
features annotated.

Safety glass, Flat Panels
in quick-jettisoning
Cupola

Trailing-Aerial
Winch

Wind Deflector

M/c Gun swung over
(stowed)

Ten 10 Kg. Bomb

Ammunition
Drums

NT GUNNER
MB AIMING

PITOT HEAD
(FROM OFF
PORT SIDE)

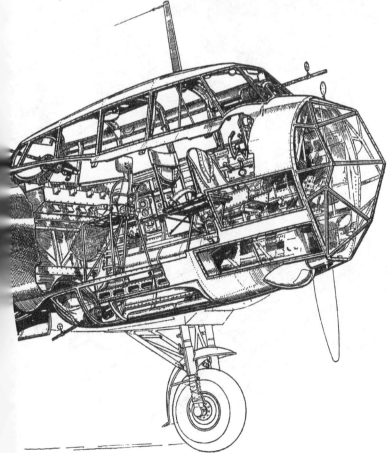

DEFENCE.—The four Brownings in the Nash and Thompson
tail gun-turret of an Armstrong Whitworth Whitley. They have
already proved to be a match for German fighters.

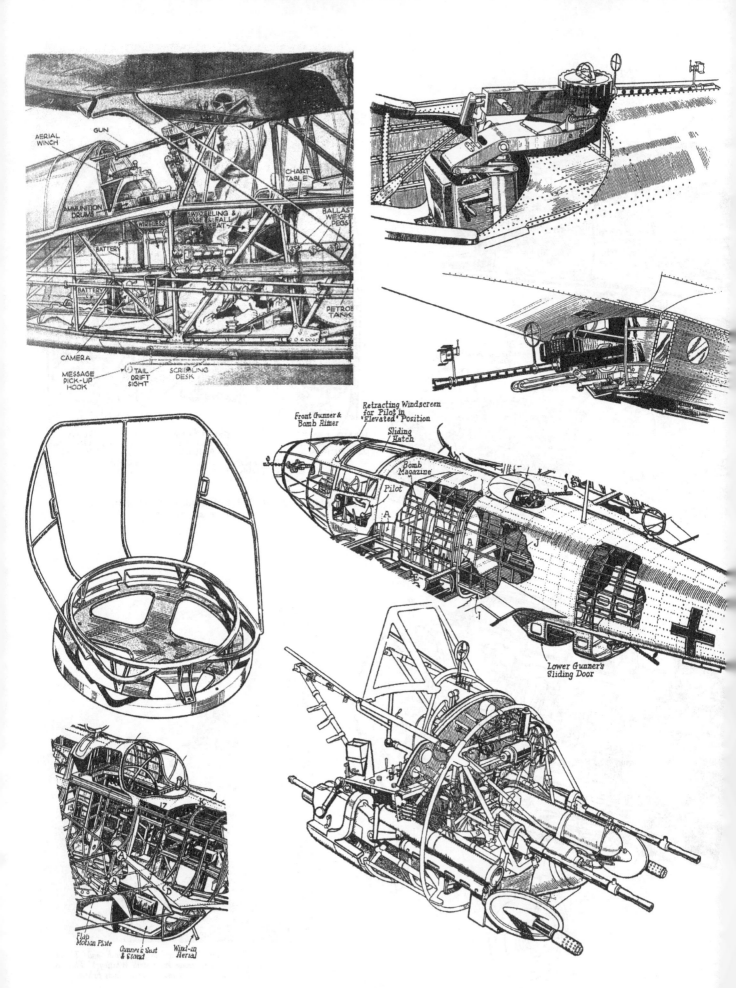

AERIAL WINCH

GUN

CHART TABLE

AMMUNITION DRUMS

BALLAST WEIGHT PEGS

WIRELESS

SWIVELLING & RISE & FALL SEAT

BATTERY

BATTERY

PETROL TANK

CAMERA

MESSAGE PICK-UP HOOK

TAIL DRIFT SIGHT

SCRIBBLING DESK

Front Gunner & Bomb Aimer

Retracting Windscreen for Pilot in 'Elevated' Position

Sliding Hatch

Bomb Magazine

Pilot

Lower Gunner's Sliding Door

Flap Motion Plate

Gunner's Seat & Stand

Wind-in Aerial

8.02

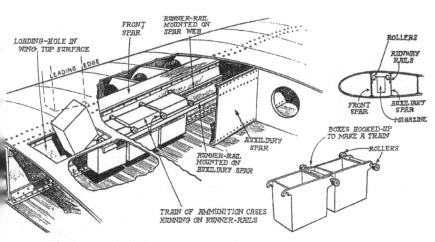

LOADING-HOLE IN
WING TOP SURFACE

LEADING EDGE

FRONT
SPAR

RUNNER-RAIL
MOUNTED ON
SPAR WEB

ROLLERS

RUNWAY
RAILS

FRONT
SPAR

AUXILIARY
SPAR

MAGAZINE

AUXILIARY
SPAR

RUNNER-RAIL
MOUNTED ON
AUXILIARY SPAR

BOXES HOOKED-UP
TO MAKE A TRAIN

ROLLERS

TRAIN OF AMMUNITION CASES
RUNNING ON RUNNER-RAILS

The installation of a 23mm. Madsen shell-gun on a Curtiss Hawk 75. The upper sketch shows how the rear part of the weapon is faired.

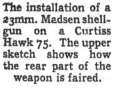

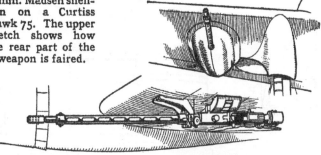

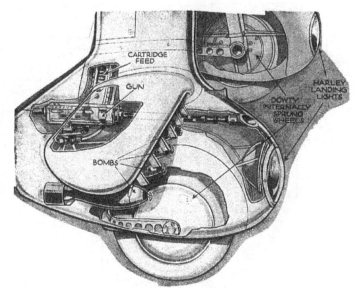

CARTRIDGE
FEED

GUN

HARLEY
LANDING
LIGHTS

DOWTY
INTERNALLY
SPRUNG
WHEELS

BOMBS

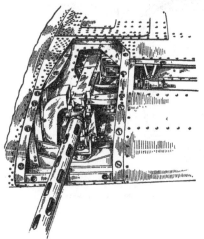

The wing gun installation shown above is typical of many in the present pursuit ships. This one, a .30 caliber, is in the wing of a Republic EP-1 pursuit and is capable of carrying 1000 rounds of ammunition. The container on the right side is the ammunition box, feeding cartridges into the gun through the chute just to the right of the gun. The link ejection chute is located just to the left of the gun and the cartridge cases are ejected through the chute in the bottom below the gun. The rear of the gun has had to be inserted through a hole in the wing spar.

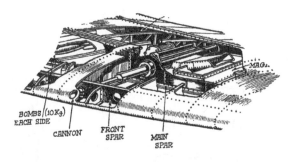

BOMBS (10 Kg)
EACH SIDE

CANNON

FRONT
SPAR

MAIN
SPAR

MAG.

Aspect en vol du Fokker G. 1 « Le Faucheur ».

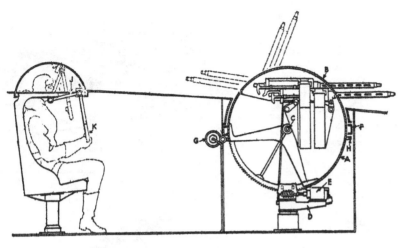

Blackburn elec-
trically controlled turret.

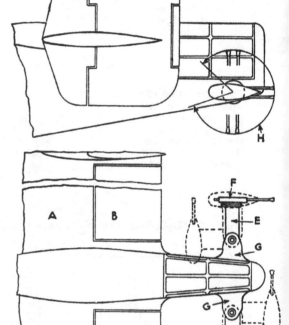

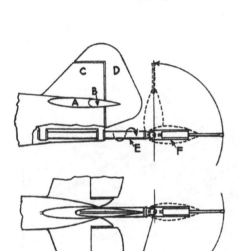

The Boulton
Paul rear gun on
rotatable outrigger.

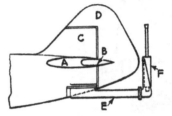

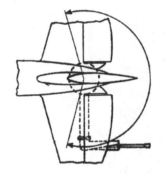

Alternative Boulton
Paul mounting with pivotal
outrigger.

Multi-gun arrangement for large aircraft.

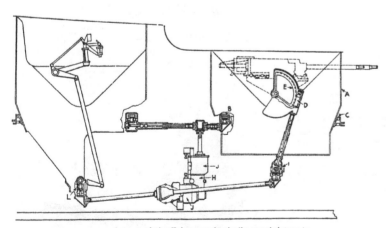

Layout of the Fairey mechanically coupled turrets.

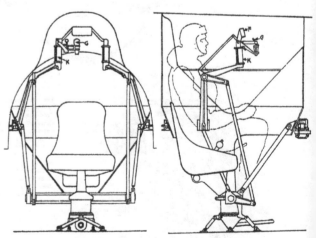

The Fairey sighting turret

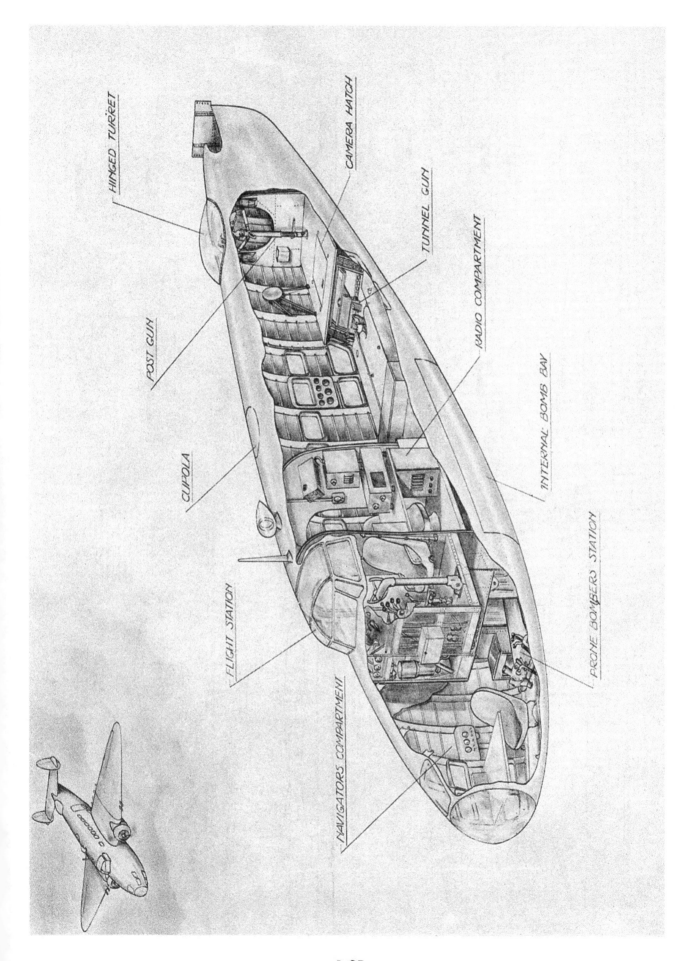

HINGED TURRET

CAMERA HATCH

POST GUN

TUNNEL GUN

RADIO COMPARTMENT

CUPOLA

INTERNAL BOMB BAY

FLIGHT STATION

PRONE BOMBERS STATION

NAVIGATORS COMPARTMENT

8.05

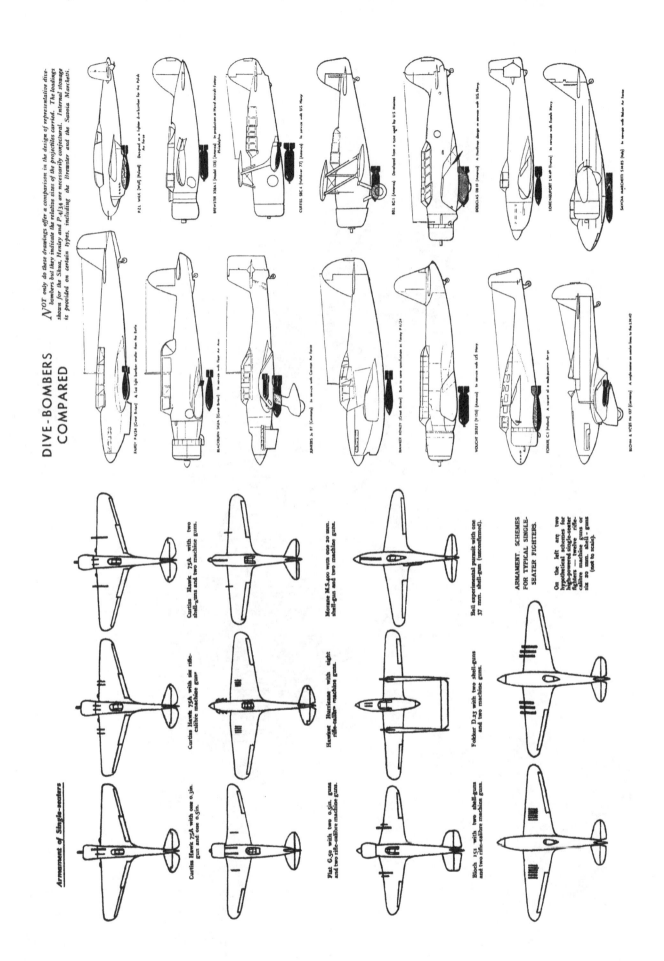

DIVE-BOMBERS COMPARED

NOT only do these drawings offer a comparison in the design of representative dive-bombers but they indicate the relative sizes of the projectiles carried. The loadings shown for the Skua, Henley and P.4/34 are necessarily conjectural. Internal stowage is provided on certain types, including the Brewster and the Savoia Marchetti.

PZL WILK [Wolf] (Poland) Designed as a fighter & co-bomber for the Polish Air Force

BREWSTER XSBA-1 (Model 138) (America) In production at Naval Aircraft Factory Philadelphia

CURTISS SBC-4 (Helldiver 77) (America) In service with U.S. Navy

BELL BC-1 (America) Developed from a type used by U.S. Navy

DOUGLAS DB19 (America) A fighter-design in service with U.S. Navy

LOIRE-NIEUPORT (1nd0 France) In service with French Navy

SAVOIA MARCHETTI S.M.85 (Italy) In service with Italian Air force

FAIREY P.4/34 (Great Britain) A less light bomber smaller than the Battle

BLACKBURN SKUA (Great Britain) In service with Fleet Air Arm

JUNKERS Ju 87 (Germany) In service with German Air force

HAWKER HENLEY (Great Britain) Built to same specification as Fairey P.4/34

VOUGHT SB2U (V-156) In service with U.S. Navy

FOKKER G-1 (Holland) A squad of a multi-purpose design

BLOHM & VOSS Ha 137 (Germany) A replacement on similar lines to the J.U-87

Armament of Single-seaters

Curtiss Hawk 75A with two shell-guns and two machine guns.

Curtiss Hawk 75A with six rifle-calibre machine guns

Curtiss Hawk 75A with one 0.5in. gun and two rifle-calibre machine guns.

Morane M.S.400 with one 20 mm. shell-gun and two machine guns.

Hawker Hurricane with eight rifle-calibre machine guns.

Flat G.50 with two 0.5in. guns and two rifle-calibre machine guns.

Bell experimental pursuit with one 37 mm. shell-gun (unconfirmed).

Fokker D.23 with two shell-guns and two machine guns.

Bloch 151 with two shell-guns and two rifle-calibre machine guns.

ARMAMENT SCHEMES FOR TYPICAL SINGLE-SEATER FIGHTERS.

On the left are two hypothetical schemes for high-powered single-seater fighters — twelve rifle-calibre machine guns or six 20 mm. shell-guns (not to scale).

MULTI-PURPOSE

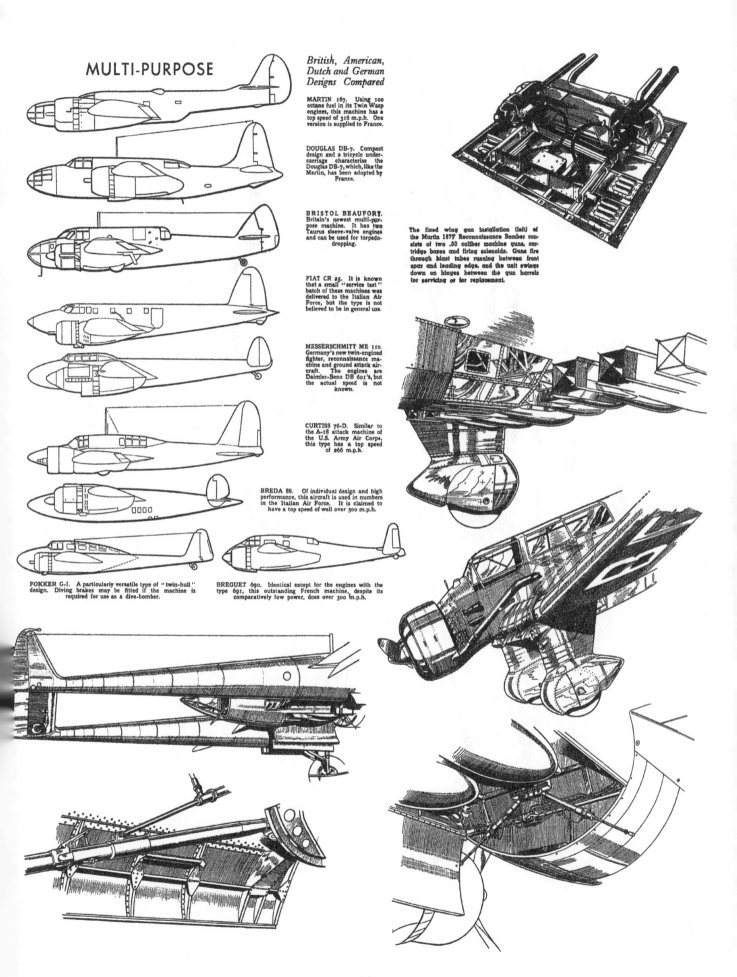

MARTIN 167. Using 100 octane fuel in its Twin Wasp engines, this machine has a top speed of 316 m.p.h. One version is supplied to France.

DOUGLAS DB-7. Compact design and a tricycle under-carriage characterise the Douglas DB-7, which, like the Martin, has been adopted by France.

BRISTOL BEAUFORT. Britain's newest multi-purpose machine. It has two Taurus sleeve-valve engines and can be used for torpedo-dropping.

FIAT CR 25. It is known that a small "service test" batch of these machines was delivered to the Italian Air Force, but the type is not believed to be in general use.

MESSERSCHMITT ME 110. Germany's new twin-engined fighter, reconnaissance machine and ground attack aircraft. The engines are Daimler-Benz DB 601's, but the actual speed is not known.

CURTISS 76-D. Similar to the A-18 attack machine of the U.S. Army Air Corps, this type has a top speed of 266 m.p.h.

BREDA 88. Of individual design and high performance, this aircraft is used in numbers in the Italian Air Force. It is claimed to have a top speed of well over 300 m.p.h.

FOKKER G-I. A particularly versatile type of "twin-hull" design. Diving brakes may be fitted if the machine is required for use as a dive-bomber.

BREGUET 690. Identical except for the engines with the type 691, this outstanding French machine, despite its comparatively low power, does over 300 m.p.h.

The fixed wing gun installation (left) of the Martin 187F Reconnaissance Bomber consists of two .30 caliber machine guns, cartridge boxes and firing solenoids. Guns fire through blast tubes running between front spar and leading edge, and the unit swings down on hinges between the gun barrels for servicing or for replacement.

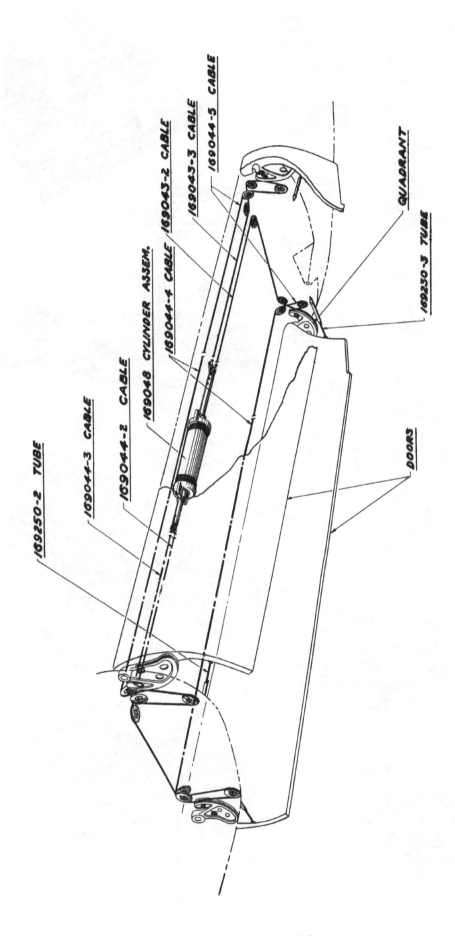

BOMB DOOR OPERATION

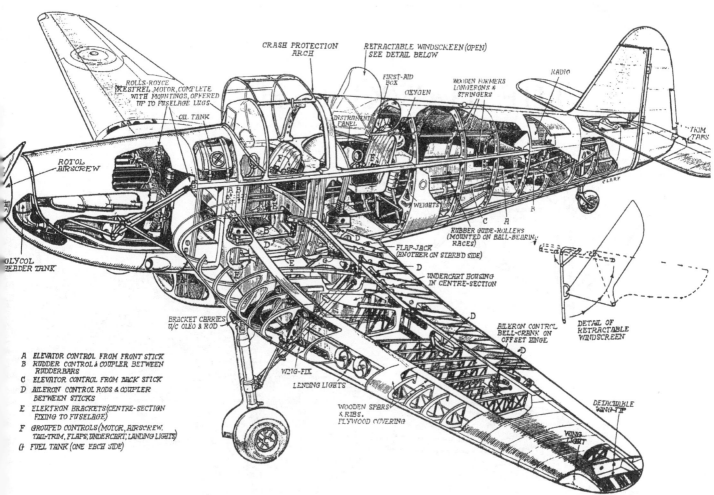

CRASH PROTECTION ARCH

RETRACTABLE WINDSCREEN (OPEN) SEE DETAIL BELOW

FIRST-AID BOX

OXYGEN

WOODEN FORMERS LONGERONS & STRINGERS

RADIO

ROLLS-ROYCE KESTREL MOTOR, COMPLETE WITH MOUNTINGS, OFFERED UP TO FUSELAGE LUGS

OIL TANK

INSTRUMENT PANEL

TRIM TABS

ROTOL AIRSCREW

GLARY

GLYCOL HEADER TANK

WEIGHTS

RUBBER GUIDE-ROLLERS (MOUNTED ON BALL-BEARING RACES)

FLAP-JACK (ANOTHER ON STARB'D SIDE)

UNDERCART HOUSING IN CENTRE-SECTION

BRACKET CARRIES U/C OLEO & ROD

WING-FIX

LANDING LIGHTS

WOODEN SPARS & RIBS, PLYWOOD COVERING

AILERON CONTROL BELL-CRANK ON OFFSET HINGE

DETAIL OF RETRACTABLE WINDSCREEN

DETACHABLE WING-TIP

WING LIGHT

A ELEVATOR CONTROL FROM FRONT STICK
B RUDDER CONTROL & COUPLER BETWEEN RUDDERBARS
C ELEVATOR CONTROL FROM BACK STICK
D AILERON CONTROL RODS & COUPLER BETWEEN STICKS
E ELEKTRON BRACKETS (CENTRE-SECTION FIXING TO FUSELAGE)
F GROUPED CONTROLS (MOTOR, AIRSCREW, TAIL-TRIM, FLAPS, UNDERCART, LANDING LIGHTS)
G FUEL TANK (ONE EACH SIDE)

The Miles "Master" Advanced Training Monoplane (Rolls-Royce "Kestrel" engine).

FOLDING AERIAL STRUT

PILOT'S OXYGEN MASK

MAIN OIL COOLER

PETROL TANK

SLIDING COWL

WIRELESS TUNING

VICKERS GUN IN FUSELAGE

AMMUNITION BOXES

SPENT AMMUNITION BOXES

OIL COOLER AND COCKPIT HEATER

BRISTOL SUPERCHARGED MERCURY ENGINE

THE HAWKER HENLEY

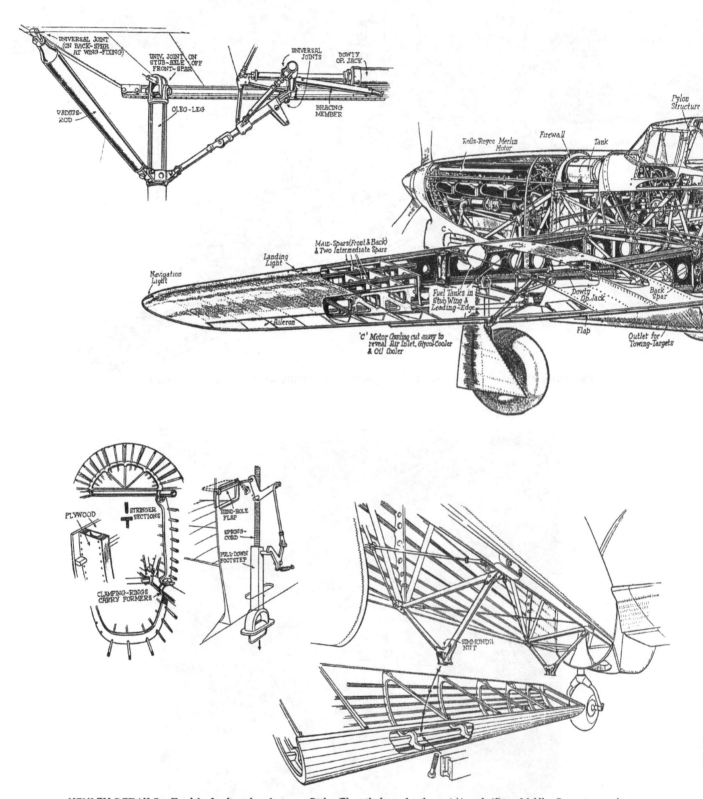

UNIVERSAL JOINT
(ON BACK-SPAR
AT WING-FIXING)

UNIV. JOINT ON
STUB-AXLE OFF
FRONT-SPAR

UNIVERSAL
JOINTS

DOWTY
OP. JACK

RADIUS-
ROD

OLEO-LEG

BRACING
MEMBER

Pylon
Structure

Rolls-Royce Merlin
Motor

Firewall

Tank

Main-Spars (Front & Back)
& Two Intermediate Spars

Landing
Light

Navigation
Light

Fuel Tanks in
Stub Wing &
Leading-Edge

Dowty
Op. Jack

Back
Spar

Aileron

'C' Motor Cowling cut away to
reveal Air Inlet, Glycol-Cooler
& Oil Cooler

Flap

Outlet for
Towing-Targets

PLYWOOD

STRINGER
SECTIONS

HAND-HOLE
FLAP

SPRING-
CORD

PULL-DOWN
FOOTSTEP

CLAMPING-RINGS
CARRY FORMERS

SIMMONDS
NUT

HENLEY DETAILS.—Top left, Leading edge of wing.   Right, The tail-plane, details at (A) and (B).   Middle, Retracting mechanism
of undercarriage.   Bottom, Left, Aft part of fuselage fairing.   Middle, Link gear of steps.   Right, Detachable fairing under end of fuselage.

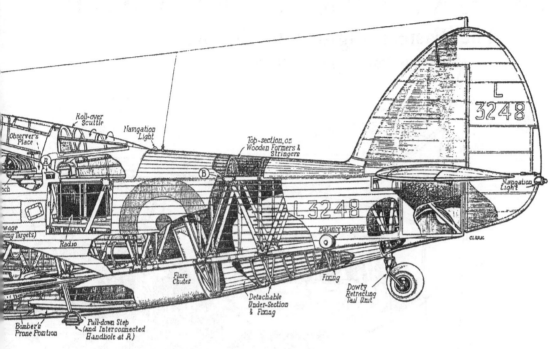

Roll-over Scuttle

Observer's Place

Navigation Light

Top-section, or Wooden Formers & Stringers

L 3248

Balance Weight(s)

Navigation Light

CLARK.

Radio

Flare Chutes

Detachable Under-Section & Fixing

Fixing

Dowty Retracting Tail Unit

Bomber's Prone Position

Pull-down Step (and Interconnected Handhole at A.)

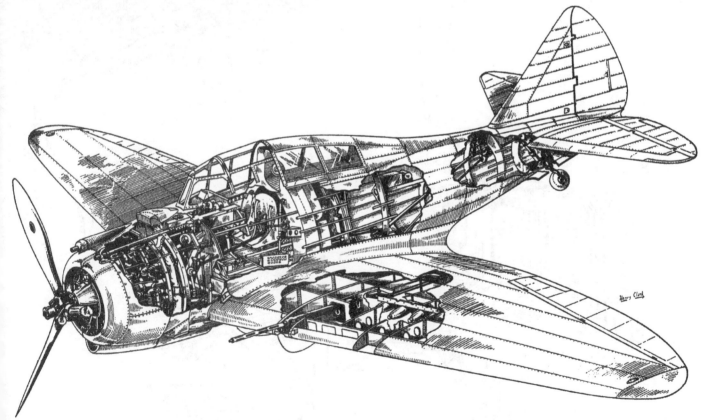

Henry Clark

THE HAWKER HURRICANE
The Fastest Fighter in Service
(Rolls-Royce 1,050 h.p. Merlin)

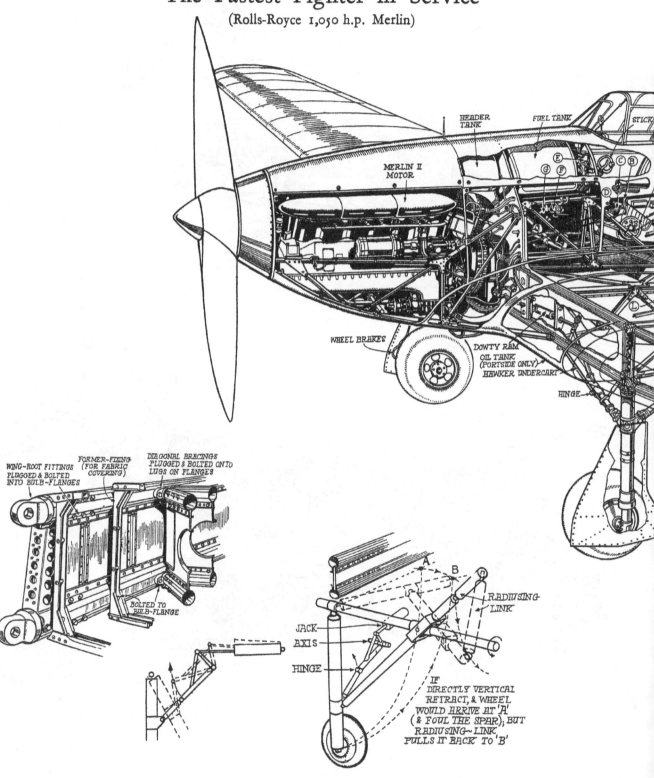

HEADER TANK

FUEL TANK

STICK

MERLIN II MOTOR

E

G F

C B

D

L

WHEEL BRAKES

DOWTY RAM OIL TANK (PORTSIDE ONLY) HAWKER UNDERCART

HINGE

WING~ROOT FITTINGS PLUGGED & BOLTED INTO BULB~FLANGES

FORMER~FIXING (FOR FABRIC COVERING)

DIAGONAL BRACINGS PLUGGED & BOLTED ONTO LUGS ON FLANGES

BOLTED TO BULB~FLANGE

A B

RADIUSING LINK

JACK

AXIS

HINGE

IF DIRECTLY VERTICAL RETRACT, & WHEEL WOULD ARRIVE AT 'A' (& FOUL THE SPAR); BUT RADIUSING~LINK PULLS IT BACK TO 'B'

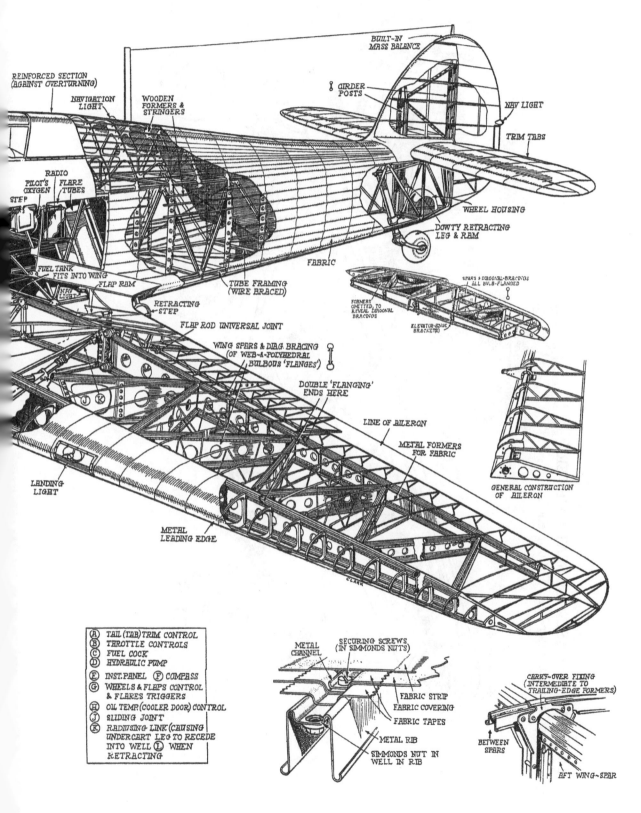

REINFORCED SECTION
(AGAINST OVERTURNING)

NAVIGATION
LIGHT

WOODEN
FORMERS &
STRINGERS

BUILT-IN
MASS BALANCE

GIRDER
POSTS

NAV LIGHT

TRIM TABS

RADIO
FLARE
TUBES

PILOT'S
OXYGEN

STEP

WHEEL HOUSING

DOWTY RETRACTING
LEG & RAM

FUEL TANK
FITS INTO WING

FLAP RAM

NAV
LIGHT

TUBE FRAMING
(WIRE BRACED)

FABRIC

SPARS & DIAGONAL-BRACINGS
ALL BULB-FLANGED

FORMERS
OMITTED, TO
REVEAL DIAGONAL
BRACINGS

ELEVATOR-HINGE
BRACKETS

RETRACTING
STEP

FLAP ROD UNIVERSAL JOINT

WING SPARS & DIAG. BRACING
(OF WEB-&-POLYHEDRAL
BULBOUS 'FLANGES')

DOUBLE 'FLANGING'
ENDS HERE

LINE OF AILERON

METAL FORMERS
FOR FABRIC

GENERAL CONSTRUCTION
OF AILERON

LANDING
LIGHT

METAL
LEADING EDGE

CLARK

A TAIL (TAB) TRIM CONTROL
B THROTTLE CONTROLS
C FUEL COCK
D HYDRAULIC PUMP
E INST. PANEL F COMPASS
G WHEELS & FLAPS CONTROL
   & FLARES TRIGGERS
H OIL TEMP. (COOLER DOOR) CONTROL
J SLIDING JOINT
K RADIUSING LINK (CAUSING
   UNDERCART LEG TO RECEDE
   INTO WELL L WHEN
   RETRACTING

METAL
CHANNEL

SECURING SCREWS
(IN SIMMONDS NUTS)

FABRIC STRIP
FABRIC COVERING
FABRIC TAPES

METAL RIB

SIMMONDS NUT IN
WELL IN RIB

CARRY-OVER FIXING
(INTERMEDIATE TO
TRAILING-EDGE FORMERS)

BETWEEN
SPARS

AFT WING-SPAR

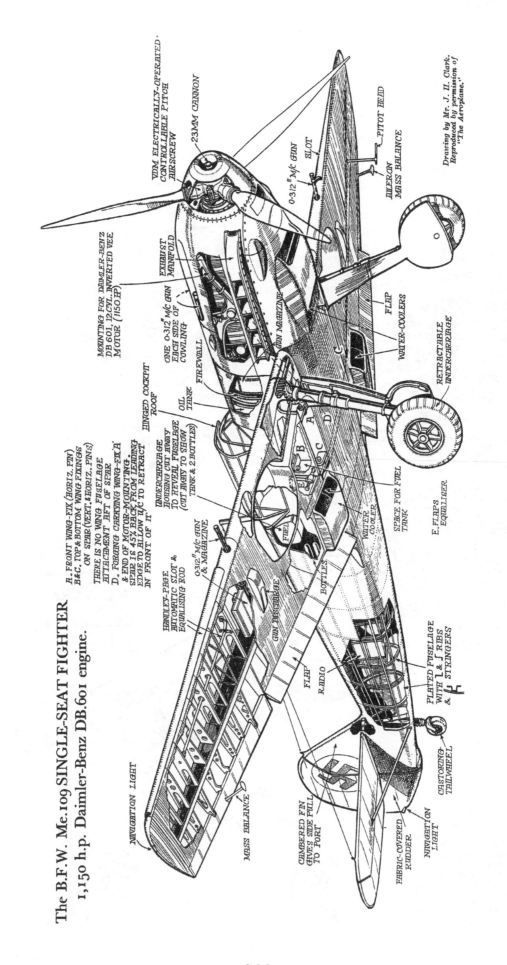

The B.F.W. Me.109 SINGLE-SEAT FIGHTER
1,150 h.p. Daimler-Benz DB.601 engine.

VDM ELECTRICALLY-OPERATED CONTROLLABLE PITCH AIRSCREW

23MM CANNON

0·3½" M/c GUN

SLOT

PITOT HEAD

AILERON MASS BALANCE

*Drawing by Mr. J. H. Clark.
Reproduced by permission of
"The Aeroplane."*

MOUNTING FOR DAIMLER-BENZ DB 601, 12.CYL. INVERTED VEE MOTOR (1150 HP)

EXHAUST MANIFOLD

GUN MAGAZINE

ONE 0·3½" M/c GUN EACH SIDE OF COWLING

FIREWALL

FLAP

WATER-COOLERS

OIL TANK

HINGED COCKPIT ROOF

RETRACTABLE UNDERCARRIAGE

A. FRONT WING-FIX (HORIZ. PIN)
B & C. TOP & BOTTOM WING-FIXINGS ON SPAR (VERT. & HORIZ. PINS)

THERE IS NO WING FUSELAGE ATTACHMENT AFT OF SPAR
D. FORMING CARRYING WING-FIX 'A'
& END OF MOTOR-MOUNTING.
SPAR IS 45% BACK FROM LEADING EDGE TO ALLOW U/C TO RETRACT IN FRONT OF IT

UNDERCARRIAGE HOUSING CUT AWAY TO REVEAL FUSELAGE (CUT AWAY TO SHOW TANK & 2 BOTTLES)

WATER COOLER

SPACE FOR FUEL TANK

E. FLAPS EQUALISER

HANDLEY-PAGE AUTOMATIC SLOT & EQUALISING ROD

0·3½" M/c GUN & MAGAZINE

FUEL

BOTTLES

GUN DISCHARGE

NAVIGATION LIGHT

MASS BALANCE

FLAP

RADIO

PLATED FUSELAGE WITH ⌐ & ⌐ RIBS & ⌐ STRINGERS

CAMBERED FIN GIVES SIDE PULL TO PORT

FABRIC-COVERED RUDDER

CASTORING TAILWHEEL

NAVIGATION LIGHT

THE HENSCHEL Hs 126 RECONNAISSANCE MONOPLANE

(870 h.p. B.M.W. 132Dc Nine-cylinder Radial Motor)

Landing Light

2-Spar Dural Wing

Safety glass, Flat Panels in quick-jettisoning Cupola

Wind Deflector

Fork & Starb'd Spars Coupling

Fixed Machine Gun & Magazine

Ball & Socket Motor Mounts to Firewall

BMW 132 Dc Motor 870 H.P. VDM Airscrews NACH Cowling

Oil Tank

Fixed Front Ring

Detachable Panels

Hydraulically Actuated Gills

Oil Cooling Air Outlet

Oil Cooler

Carburetter Air Intake

Aerodynamically clean Fairing (undercarriage/fuselage)

Swing-out Steps for Motor servicing

Wheels have Hydraulic Brakes

Trailing-Aerial Winch

Ten 10Kg. Bombs

M/c Gun swung over (stowed)

Ammunition Drums

Wireless Generator

Trailing Aerial Lead-in

Fuel Tank

Longeron

Longeron

Step

Fabric-covered Rudder

Trim & Balance Tabs

Elevator adjustable on ground

Elevator Actuating Links

Fabric-covered Elevator

Rudder Lower Bearing

Castoring Tailwheel

2-Spar Two-Piece Fin

2-Spar Tailplane

Skin Plating in Large Panels (detachable for easy assembly & maintenance)

Hydraulic Camber-changing Flaps

Fabric-covered Aileron with Trim & Balance Tabs

Spars

II

Rib Pressures (Nose, Middle & Trailing) rivetted to Spars

Sheet metal spars with Pressed Profile Flanges

A = Radio
B = Gunner's Stand & Folding Seat
C = M/c Gun Spent Cases exit
D = Camera   E = Footstep
F = All Pilot's Controls are on Port & Starboard sides
G = Detail of Monocoque formers & Stringers
H = Depress top of Rudder Pedals to operate Hydraulic Wheelbrakes

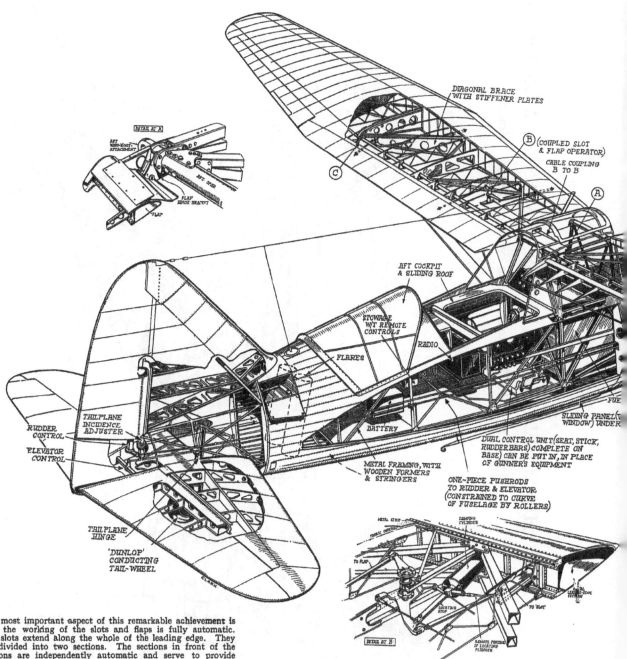

DETAIL AT A

AFT WING-ROOT ATTACHMENT

AFT SPAR

FLAP HINGE BRACKET

FLAP

DIAGONAL BRACE WITH STIFFENER PLATES

Ⓑ (COUPLED SLOT & FLAP OPERATOR)

CABLE COUPLING B TO B

Ⓒ

Ⓐ

AFT COCKPIT & SLIDING ROOF

STOWAGE W/T REMOTE CONTROLS

RADIO

FLARES

BATTERY

SLIDING PANEL (WINDOW) UNDER

FUE

DUAL CONTROL UNIT (SEAT, STICK, RUDDER BARS) COMPLETE ON BASE) CAN BE PUT IN, IN PLACE OF GUNNER'S EQUIPMENT

ONE-PIECE PUSHRODS TO RUDDER & ELEVATOR (CONSTRAINED TO CURVE OF FUSELAGE BY ROLLERS)

METAL FRAMING, WITH WOODEN FORMERS & STRINGERS

RUDDER CONTROL

ELEVATOR CONTROL

TAILPLANE INCIDENCE ADJUSTER

TAILPLANE HINGE

'DUNLOP' CONDUCTING TAIL-WHEEL

CLARK

METAL STRIP

RAMMING CYLINDER

TO FLAP

TO 'SLOT'

LOCATING STOP

DETAIL AT B

REMOTE CONTROL OF LOCATING PLUNGER

A most important aspect of this remarkable achievement is that the working of the slots and flaps is fully automatic. The slots extend along the whole of the leading edge. They are divided into two sections. The sections in front of the ailerons are independently automatic and serve to provide lateral stability and lateral control at large angles of incidence and slow speeds.

The inner sections of the slots are coupled together and also coupled to the slotted flaps which extend inwards along the trailing edges of the wings from the ailerons to the fuselage. As the slots open, so they pull down the flaps. The action is completely automatic and completely independent of the pilot except in so far as movement of the normal controls by the pilot controls the attitude of the aeroplane.

A further idea of the improvements conferred by the use of slots and flaps is given by the relative performances with the slots and flaps open, or free to open, and with slots and flaps locked shut. Loaded to a weight of 5,500 lb. the minimum speed is 61 m.p.h. with the slots and flaps open. If these are locked shut, the speed goes up to 82 m.p.h.

At this weight the take-off is 103 yds. This becomes 226 yds. with the slots and flaps locked shut. The normal landing run with brakes is 160 yds. Without slots and flaps the run becomes 298 yds.

Some tests were made to determine how much these qualitie could be attributed to the slots, how much to the flaps, an also how much to the variable-pitch airscrew. With the slot closed and the flaps pulled down, the minimum speed becam 69 m.p.h.—only 13 m.p.h. better than the speed with bot slots and flaps shut.

By taking off with the airscrew in coarse pitch instead of i fine pitch, the take-off was increased from 103 to 172 yds So the controllability of the airscrew-pitch does not accoun for the whole of the excellent take-off.

This 103 yds. to take-off could be even further decreased b holding the flaps right down in the locked-open position instea of allowing them to work automatically. The take-off ru was then reduced to 80 yds. but the climb was not so good.

WESTLAND LYSANDER

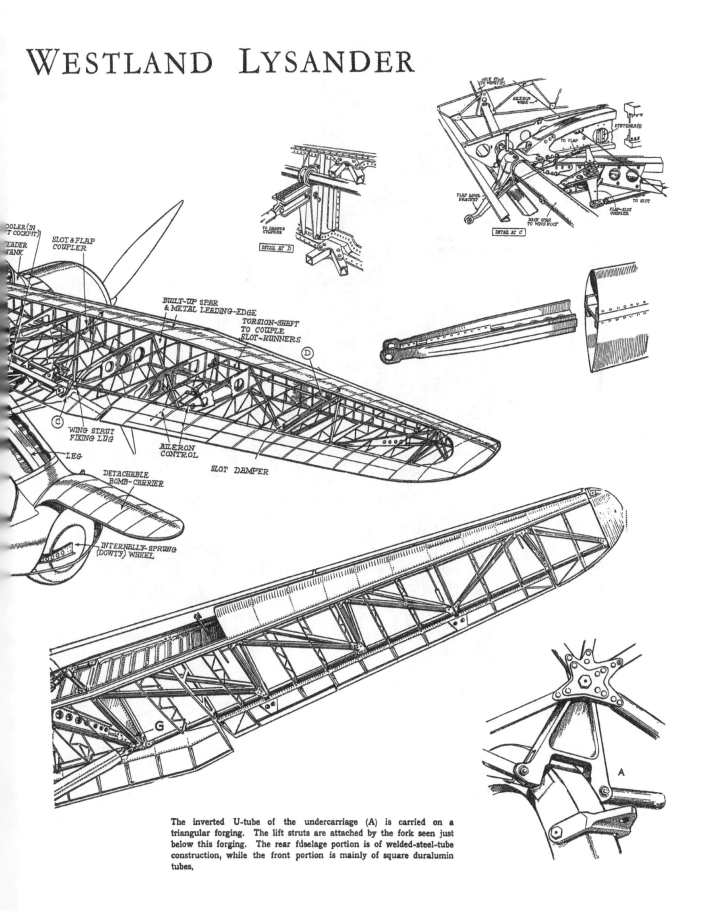

DETAIL AT D

ROCK STRUT (TO WINGTIP)

AILERON WIRE

STIFFENER(S)

TO FLAP

FLAP ANGLE BRACKET

TO SLOT

BACK SPAR TO WING ROOT

FLAP-SLOT COUPLER

DETAIL AT C

COOLER (IN T COCKPIT)

LEADER TANK

SLOT & FLAP COUPLER

BUILT-UP SPAR & METAL LEADING-EDGE

TORSION-SHAFT TO COUPLE SLOT-RUNNERS

D

C

WING STRUT FIXING LUG

AILERON CONTROL

LEG

SLOT DAMPER

DETACHABLE BOMB-CARRIER

INTERNALLY-SPRUNG (DOWTY) WHEEL

G

A

The inverted U-tube of the undercarriage (A) is carried on a triangular forging. The lift struts are attached by the fork seen just below this forging. The rear fuselage portion is of welded-steel-tube construction, while the front portion is mainly of square duralumin tubes.

THE BLACKBURN SKUA FIGHTER DIVE-BOMBER

(830 h.p. Bristol Perseus Sleeve-valve Motor)

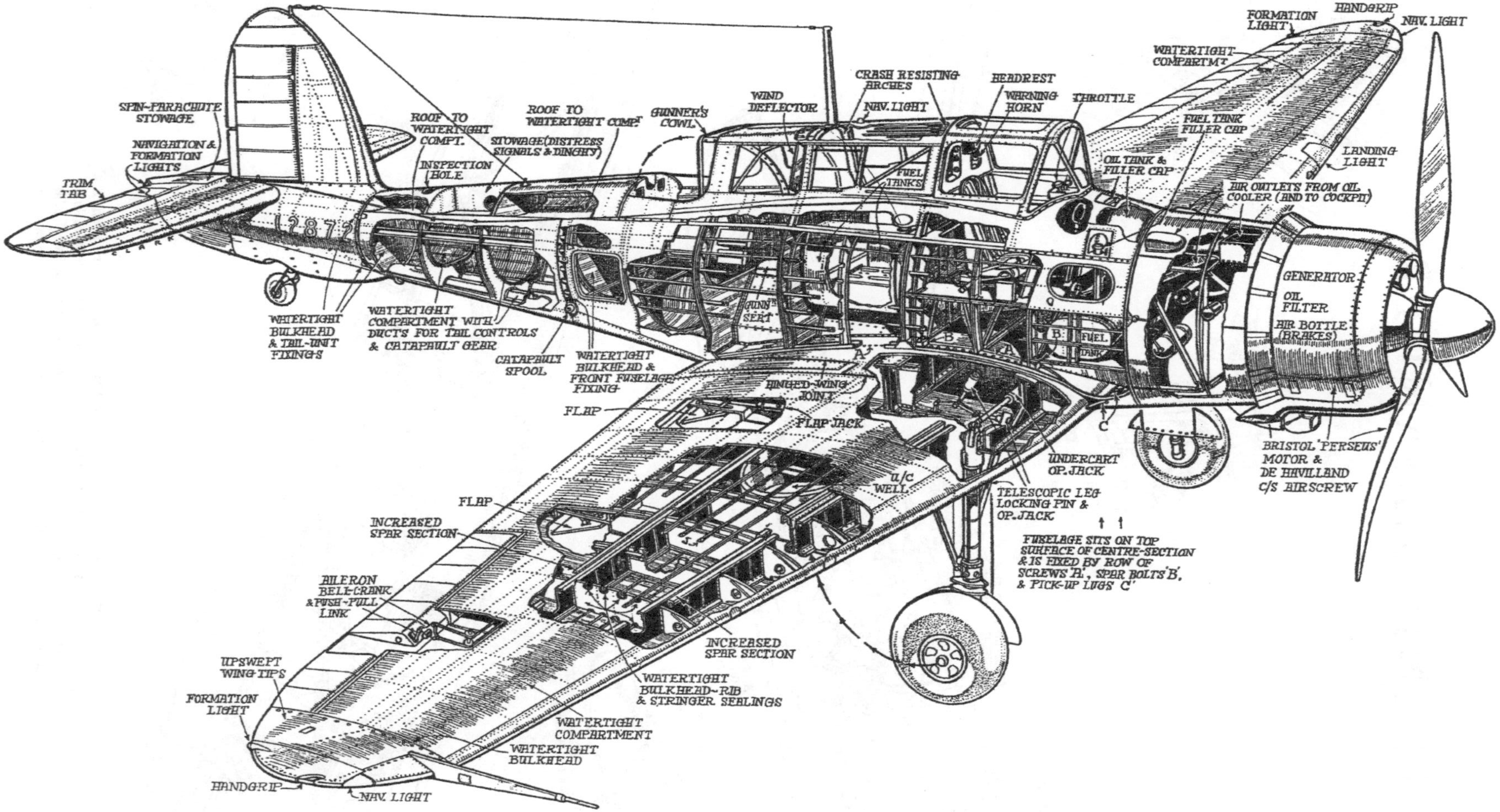

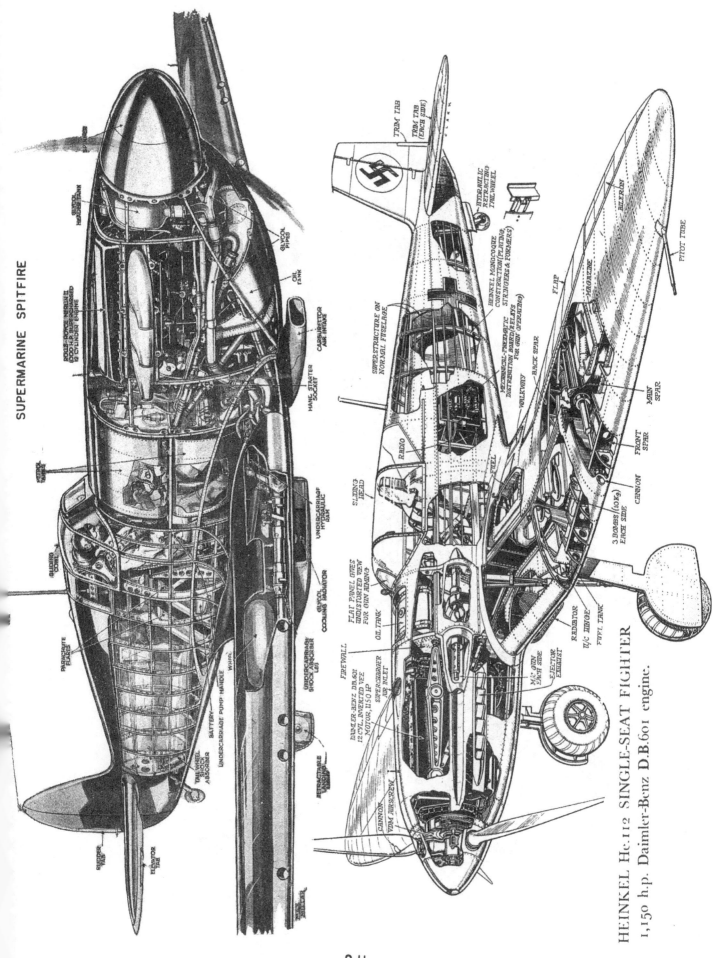

SUPERMARINE SPITFIRE

GLYCOL HEADER TANK

OIL TANK

ROLLS-ROYCE MERLIN II 1000 H.P. SUPERCHARGED 12 CYLINDER ENGINE

CARBURETTOR AIR INTAKE

HAND STARTER SOCKET

UNDERCARRIAGE HYDRAULIC RAM

GLYCOL COOLING RADIATOR

SLIDING COWL

PARACHUTE FLARES

BATTERY

UNDERCARRIAGE PUMP HANDLE

WHEEL

UNDERCARRIAGE SHOCK ABSORBER LEG

TAIL WHEEL SHOCK ABSORBER

RETRACTABLE LANDING

RUDDER TAB

ELEVATOR TAB

TRIM TAB

TRIM TAB (EACH SIDE)

HYDRAULIC RETRACTING TAIL WHEEL

HEINKEL MONOCOQUE CONSTRUCTION (PLATING, STRINGERS & FORMERS)

MECHANICAL-PNEUMATIC DISTRIBUTION BOARD (RELAYS FOR GUN OPENING)

SUPERSTRUCTURE ON NORMAL FUSELAGE

WALKWAY

BACK SPAR

AILERON

FLAP

MAGAZINE

FUEL

MAIN SPAR

FRONT SPAR

PITOT TUBE

RADIO

SLIDING HEAD

FLAT PANEL GIVES UNDISTORTED VIEW FOR GUN AIMING

OIL TANK

FIREWALL

DAIMLER-BENZ DB.601 12 CYL. INVERTED VEE MOTOR, 1150 HP

SUPERCHARGER AIR INLET

CANNON

3 BOMBS (10 Kg.) EACH SIDE

CANNON

RADIATOR

U/c HINGE

FUEL TANK

M/c GUN EACH SIDE

EJECTOR EXHAUST

VDM AIRSCREW

HEINKEL He.112 SINGLE-SEAT FIGHTER
1,150 h.p. Daimler-Benz D.B.601 engine.

9.11

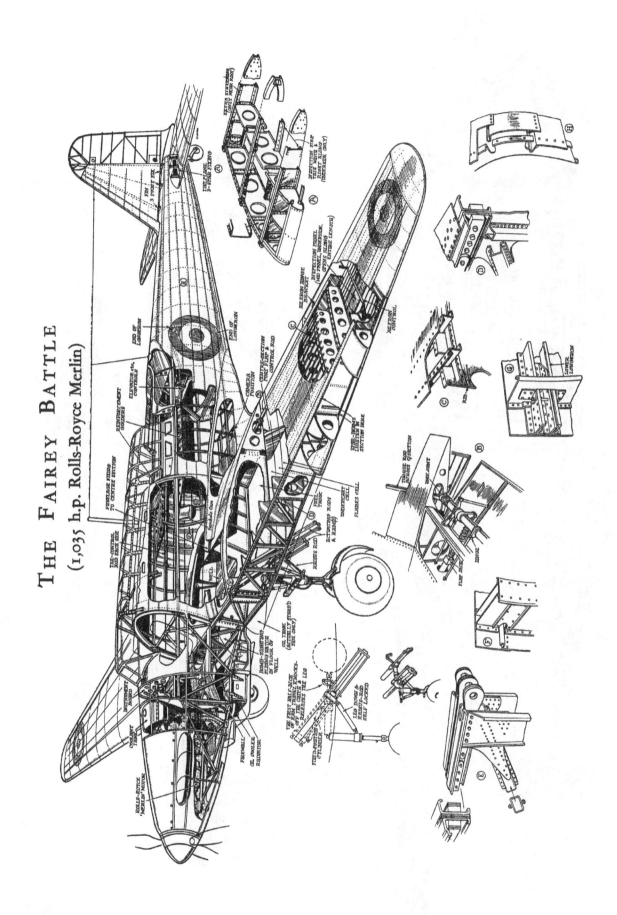

THE FAIREY BATTLE
(1,035 h.p. Rolls-Royce Merlin)

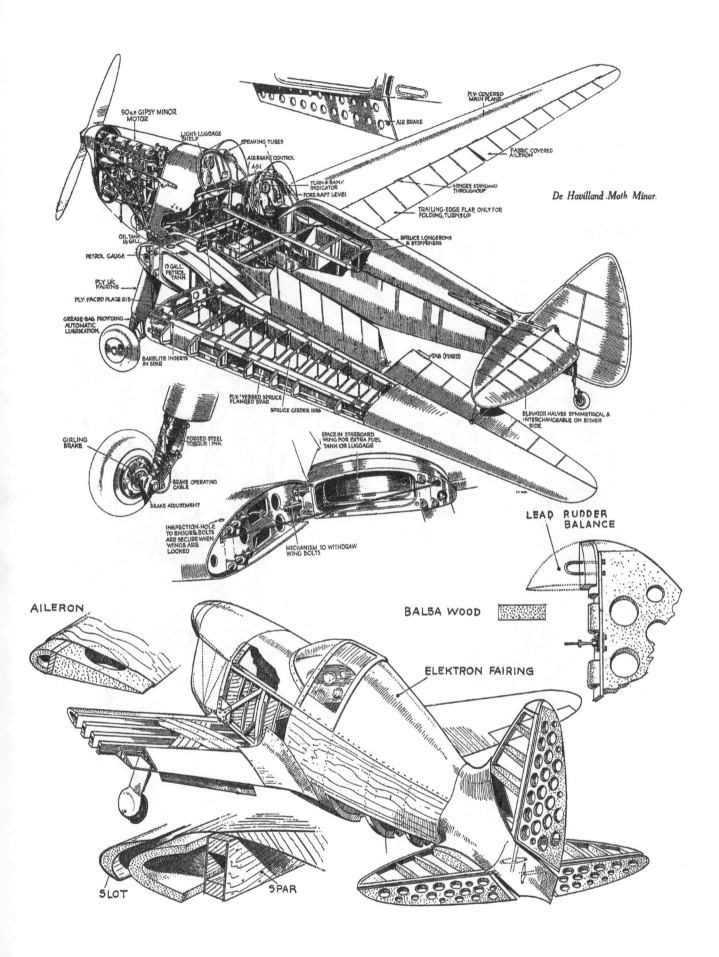

90 H.P. GIPSY MINOR MOTOR

LIGHT-LUGGAGE SHELF

SPEAKING TUBES

AIR-BRAKE CONTROL A.S.I

TURN & BANK INDICATOR

FORE & AFT LEVEL

OIL TANK ½ GALL

PETROL GAUGE

PLY U/C FAIRING

PLY-FACED PLATE RIB

GREASE-BAG PROVIDING AUTOMATIC LUBRICATION

BAKELITE INSERTS IN SPAR

15 GALL. PETROL TANK

PLY-WEBBED SPRUCE FLANGED SPAR

SPRUCE GIRDER RIBS

PLY-COVERED MAIN PLANE

AIR BRAKE

FABRIC COVERED AILERON

HINGES STANDARD THROUGHOUT

TRAILING-EDGE FLAP, ONLY FOR FOLDING, TURNS UP

SPRUCE LONGERONS & STIFFENERS

De Havilland Moth Minor.

TAB (FIXED)

ELEVATOR HALVES SYMMETRICAL & INTERCHANGEABLE ON EITHER SIDE

GIRLING BRAKE

FORGED STEEL TORQUE LINK

BRAKE OPERATING CABLE

BRAKE ADJUSTMENT

INSPECTION-HOLE TO ENSURE BOLTS ARE SECURE WHEN WINGS ARE LOCKED

MECHANISM TO WITHDRAW WING BOLTS

SPACE IN STARBOARD WING FOR EXTRA FUEL TANK OR LUGGAGE

LEAD RUDDER BALANCE

AILERON

BALSA WOOD

ELEKTRON FAIRING

SLOT

SPAR

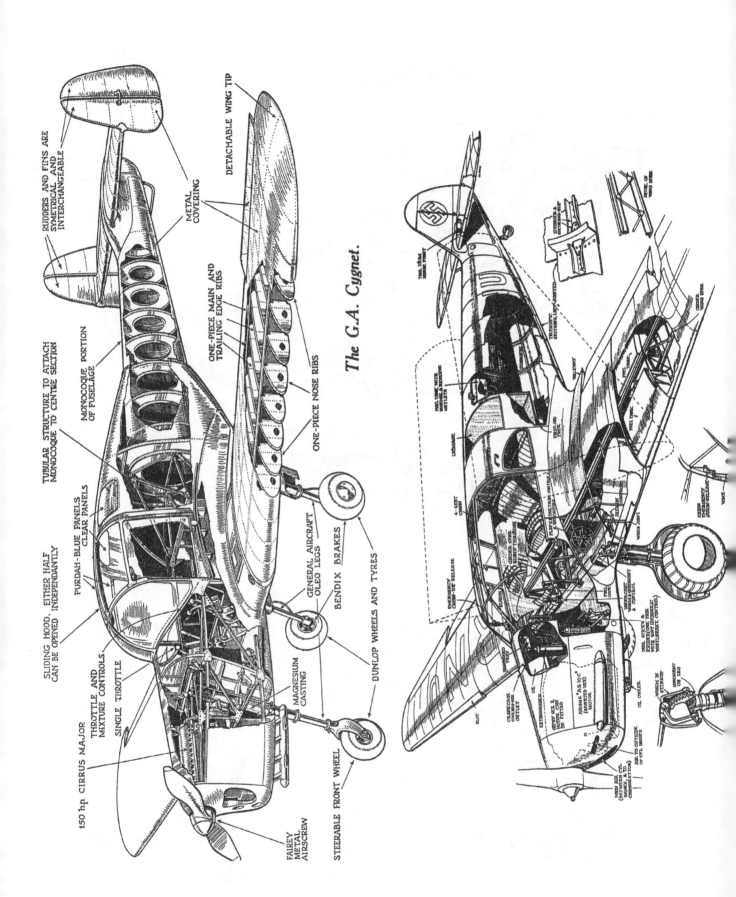

The G.A. Cygnet.

RUDDERS AND FINS ARE SYMETRICAL AND INTERCHANGEABLE

DETACHABLE WING TIP

METAL COVERING

ONE-PIECE MAIN AND TRAILING EDGE RIBS

ONE-PIECE NOSE RIBS

TUBULAR STRUCTURE TO ATTACH MONOCOQUE TO CENTRE SECTION

MONOCOQUE PORTION OF FUSELAGE

PURDAH-BLUE PANELS CLEAR PANELS

SLIDING HOOD, EITHER HALF CAN BE OPENED INDEPENDANTLY

THROTTLE AND MIXTURE CONTROLS

SINGLE THROTTLE

150 h.p. CIRRUS MAJOR

GENERAL AIRCRAFT OLEO LEGS

BENDIX BRAKES

DUNLOP WHEELS AND TYRES

MAGNESIUM CASTING

FAIREY METAL AIRSCREW

STEERABLE FRONT WHEEL

THE JUNKERS JU 86K. BOMBER

(Two 700 h.p. Junkers Jumo 205c. motors)

Labels on drawing:

MASS BALANCE
MASS BALANCE
MASS BALANCE
JUNKERS JUMO 205 DIESEL HEAVY-OIL MOTORS
JUNKERS-HAMILTON CONTROLLABLE-PITCH AIR-SCREWS
FRONT GUNNER & BOMB AIMING
PITOT HEAD (FROM OFF PORT SIDE)
RADIO
PILOT
BOMB DOORS
OIL TANKS
OIL TANK
FULL TANK
BCL FUEL TANK (40 GALLONS)
MAGAZINE FOR EIGHT 275k.(1o3k.) BOMBS
LONGERON
STRINGER
BULKHEAD FRAME
D.F. LOOP
RUDDER MASS-BALANCE (SWINGS THRO' FIN)
TRIM TAB
ELEVATOR MASS BALANCE
TRIM TAB
ADJUSTABLE TAIL-PLANE
MASS BALANCE
FULLY CASTERING SELF-CENTREING TAILWHEEL
TOP AFT GUNNER WITH SLIDING COWL
BULKHEAD FRAME WITH CORRUGATED PANELLING
LOWER AFT GUNNER'S RETRACTING TURRET
LONGERONS
BCL FUEL TANK (40 GALS)
RIBS N.
FUEL TANKS WITH RETAINING DEVICE (& INSPECTION PANELS IN UNDERSIDE SURFACE)
CORRUGATED PANELS ON WARREN-GIRDER WING SPAR (TUBULAR BOOMS)
WATER RADIATOR & OIL COOLER
FUEL 55 GAL
FUEL 70 GAL
STRINGER
AILERON MASS BALANCE
PET-STSP END
JUNKERS "DOUBLE WING" FLAP
MASS BALANCE

A.- 7 SCREW-UP WING FIXINGS (BALL AND SOCKET)
B.- UNDERCARRIAGE FAIRING
C.- CENTRE-SECTION SPARS ACROSS FUSELAGE
D.- UNDERCARRIAGE HOUSING
F.- MOTOR MOUNTINGS
G.- OLEO LEG SLIDING HINGE CONNECTION SLIDES IN TOWARDS FUSELAGE ALONG E. UNDERCARRIAGE IS ELECTRICALLY OPERATED WITH EMERGENCY HAND GEAR
H.- UNDERCARRIAGE RADIUS ROD

Characteristics of the Ju 86K. (Junkers Jumo 205c. motors).

DIMENSIONS:—Span 22.5 m. (78 ft. 9 ins.). Length 17.0 m. (58 ft. 8 ins.). Wing area 82 sq. m. (882.3 sq. ft.). Aspect ratio 6.18.

WEIGHTS:—Empty 5,150 kg. (11,354 lb.). Crew (4) 360 kg. (800 lb.). Fuel 1,290 kg. (2,840 lb.). Oil 60 kg. (132 lb.). Bombs 1,000 kg. (2,205 lb.). Equipment, etc., 200 kg. (440 lb.). Disposable load 2,910 kg. (6,416 lb.). Loaded weight 8,060 kg. (17,770 lb.).

LOADINGS:—Wing 98.4 kg. per sq. m. (20.02 lb. per sq. ft.). Power 5.75 kg. per h.p. (12.7 lb. per h.p.). Span 15.9 kg. per sq. m. (3.25 lb. per sq. ft.).

PERFORMANCE:—Maximum speed 360 km.h. (224 m.p.h.). Cruising speed 280 km.h. (174 m.p.h.) at 2,000 m. (6,562 ft.). Stalling speed 106 km.h. (66 m.p.h.). Range 2,500 km. (1,555 miles) at 280 km.h. (174 m.p.h.).

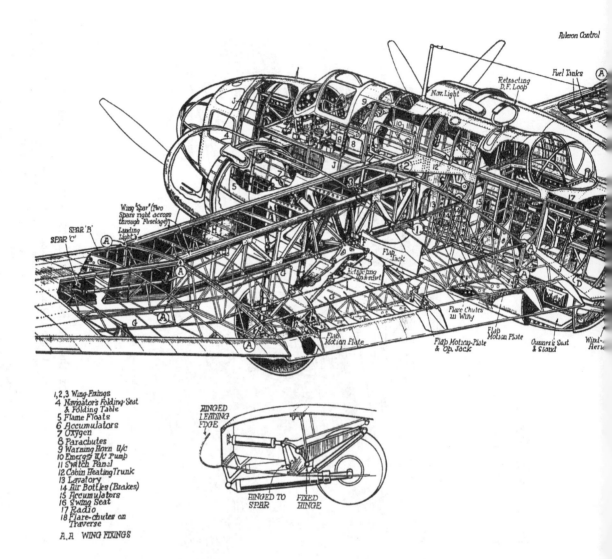

Aileron Control

Fuel Tanks (A)

Retracting
D.F. Loop

Nav. Light

Wing 'Spar' (Two
Spars right across
through 'Fuselage')

SPAR 'B'
SPAR 'C' (A)

Landing
Light'3

Flap
Jack

Retracting
Jack'ment

Flare Chutes
in Wing

Flap
Motion Plate

Flap
Motion Plate

Flap Motion Plate
& Op. Jack

Gunner's Seat
& Stand

Wind-
Aeria

1,2,3 *Wing-Fixings*
4 *Navigator's Folding Seat*
  & Folding Table
5 *Flame Floats*
6 *Accumulators*
7 *Oxygen*
8 *Parachutes*
9 *Warning Horn U/c*
10 *Emerg? U/c Pump*
11 *Switch Panel*
12 *Cabin Heating Trunk*
13 *Lavatory*
14 *Air Bottles (Brakes)*
15 *Accumulators*
16 *S'wing Seat*
17 *Radio*
18 *Flare-chutes on*
  Traverse

A,A *WING FIXINGS*

HINGED
LEADING
EDGE

HINGED TO   FIXED
SPAR   HINGE

SPARS
B, C, H

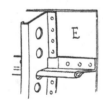

E

G

POWER PLANT.—Two 1,000 h.p. Bristol "Pegasus XVIII" nine-cylinder radial air-cooled engines in N.A.C.A. type cowling. Three-bladed De Havilland constant-speed airscrews. Six fuel tanks, three to each engine, in centre-section. Tanks are easily removed through panels in underside of wing. Maximum fuel capacity 654 Imp. gallons (2,975 litres), Maximum oil capacity 36 Imp. gallons (164 litres).

ACCOMMODATION.—Totally-enclosed accommodation for crew of four. Three gunner's positions, one in nose, one above fuselage over trailing-edge of wings and one below fuselage at break in lower fuselage line. In addition to these three moveable guns, pilot is provided with one fixed forward-firing gun in decking of fuselage. Internal bomb-stowage in fuselage below wings.

DIMENSIONS.—Span 69 ft. 2 in. (21.08 m.), Length 53 ft. 7 in. (16.33 m.), Height 14 ft. 11 in. (4.55 m.), Total wing area 668 sq. ft. (62.1 sq. m.), Track 17 ft. 4 in. (5.28 m.), Chord (root) 16.29 ft. (4.96 m.), Chord (tip) 3.85 ft. (1.17 m.), Aspect ratio 6.58 : 1.

WEIGHTS AND LOADINGS.—Weight empty 11,780 lbs. (5,354 kg.), Fuel 3,173 lbs. (1,442 kg.), Oil 216 lbs. (98 kg.), Service load (including crew) 3,587 lbs. (1,631 kg.), Weight loaded 18,756 lbs. (8,525 kg.), Maximum permissible loaded weight 21,000 lbs. (9,550 kg.), Wing loading (normal) 28.1 lbs./sq. ft. (137 kg./sq. m.), Power loading (normal take-off) 9.77 lbs. (4.4 kg.) per h.p.

The
HANDLEY PAGE "HAMPDEN"
(two Bristol "Pegasus" XVIII engines).

Drawing by Mr. J. H. Clark.
Reproduced by permission of "The Aeroplane."

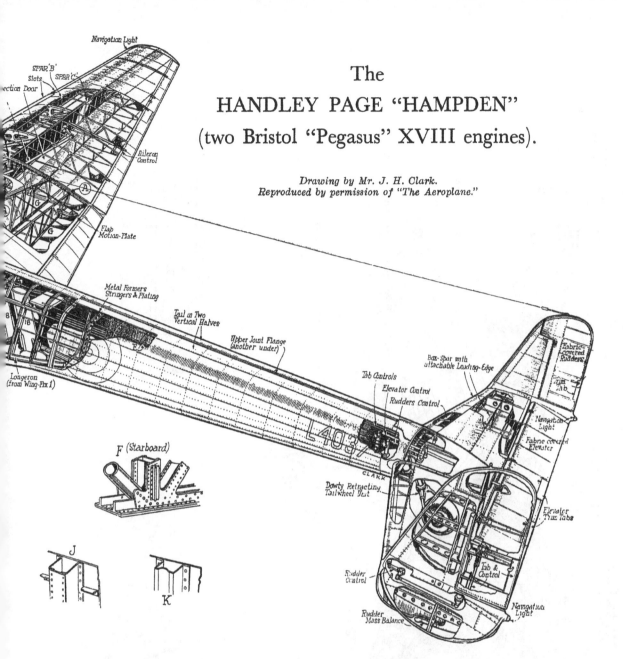

PERFORMANCE (at 18,750 lbs. = 8,525 kg. loaded weight).—Maximum speed at 15,500 ft. (4,730 m.) 265 m.p.h. (427 km.h.), Cruising speed at 2,250 r.p.m. at 15,000 ft. (4,580 m.) 217 m.p.h. (350 km.h.), Economical cruising speed at 1,800 r.p.m. at 15,000 ft. (4,580 m.) 167 m.p.h. (269 km.h.), Service ceiling 22,700 ft. (6,920 m.), Climb to 15,000 ft. (4,580 m.) 18.9 min., Rate of climb to sea-level 980 ft./min. (298.8 m./min.), Landing speed 73 m.p.h. (117 km.h.).

PERFORMANCE (at 21,000 lbs. = 9,550 kg. loaded weight).—Cruising speed at 2,250 r.p.m. at 15,000 ft. (4,580 m.) 212 m.p.h. (341 km.h.), Economical speed at 1,800 r.p.m. at 15,000 ft. (4,580 m.) 172 m.p.h. (277 km.h.), Service ceiling 19,500 ft. (5,950 m.), Time to 15,000 ft. (4,580 m.) 27.2 min., Rate of climb at sea-level 760 ft./min. (232.2 m./min.).

RANGES (at 2,250 r.p.m. and at 18,750 lbs.).—Service load 2,587 lbs. (1,176 kg.) range 1,475 miles (2,380 km.), Service load 3,587 lbs. (1,631 kg.) range 1,095 miles (1,760 km.), Service load 5,587 lbs. (2,540 kg.) range 360 miles (580 km.), At 1,800 r.p.m. for same service loads ranges are 1,790 miles (2,880 km.), 1,335 miles (2,150 km.), 440 miles (710 km.).

RANGES (at 2,250 r.p.m. and at 21,000 lbs.).—Service load 3,587 lbs. (1,631 kg.) range 1,725 miles (2,780 km.), Service load 5,587 lbs. (2,540 kg.) range 1,165 miles (1,875 km.), Service load 6,587 lbs.

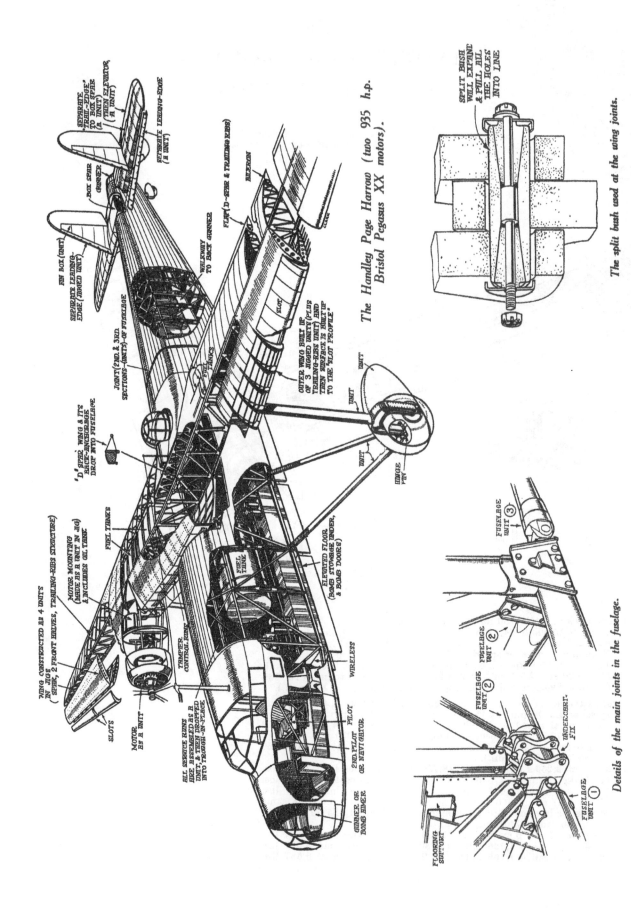

The Handley Page Harrow (two 935 h.p. Bristol Pegasus XX motors).

SPLIT BUSH WILL EXPAND & PULL ALL THE HOLES INTO LINE

The split bush used at the wing joints.

FUSELAGE UNIT ③

FUSELAGE UNIT ②

FUSELAGE UNIT ②

UNDER-CART-FIX

FUSELAGE UNIT ①

FLOORING SUPPORT

Details of the main joints in the fuselage.

SEPARATE TRAIL-EDGE TO BOX SPAR (A UNIT)

THEN ELEVATOR (A UNIT)

SEPARATE LEADING-EDGE (A UNIT)

BOX SPAR GUNNER

FIN BOX (UNIT)

SEPARATE LEADING-EDGE (JIGGED UNIT)

JOINT (2ND & 3RD SECTIONS (UNITS) OF FUSELAGE

WALKWAY TO BACK GUNNER

FLAP (D-SPAR & TRAILING RIBS)

AILERON

SLOT

OUTER WING BUILT UP OF 3 JIGGED UNITS (PLUS TRAILING-RIBS UNIT) AND THEN SURFACE IS BUILT UP TO THE "SLOT PROFILE".

FUEL TANKS

'D' SPAR WING & IT'S BACK-ANCHORAGE DROP INTO FUSELAGE

UNIT

UNIT

UNIT

HINGE PIN

WING CONSTRUCTED AS 4 UNITS IN JIGS (SPAR, 2 FRONT HALVES, TRAILING-RIBS STRUCTURE)

MOTOR MOUNTING (MADE AS A UNIT IN JIG) & INCLUDES OIL TANK

FUEL TANKS

FUEL TANK

ELEVATED FLOOR (BOMB STOWAGE UNDER, & BOMB DOORS)

TRIMMER CONTROL RUNS

WIRELESS

SLOTS

MOTOR AS A UNIT

ALL SERVICE RUNS ARE ASSEMBLED AS A UNIT, & THEN DROPPED INTO TROUGH-IN-PLACE

2ND PILOT PILOT OR NAVIGATOR

GUNNER OR BOMB AIMER

10.04

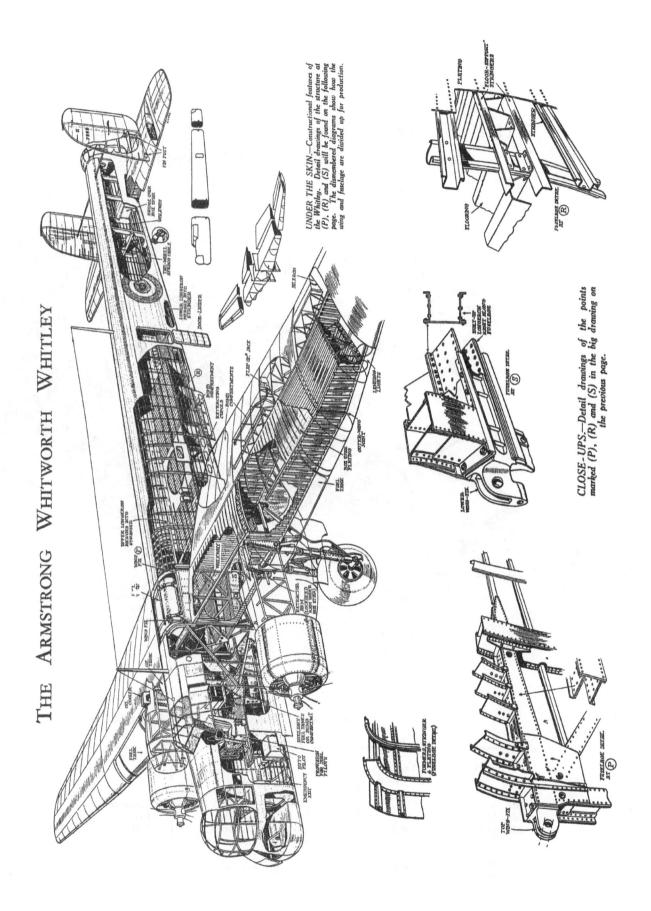

THE ARMSTRONG WHITWORTH WHITLEY

UNDER THE SKIN.—Constructional features of the Whitley. Detail drawings of the structure at (P), (R) and (S) will be found on the following page. The dismembered diagrams show how the wing and fuselage are divided up for production.

CLOSE-UPS.—Detail drawings of the points marked (P), (R) and (S) in the big drawing on the previous page.

THE HEINKEL He.111K. Mk. V. BOMBER
(two Daimler-Benz D.B.601A engines).

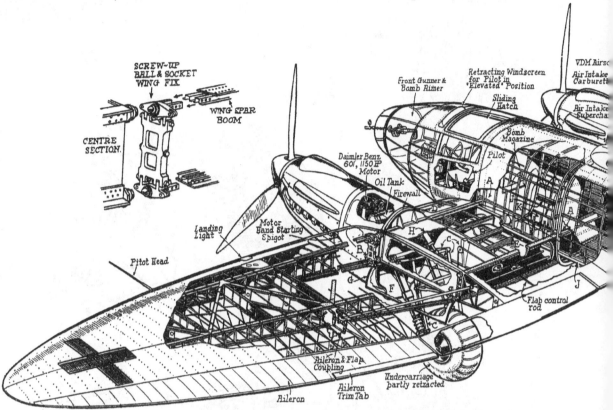

A. Centre-section spar is inset in fuselage between frames
B. Wing fix (screw-ub, ball & socket)
C. Undercarriage Links, radius rods & wheelbrake cable
D. Oil cooler   E. Fuel tank (each side)
F. Controlled air outlet from radiator
G. Undercarriage doors
H. Undercarriage hydraulic op. jack
J. Longerons   K. Bomb doors

THE DEVELOPMENT OF THE HEINKEL He.111K.

He.111K	Year Appeared	Engines	Remarks
Mk. I	1935	2—660 h.p. B.M.W. VI	Long nose
Mk. II	1936	2—950 h.p. DB.600	Long nose
Mk. IIA	1937	2—1,050 h.p. DB.600G	Long nose (improved)
Mk. III	1937	2—1,050 h.p. "Jumo 211"	Long nose (improved)
Mk. IV	1938	2—1,150 h.p. DB.601	Long nose (improved)
Mk. V	1938	2—1,150 h.p. DB.601A	Short nose

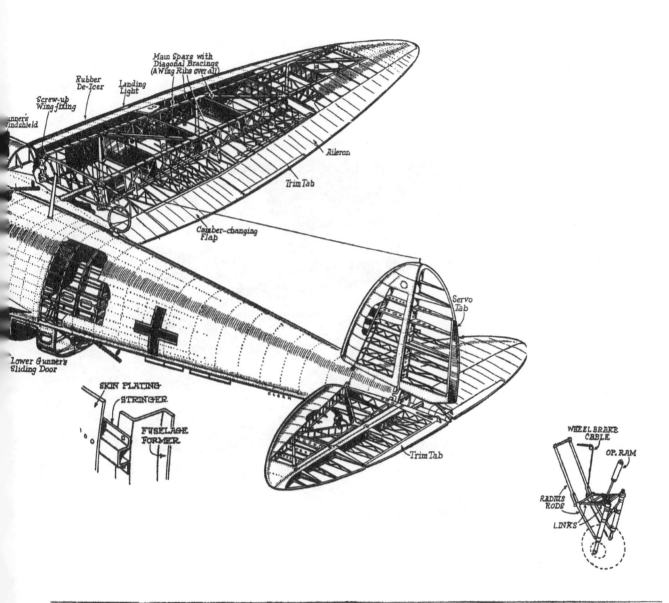

Screw-up
Wing fixing

Rubber
De-Icer

Landing
Light

Main Spars with
Diagonal Bracings
(& Wing Ribs over all)

Gunner's
Windshield

Aileron

Trim Tab

Camber-changing
Flap

Servo
Tab

Lower Gunner's
Sliding Door

SKIN PLATING

STRINGER

FUSELAGE
FORMER

Trim Tab

WHEEL BRAKE
CABLE

OP. RAM

RADIUS
RODS

LINKS

Max. Speed Armament Retracted	Max. Speed Armament Extended
337.6 km.h. (211 m.p.h.) at sea level	308.8 km.h. (193 m.p.h.) at sea level
372.8 km.h. (233 m.p.h.) at 3,600 m. (11,800 ft.)	342.4 km.h. (214 m.p.h.) at 3,600 m. (11,800 ft.)
403.2 km.h. (252 m.p.h.) at 3,600 m. (11,800 ft.)	368 km.h. (230 m.p.h.) at 3,600 m. (11,800 ft.)
408 km.h. (255 m.p.h.) at 4,000 m. (13,120 ft.)	377.6 km.h. (236 m.p.h.) at 4,000 m. (13,120 ft.)
417.6 km.h. (261 m.p.h.) at 3,750 m. (12,300 ft.)	393.6 km.h. (246 m.p.h.) at 3,750 m. (12,300 ft.)
	438.4 km.h. (274 m.p.h.) at 3,750 m. (12,300 ft.)

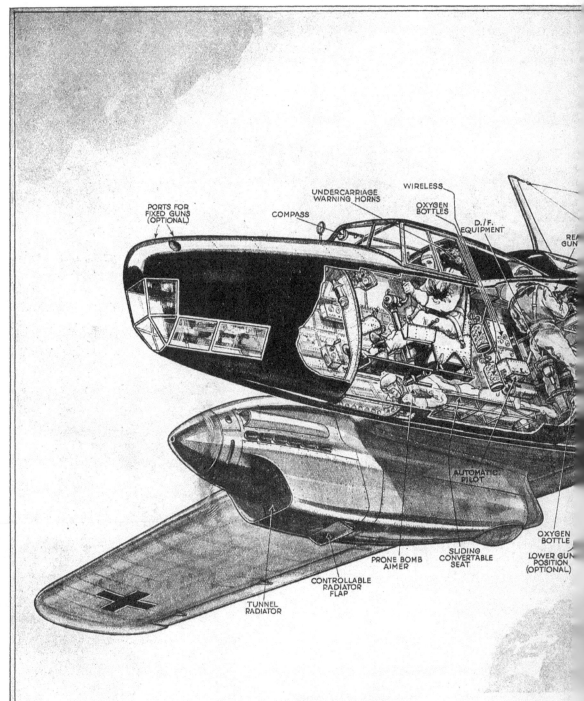

PORTS FOR
FIXED GUNS
(OPTIONAL)

UNDERCARRIAGE
WARNING HORNS

WIRELESS

OXYGEN
BOTTLES

COMPASS

D./F.
EQUIPMENT

REA
GUN

AUTOMATIC
PILOT

OXYGEN
BOTTLE

PRONE BOMB
AIMER

SLIDING
CONVERTABLE
SEAT

LOWER GUN
POSITION
(OPTIONAL)

CONTROLLABLE
RADIATOR
FLAP

TUNNEL
RADIATOR

This specially prepared *Flight* drawing presents at a glance the layout of the Do.17 bomber-fighter. Actually the machine represented here is to some extent a "cocktail" version, embodying various optional features such as twin fixed guns in the top front fuselage decking. If need be, bombs may be carried externally, low on the sides of the fuselage. The inverted Daimler-Benz engines may be regarded as opposite numbers of our Merlin, though current ratings are slightly lower than for the Rolls-Royces. On the right, Gnôme-engined version.

Do.17 BOMBER - FIGHTER and its EQUIPMENT

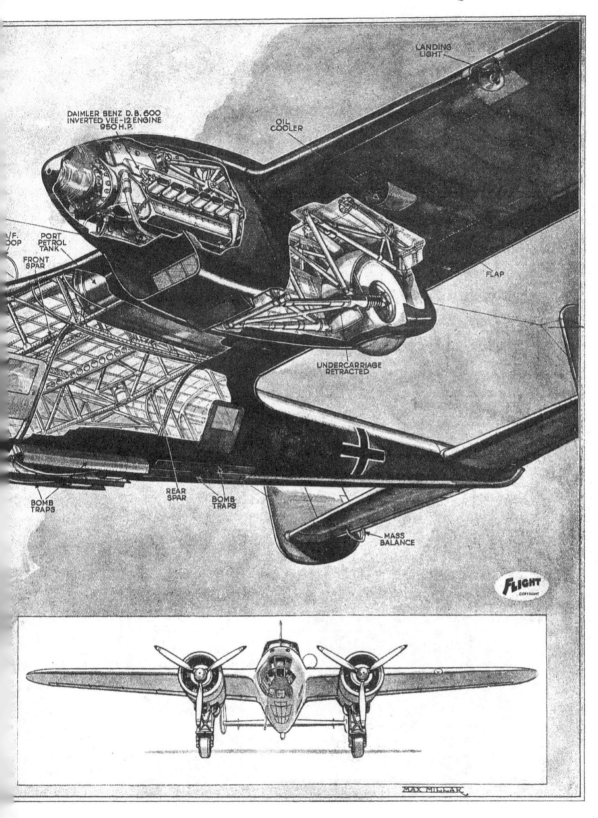

LANDING LIGHT
DAIMLER BENZ D.B. 600 INVERTED VEE-12 ENGINE 950 H.P.
OIL COOLER
/F. OOP
PORT PETROL TANK
FRONT SPAR
FLAP
UNDERCARRIAGE RETRACTED
BOMB TRAPS
REAR SPAR
BOMB TRAPS
MASS BALANCE
FLIGHT COPYRIGHT
MAX MILLAR

THE BRISTOL BLENHEIM.

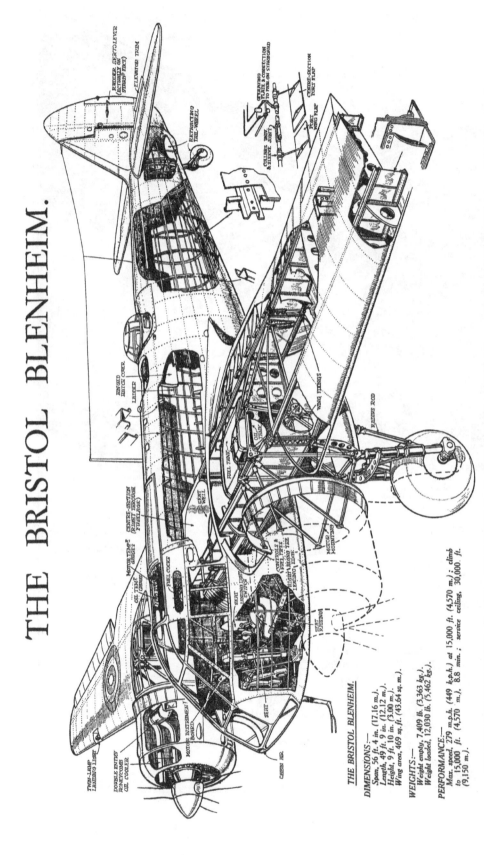

THE BRISTOL BLENHEIM.

DIMENSIONS:—
Span, 56 ft. 4 in. (17.16 m.).
Length, 49 ft. 9 in. (12.12 m.).
Height, 9 ft. 10 in. (3.00 m.).
Wing area, 469 sq.ft. (43.64 sq. m.).

WEIGHTS:—
Weight empty, 7,409 lb. (3,363 kg.).
Weight loaded, 12,030 lb. (5,462 kg.).

PERFORMANCE:—
Max. speed, 279 m.p.h. (449 k.p.h.) at 15,000 ft.; climb
to 15,000 ft. (4,570 m.), 8.8 min.; service ceiling, 30,000 ft.
(9,150 m.).

THE WORLD'S FASTEST BOMBER.—The official speed of the Bristol Blenheim (two 840 h.p. Bristol Mercury VIIIs) is given as 279 m.p.h. at 15,000 feet, but there is a general belief that lower down, with everything wide open regardless of consequences, it can go very nearly as fast as Mr. Howard Hughes's Land-plane Record.

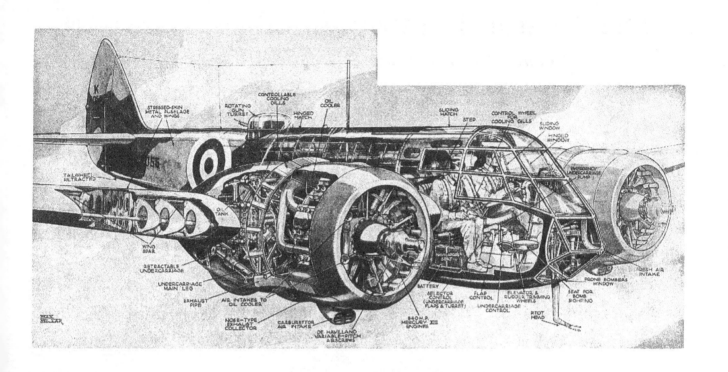

BRISTOL BLENHEIM

AVRO ANSON

The Bristol Bombay Bomber-Transport

(Two 1,010 h.p. Bristol Pegasus XXII motors).

Built by Short and Harland Ltd. in Belfast.

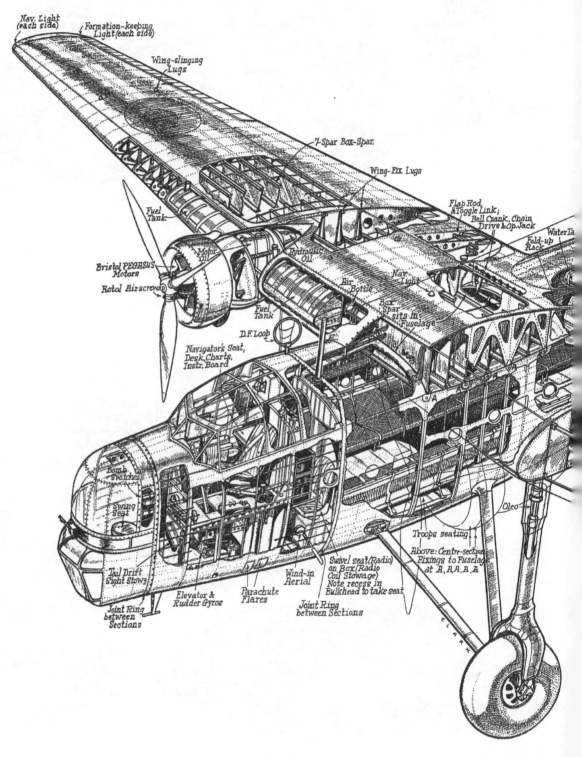

Nav. Light (each side)

Formation-keeping Light (each side)

Wing-slinging Lugs

7-Spar Box-Spar.

Wing-Fix Lugs

Flap Rod & Toggle Link;

Bell Crank, Chain Drive & Op.Jack

Water Ta

Fold-up Rack

Fuel Tank

Motor XXI

Hydraulic Oil

Air Bottle

Nav. Light

Box Spar sits in Fuselage

Bristol PEGASUS Motors

Rotol Airscrews

Fuel Tank

D.F. Loop

Navigator's Seat, Desk, Charts, Instr. Board

Bomb Switches

Swing Seat

Olco

Troops seating

Above: Centre-section Fixings to Fuselage at A, A, A, A

Tail Drift Sight Stows

Swivel seat (Radio) on Box (Radio Coil Stowage) Note recess in Bulkhead to take seat

Wind-in Aerial

Elevator & Rudder Gyros

Parachute Flares

Joint Ring between Sections

Joint Ring between Sections

CLARK

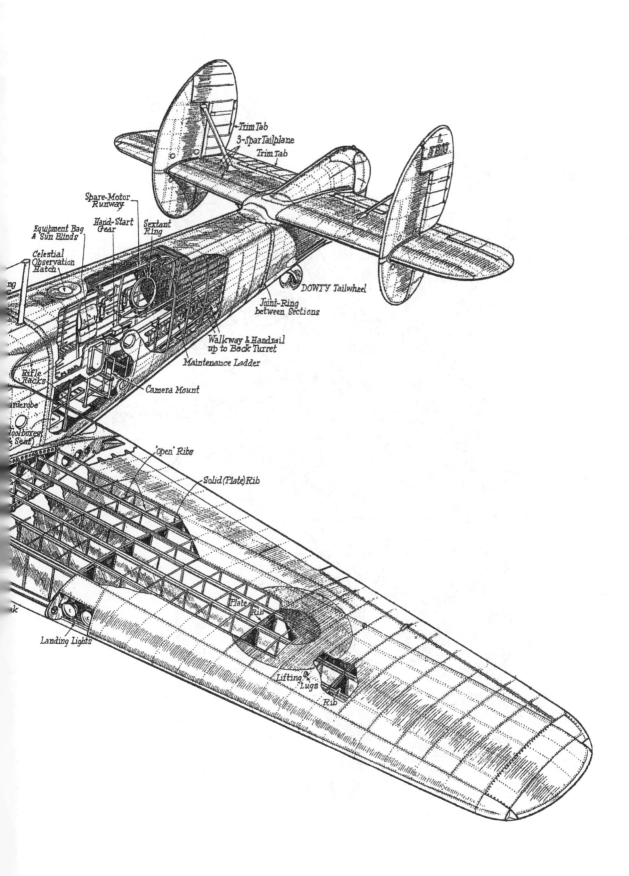

Trim Tab
3-Spar Tailplane
Trim Tab

Spare-Motor Runway
Equipment Bag & 'Sun Blinds'
Hand-Start Gear
Sextant Ring
Celestial Observation Hatch

DOWTY Tailwheel
Joint-Ring between Sections

Walkway & Handrail up to Back Turret
Maintenance Ladder

Rifle Racks

Camera Mount

Wardrobe

Toolboxes & Seat

'Open' Ribs

Solid (Plate) Rib

Plate Rib

Landing Lights

Lifting Lugs
Rib

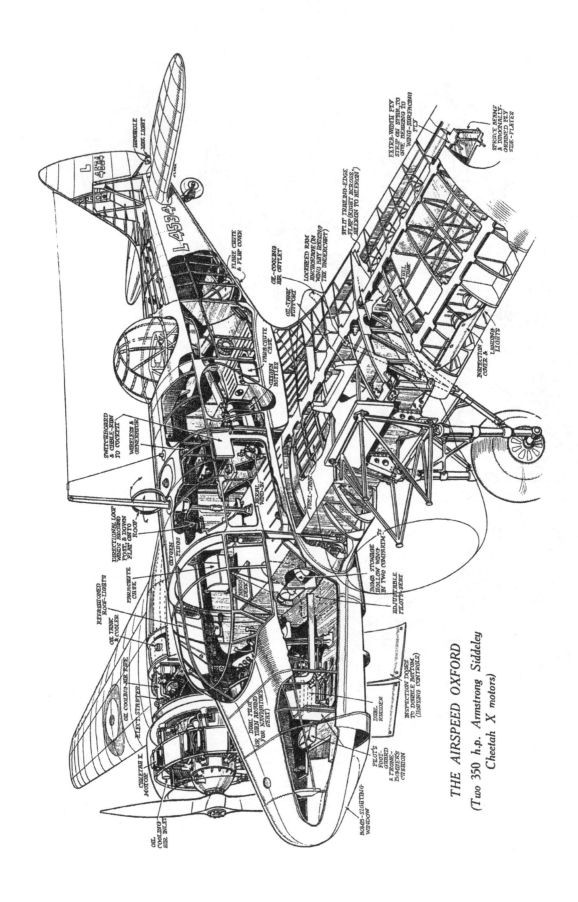

THE AIRSPEED OXFORD

(Two 350 h.p. Armstrong Siddeley
Cheetah X motors)

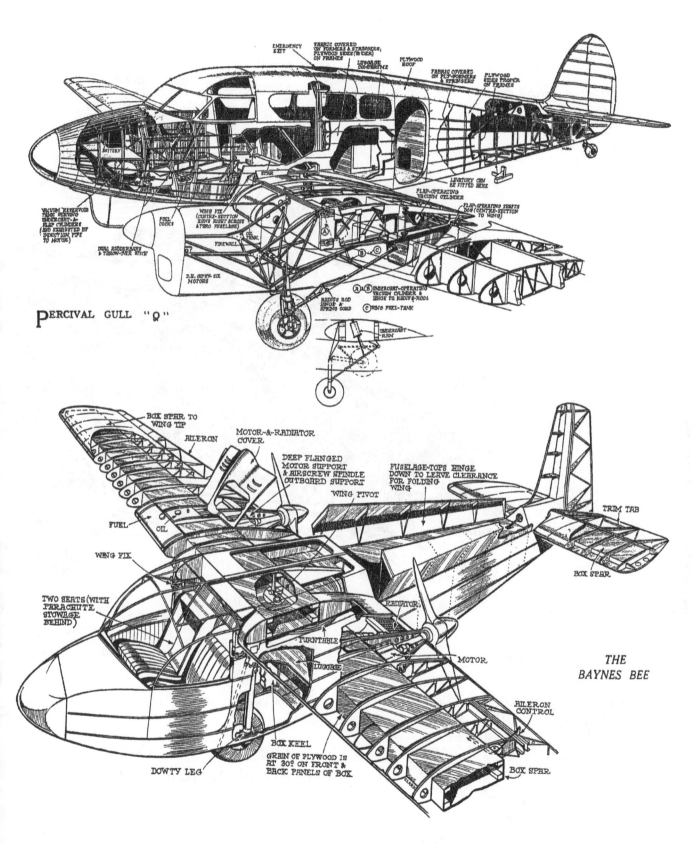

PERCIVAL GULL "Q"

THE
BAYNES BEE

The Carden-Baynes Bee is of interest not only because of its
unusual layout but because it incorporates a number of
unusual structural features, particularly, as visible in this
sketch, in the wing. Petrol is carried in leading edge tanks.
The accessibility of the cabin is particularly commendable :
the doors are large and the fuselage low.

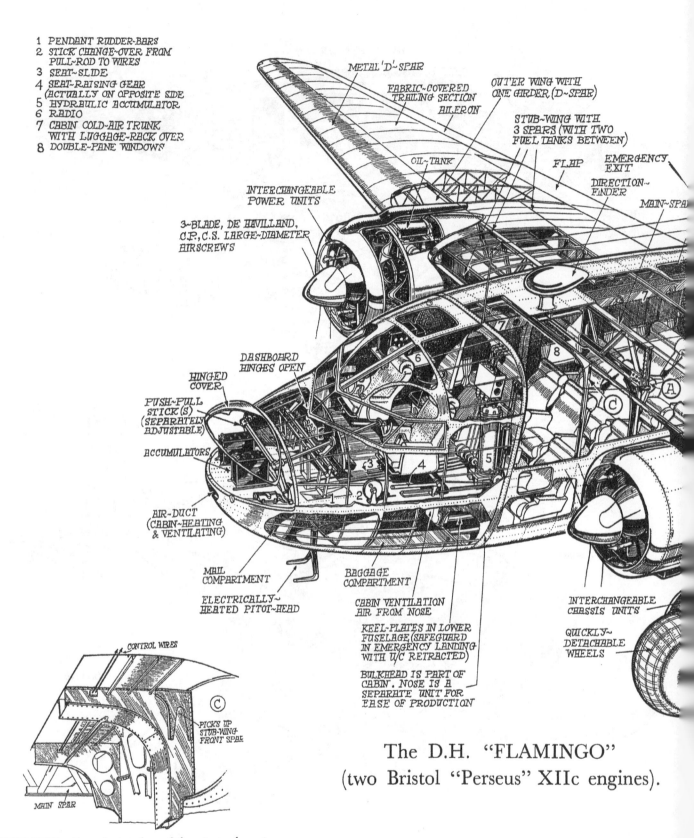

1 PENDANT RUDDER-BARS
2 STICK CHANGE-OVER FROM PULL-ROD TO WIRES
3 SEAT-SLIDE
4 SEAT-RAISING GEAR (ACTUALLY ON OPPOSITE SIDE
5 HYDRAULIC ACCUMULATOR
6 RADIO
7 CABIN COLD-AIR TRUNK WITH LUGGAGE-RACK OVER
8 DOUBLE-PANE WINDOWS

METAL 'D'-SPAR

FABRIC-COVERED TRAILING SECTION
AILERON

OUTER WING WITH ONE GIRDER (D-SPAR)

STUB-WING WITH 3 SPARS (WITH TWO FUEL TANKS BETWEEN)

OIL-TANK

FLAP

EMERGENCY EXIT

DIRECTION-FINDER

MAIN-SPAR

INTERCHANGEABLE POWER UNITS

3-BLADE, DE HAVILLAND, C.P., C.S. LARGE-DIAMETER AIRSCREWS

DASHBOARD HINGES OPEN

HINGED COVER

PUSH-PULL STICK (S) (SEPARATELY ADJUSTABLE)

ACCUMULATORS

AIR-DUCT (CABIN-HEATING & VENTILATING)

MAIL COMPARTMENT

ELECTRICALLY-HEATED PITOT-HEAD

BAGGAGE COMPARTMENT

CABIN VENTILATION AIR FROM NOSE

KEEL-PLATES IN LOWER FUSELAGE (SAFEGUARD IN EMERGENCY LANDING WITH U/C RETRACTED)

BULKHEAD IS PART OF CABIN. NOSE IS A SEPARATE UNIT FOR EASE OF PRODUCTION

INTERCHANGEABLE CHASSIS UNITS

QUICKLY-DETACHABLE WHEELS

CONTROL WIRES

C

PICKS UP STUB-WING FRONT SPAR

MAIN SPAR

The D.H. "FLAMINGO"
(two Bristol "Perseus" XIIc engines).

SIMPLICITY.—Above, the top of one of the main spar-frames in the cabin. Right, how extrusions are used for longitudinal stiffening of the skin.

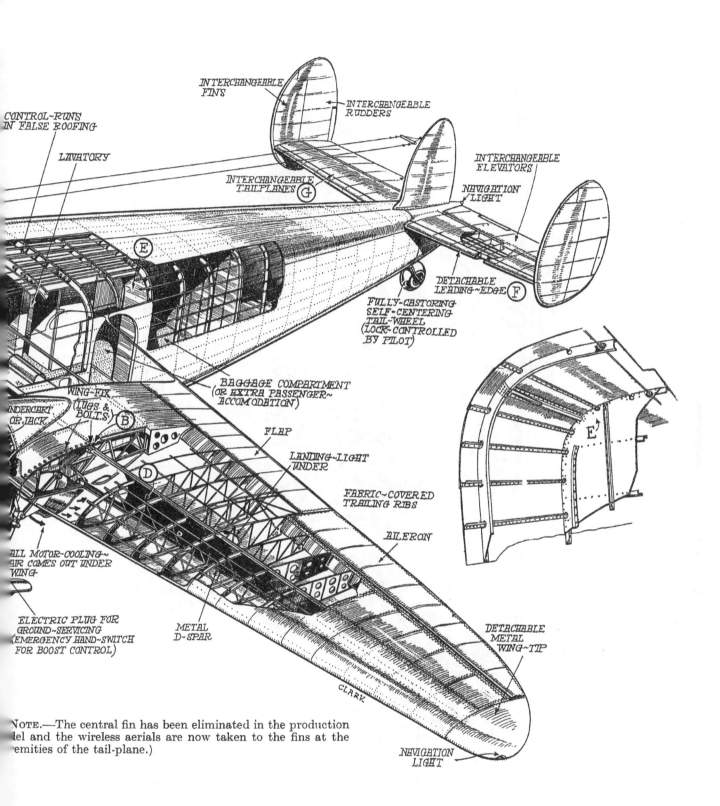

CONTROL~RUNS IN FALSE ROOFING

LAVATORY

INTERCHANGEABLE FINS

INTERCHANGEABLE RUDDERS

INTERCHANGEABLE TAILPLANES (G)

INTERCHANGEABLE ELEVATORS

NAVIGATION LIGHT

DETACHABLE LEADING~EDGE (F)

(E)

FULLY~CASTORING SELF~CENTERING TAIL~WHEEL (LOCK~CONTROLLED BY PILOT)

WING~FIX (LUGS & BOLTS) (B)

UNDERCART OR JACK

(D)

BAGGAGE COMPARTMENT (OR EXTRA PASSENGER~ ACCOMODATION)

FLAP

LANDING~LIGHT UNDER

FABRIC~COVERED TRAILING RIBS

AILERON

ALL MOTOR~COOLING~ AIR COMES OUT UNDER WING

ELECTRIC PLUG FOR GROUND~SERVICING (EMERGENCY HAND~SWITCH FOR BOOST CONTROL)

METAL D~SPAR

CLARK

DETACHABLE METAL WING~TIP

NAVIGATION LIGHT

E

(NOTE.—The central fin has been eliminated in the production model and the wireless aerials are now taken to the fins at the extremities of the tail-plane.)

10.53

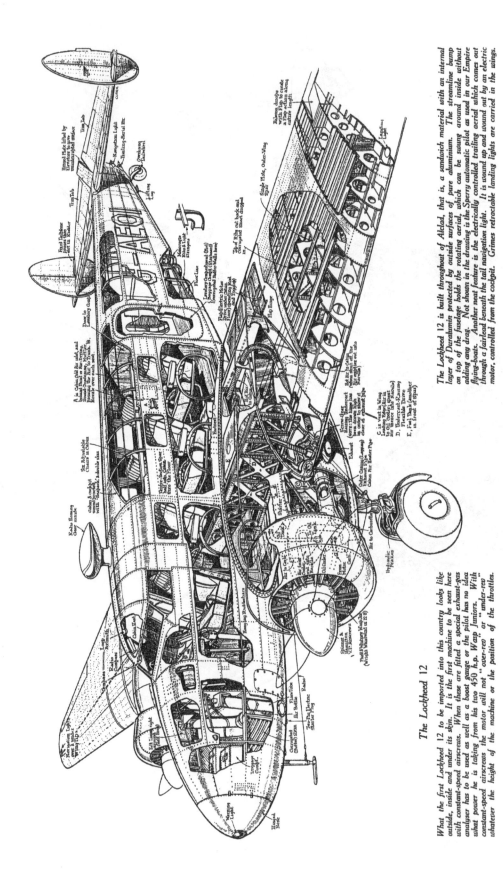

The Lockheed 12

What the first Lockheed 12 to be imported into this country looks like outside, inside and under its skin. It is the first machine to be seen here with constant-speed airscrews. When these are fitted a special exhaust-gas analyser has to be used as well as a boost gauge or the pilot has no idea what power he is taking from his two 450 h.p. Wasp Juniors. With constant-speed airscrews the motor will not "over-rev" or "under-rev" whatever the height of the machine or the position of the throttles.

The Lockheed 12 is built throughout of Alclad, that is, a sandwich material with an internal layer of Duralumin protected by outside surfaces of pure aluminium. The streamline bump on top of the fuselage holds the rotating aerial, which can be swung around inside without adding any drag. Not shown in the drawing is the Sperry automatic pilot as used in our Empire flying-boats. Another neat feature is the electrically controlled trailing aerial which comes out through a fairlead beneath the tail navigation light. It is wound up and wound out by an electric motor, controlled from the cockpit. Grimes retractable landing lights are carried in the wings.

Navigation Light

Landing Light

Oil Tank

Servo Flap On Aileron

Main Box Spar Structure

Split Flap

Undercarriage (Retracted)

Aft Passenger Cabin (9 Passengers)

Rear Main Door

Freight Hold

the degree of comfort and safety it affords its passengers) yet ordered by an airline.   Powered with four Armstrong Siddeley Tiger IX,
200 m.p.h., the normal cruising speed being about 160 m.p.h.   The total loaded weight is over 20 tons.

THE ARMSTRONG

(Four 800 h.p. Armstrong

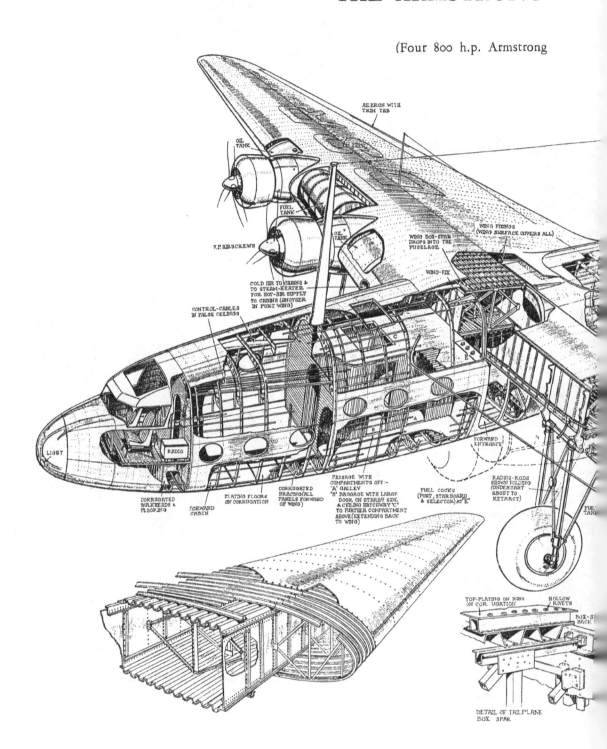

AILERON WITH
TRIM TAB

OIL
TANK

FUEL
TANK

OIL
TANK

WING FIXINGS
(WING SURFACE COVERS ALL)

V.P. AIRSCREWS

WING BOX-SPAR
DROPS INTO THE
FUSELAGE

WING-FIX

COLD AIR TO CABINS &
TO STEAM-HEATER
FOR HOT-AIR SUPPLY
TO CABINS (ANOTHER
IN PORT WING)

CONTROL-CABLES
IN FALSE CEILINGS

C

RADIO

LIGHT

B

A

FORWARD
ENTRANCE

PASSAGE WITH
COMPARTMENTS OFF:-
'A' GALLEY
'B' BAGGAGE WITH LARGE
DOOR ON STARB'D SIDE
& CEILING HATCHWAY 'C'
TO FURTHER COMPARTMENT
ABOVE (EXTENDING BACK
TO WING)

FUEL COCKS
(PORT, STARBOARD
& SELECTOR) AT 'E'

RADIUS-RODS
SHOWN FOLDING
(UNDERCART
ABOUT TO
RETRACT)

CORRUGATED
BULKHEADS &
FLOORING

FORWARD
CABIN

PLATING FLOORS
ON CORRUGATION

CORRUGATED
BRACING (ALL
PANELS FORWARD
OF WING)

FUEL
TANK

TOP-PLATING ON RIBS
ON CORRUGATION

HOLLOW
RIVETS

BOX-S
BACK

DETAIL OF TAILPLANE
BOX SPAR

11.54

WHITWORTH ENSIGN

Siddeley Tiger IX Motors)

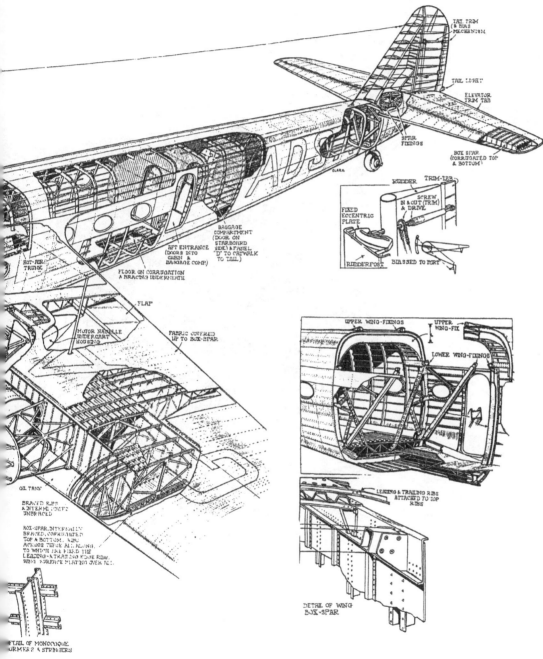

TAIL TRIM
(& BIAS
MECHANISM)

TAIL LIGHT

ELEVATOR
TRIM TAB

SPAR
FIXINGS

BOX SPAR
(CORRUGATED TOP
& BOTTOM)

RUDDER TRIM-TAB

SCREW
IN & OUT (TRIM)
& DRIVE

FIXED
ECCENTRIC
PLATE

RUDDERPOST BIASSED TO PORT

BAGGAGE
COMPARTMENT
(DOOR ON
STARBOARD
SIDE) & PANEL
'D' TO CATWALK
TO TAIL)

AFT ENTRANCE
(DOORS INTO
CABIN &
BAGGAGE COMP)

HOT-AIR
TRUNK

FLOOR ON CORRUGATION
& BRACING UNDERNEATH

FLAP

MOTOR NACELLE
UNDERCART
HOUSING

FABRIC COVERED
UP TO BOX-SPAR

UPPER WING-FIXINGS

UPPER
WING-FIX

LOWER WING-FIXINGS

OIL TANK

BRACED RIBS
& INTERMEDIATE
UNBRACED

BOX-SPAR, INTERNALLY
BRACED, CORRUGATED
TOP & BOTTOM. RIBS
ACROSS THESE ALL ALONG
TO WHICH ARE FIXED THE
LEADING & TRAILING EDGE RIBS
WING SURFACE PLATING OVER ALL

LEADING & TRAILING RIBS
ATTACHED TO TOP
RIBS

DETAIL OF WING
BOX-SPAR

DETAIL OF MONOCOQUE
FORMERS & STRINGERS

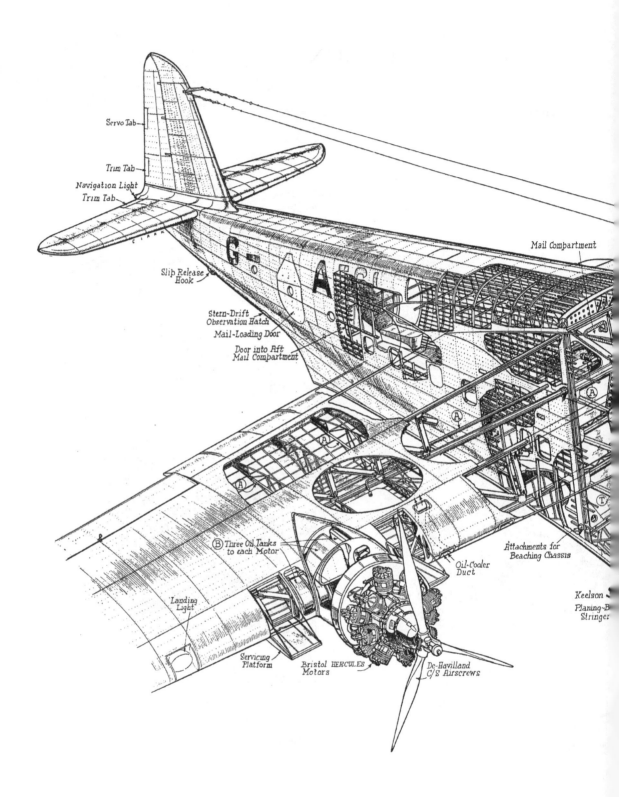

Servo Tab

Trim Tab
Navigation Light
Trim Tab

Slip Release
Hook

Stern-Drift
Observation Hatch
Mail-Loading Door
Door into Aft
Mail Compartment

Mail Compartment

Ⓑ Three Oil Tanks
to each Motor

Oil-Cooler
Duct

Attachments for
Beaching Chassis

Keelson
Planing-B
Stringer

Landing
Light

Servicing
Platform

Bristol HERCULES
Motors

De-Havilland
C/S Airscrews

G-A

11.56

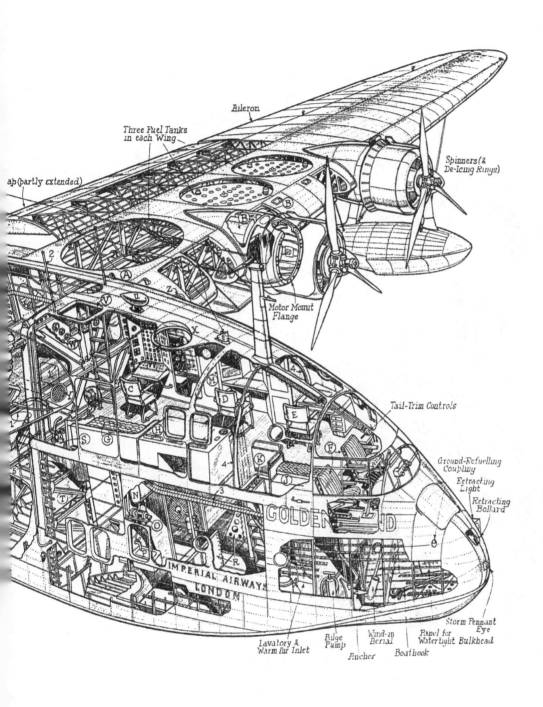

Aileron

Three Fuel Tanks in each Wing

ap (partly extended)

Spinners (& De-Icing Rings)

Motor Mount Flange

Tail-Trim Controls

Ground-Refuelling Coupling

Retracting Light

Retracting Bollard

GOLDEN HIND

IMPERIAL AIRWAYS
LONDON

Storm Pennant Eye

Panel for Watertight Bulkhead

Lavatory & Warm Air Inlet

Bilge Pump

Wind-in Aerial

Anchor

Boathook

The SHORT "G" CLASS FLYING-BOAT
(four Bristol "Hercules" engines)

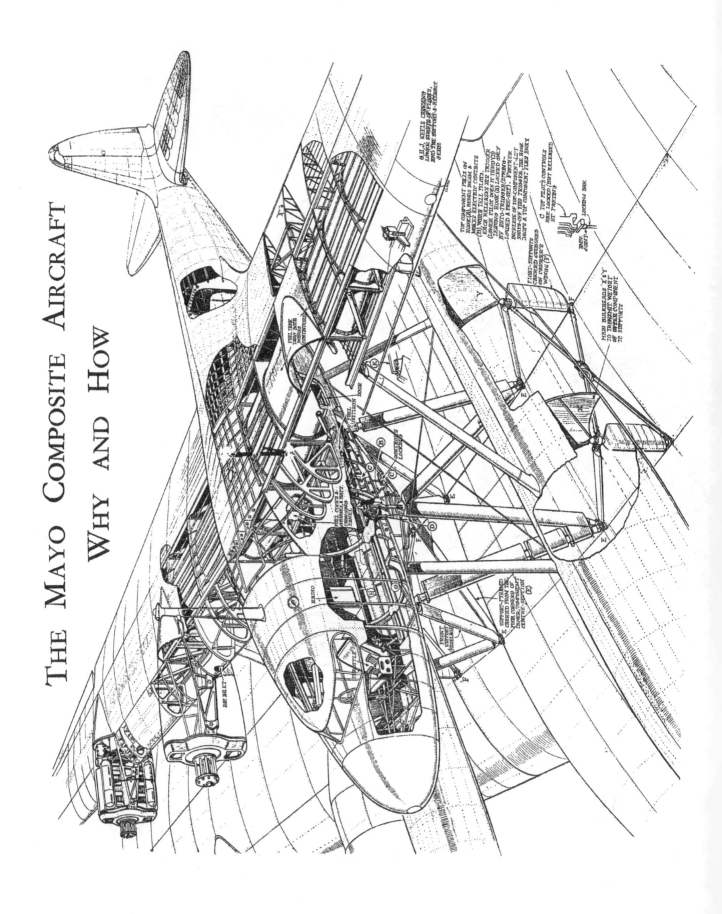

The Mayo Composite Aircraft
Why and How

A CATALOG OF SELECTED DOVER
BOOKS IN ALL FIELDS OF INTEREST

100 BEST-LOVED POEMS, Edited by Philip Smith. *"The Passionate Shepherd to His Love," "Shall I compare thee to a summer's day?" "Death, be not proud," "The Raven," "The Road Not Taken,"* plus works by Blake, Wordsworth, Byron, Shelley, Keats, many others. Includes *13 selections from the Common Core State Standards Initiative.* 112pp.
0-486-28553-7

1000 TURN-OF-THE-CENTURY HOUSES: With Illustrations and Floor Plans, Herbert C. Chivers. Reproduced from a rare edition, this showcase of homes ranges from cottages and bungalows to sprawling mansions. Each house is meticulously illustrated and accompanied by complete floor plans. 256pp.   0-486-45596-3

101 GREAT AMERICAN POEMS, Edited by The American Poetry & Literacy Project. Rich treasury of verse from the 19th and 20th centuries includes works by Edgar Allan Poe, Robert Frost, Walt Whitman, Langston Hughes, Emily Dickinson, T. S. Eliot, other notables. Includes 13 selections from the Common Core State Standards Initiative. 96pp.   0-486-40158-8

20TH-CENTURY FASHION ILLUSTRATION: The Feminine Ideal, Rosemary Torre. Introduction by Harold Koda. This captivating retrospective explores the social context of fashion with informative text and over 70 striking images. Profiles include flappers, glamour girls, flower children, and the modern obsession with celebrity styles. 176pp.   0-486-46963-8

3200 OLD-TIME CUTS AND ORNAMENTS, Edited by Blanche Cirker. Royalty-free pictures from 1909 French typography catalog: plants, animals, religious motifs, music, carriages, boats, sports, furniture, clothing; plus borders, banners, wreaths, and other ornaments. Over 3,200 black-and-white illustrations. 112pp.
0-486-41732-8

500 YEARS OF ILLUSTRATION: From Albrecht Dürer to Rockwell Kent, Howard Simon. Unrivaled treasury of art from the 1500s through the 1900s includes drawings by Goya, Hogarth, Dürer, Morris, Doré, Beardsley, others. Hundreds of illustrations, brief introductions. Ideal as reference and browsing book. 512pp.
0-486-48465-3

ABC BOOK OF EARLY AMERICANA, Eric Sloane. Artist and historian Eric Sloane presents a wondrous A-to-Z collection of American innovations, including hex signs, ear trumpets, popcorn, and rocking chairs. Illustrated, hand-lettered pages feature brief captions explaining objects' origins and uses. 64pp.
0-486-49808-5

ADVENTURES OF HUCKLEBERRY FINN, Mark Twain. Join Huck and Jim as their boyhood adventures along the Mississippi River lead them into a world of excitement, danger, and self-discovery. Humorous narrative, lyrical descriptions of the Mississippi valley, and memorable characters. 224pp.   0-486-28061-6

ALICE STARMORE'S BOOK OF FAIR ISLE KNITTING, Alice Starmore. A noted designer from the region of Scotland's Fair Isle explores the history and techniques of this distinctive, stranded-color knitting style and provides copious illustrated instructions for 14 original knitwear designs. 208pp.   0-486-47218-3

ALICE'S ADVENTURES IN WONDERLAND, Lewis Carroll. Beloved classic about a little girl lost in a topsy-turvy land and her encounters with the White Rabbit, March Hare, Mad Hatter, Cheshire Cat, and other delightfully improbable characters. 42 illustrations by Sir John Tenniel. A selection of the Common Core State Standards Initiative. 96pp.   0-486-27543-4

AMERICAN BALLADS AND FOLK SONGS, John A. Lomax and Alan Lomax. Music and lyrics for over 200 songs. *John Henry, Goin' Home, Little Brown Jug, Alabama-Bound, Black Betty, The Hammer Song, Jesse James, Down in the Valley, The Ballad of Davy Crockett,* and many more. 672pp.   0-486-28276-7

AMERICAN LOCOMOTIVES IN HISTORIC PHOTOGRAPHS: 1858 to 1949, Ron Ziel. A rare collection of 126 meticulously detailed official photographs, called "builder portraits," majestically chronicle the rise of steam locomotive power in America. Introduction. Detailed captions. 140pp.   0-486-27393-8

ANIMALS: 1,419 Copyright-Free Illustrations of Mammals, Birds, Fish, Insects, etc, Selected by Jim Harter. Selected for its visual impact and ease of use, this outstanding collection of wood engravings presents over 1,000 species of animals in extremely lifelike poses. Includes mammals, birds, reptiles, amphibians, fish, insects, and other invertebrates. 284pp.   0-486-23766-4

THE ANNOTATED INNOCENCE OF FATHER BROWN, G. K. Chesterton. Twelve of the popular Father Brown mysteries appear in this copiously annotated edition. Includes "The Blue Cross," "The Hammer of God," "The Eye of Apollo," and more. 352pp.   0-486-29859-0

ANTIGONE, Sophocles. Filled with passionate speeches and sensitive probing of moral and philosophical issues, this powerful and often-performed Greek drama reveals the grim fate that befalls the children of Oedipus. Footnotes. 64pp.   0-486-27804-2

ART FORMS IN NATURE, Ernst Haeckel. Multitude of strangely beautiful natural forms: Radiolaria, Foraminifera, Ciliata, diatoms, calcareous sponges, Tubulariidae, Siphonophora, Semaeostomeae, star corals, starfishes, much more. All images in black and white. 100pp.   0-486-22987-4

THE ART OF WAR, Sun Tzu. Widely regarded as "The Oldest Military Treatise in the World," this landmark work covers principles of strategy, tactics, maneuvering, communication, and supplies; the use of terrain, fire, and the seasons of the year; much more. 96pp.   0-486-42557-6

THE ARTHUR RACKHAM TREASURY: 86 Full-Color Illustrations, Arthur Rackham. Selected and Edited by Jeff A. Menges. A stunning treasury of 86 full-page plates span the famed English artist's career, from *Rip Van Winkle* (1905) to masterworks such as *Undine, A Midsummer Night's Dream,* and *Wind in the Willows* (1939). 96pp.
0-486-44685-9

THE AUTHENTIC GILBERT & SULLIVAN SONGBOOK, W. S. Gilbert and A. S. Sullivan. The most comprehensive collection available, this songbook includes selections from every one of Gilbert and Sullivan's light operas. Ninety-two numbers are presented uncut and unedited, and in their original keys. 410pp.
0-486-23482-7

THE AUTOCRAT OF THE BREAKFAST-TABLE, Oliver Wendell Holmes. Witty, easy-to-read philosophical essays, written by the poet, essayist, and professor. Holmes drew upon his experiences as a resident of a New England boardinghouse to add color and humor to these reflections. 240pp.   0-486-79028-2

THE AWAKENING, Kate Chopin. First published in 1899, this controversial novel of a New Orleans wife's search for love outside a stifling marriage shocked readers. Today, it remains a first-rate narrative with superb characterization. New introductory note. 128pp.   0-486-27786-0

Browse over 10,000 books at www.doverpublications.com

BASEBALL IS . . .: Defining the National Pastime, Edited by Paul Dickson. Wisecracking, philosophical, nostalgic, and entertaining, these hundreds of quips and observations by players, their wives, managers, authors, and others cover every aspect of our national pastime. It's a great any-occasion gift for fans! 256pp.
0-486-48209-X

BEETHOVEN'S LETTERS, Ludwig van Beethoven. Edited by Dr. A. C. Kalischer. Features 457 letters to fellow musicians, friends, greats, patrons, and literary men. Reveals musical thoughts, quirks of personality, insights, and daily events. Includes 15 plates. 410pp.
0-486-22769-3

BOUND & DETERMINED: A Visual History of Corsets, 1850–1960, Kristina Seleshanko. This revealing history of corsetry ranges from the 19th through the mid-20th centuries to show how simple laced bodices developed into corsets of cane, whalebone, and steel. Lavish illustrations include line drawings and photographs. 128pp.
0-486-47892-0

THE BUILDING OF MANHATTAN, Written and Illustrated by Donald A. Mackay. Meticulously accurate line drawings and fascinating text explain construction above and below ground, including excavating subway lines and building bridges and skyscrapers. Hundreds of illustrations reveal intricate details of construction techniques. A selection of the Common Core State Standards Initiative. 160pp.
0-486-47317-1

THE BUNGALOW BOOK: Floor Plans and Photos of 112 Houses, 1910, Henry L. Wilson. Here are 112 of the most popular and economic blueprints of the early 20th century — plus an illustration or photograph of each completed house. A wonderful time capsule that still offers a wealth of valuable insights. 160pp.
0-486-45104-6

THE CALL OF THE WILD, Jack London. A classic novel of adventure, drawn from London's own experiences as a Klondike adventurer, relating the story of a heroic dog caught in the brutal life of the Alaska Gold Rush. Note. 64pp.   0-486-26472-6

CANDIDE, Voltaire. Edited by Francois-Marie Arouet. One of the world's great satires since its first publication in 1759. Witty, caustic skewering of romance, science, philosophy, religion, government — nearly all human ideals and institutions. A selection of the Common Core State Standards Initiative. 112pp.
0-486-26689-3

THE CARTOON HISTORY OF TIME, Kate Charlesworth and John Gribbin. Cartoon characters explain cosmology, quantum physics, and other concepts covered by Stephen Hawking's *A Brief History of Time*. Humorous graphic novel–style treatment, perfect for young readers and curious folk of all ages. 64pp.
0-486-49097-1

THE CHERRY ORCHARD, Anton Chekhov. Classic of world drama concerns passing of semifeudal order in turn-of-the-century Russia, symbolized in the sale of the cherry orchard owned by Madame Ranevskaya. Showcases Chekhov's rich sensitivities as an observer of human nature. 64pp.   0-486-26682-6

A CHRISTMAS CAROL, Charles Dickens. This engrossing tale relates Ebenezer Scrooge's ghostly journeys through Christmases past, present, and future and his ultimate transformation from a harsh and grasping old miser to a charitable and compassionate human being. 80pp.   0-486-26865-9

COMMON SENSE, Thomas Paine. First published in January of 1776, this highly influential landmark document clearly and persuasively argued for American separation from Great Britain and paved the way for the Declaration of Independence. A selection of the Common Core State Standards Initiative. 64pp.
0-486-29602-4

THE COMPLETE SHORT STORIES OF OSCAR WILDE, Oscar Wilde. Complete texts of "The Happy Prince and Other Tales," "A House of Pomegranates," "Lord Arthur Savile's Crime and Other Stories," "Poems in Prose," and "The Portrait of Mr. W. H." 208pp.
0-486-45216-6

COMPLETE SONNETS, William Shakespeare. Over 150 exquisite poems deal with love, friendship, the tyranny of time, beauty's evanescence, death, and other themes in language of remarkable power, precision, and beauty. Glossary of archaic terms. Includes a selection from the Common Core State Standards Initiative. 80pp.
0-486-26686-9

THE COUNT OF MONTE CRISTO: Abridged Edition, Alexandre Dumas. Falsely accused of treason, Edmond Dantès is imprisoned in the bleak Chateau d'If. After a hair-raising escape, he launches an elaborate plot to extract a bitter revenge against those who betrayed him. 448pp.   0-486-45643-9

CRAFTSMAN BUNGALOWS: 59 Homes from "The Craftsman," Edited by Gustav Stickley. Best and most attractive designs from the Arts and Crafts Movement publication from 1903 to 1916 includes sketches, photographs of homes, floor plans, and descriptive text. 128pp.   0-486-25829-7

CRIME AND PUNISHMENT, Fyodor Dostoyevsky. Translated by Constance Garnett. Supreme masterpiece tells the story of Raskolnikov, a student tormented by his own thoughts after he murders an old woman. Overwhelmed by guilt and terror, he confesses and goes to prison. A selection of the Common Core State Standards Initiative. 448pp.   0-486-41587-2

CYRANO DE BERGERAC, Edmond Rostand. A quarrelsome, hot-tempered, and unattractive swordsman falls hopelessly in love with a beautiful woman and woos her for a handsome but slow-witted suitor. A witty and eloquent drama. 144pp.
0-486-41119-2

DANIEL BOONE'S OWN STORY & THE ADVENTURES OF DANIEL BOONE, Daniel Boone and Francis Lister Hawks. This two-part tale features reminiscences in the legendary frontiersman's own words and a profile of his entire life, with exciting accounts of blazing the Wilderness Road and serving as a militiaman during the Revolutionary War. 128pp.   0-486-47690-1

THE DECLARATION OF INDEPENDENCE AND OTHER GREAT DOCUMENTS OF AMERICAN HISTORY: 1775-1865, Edited by John Grafton. Thirteen compelling and influential documents: Henry's "Give Me Liberty or Give Me Death," Declaration of Independence, The Constitution, Washington's First Inaugural Address, The Monroe Doctrine, The Emancipation Proclamation, Gettysburg Address, more. Includes 3 selections from the Common Core State Standards Initiative. 64pp.   0-486-41124-9

A DOLL'S HOUSE, Henrik Ibsen. Ibsen's best-known play displays his genius for realistic prose drama. An expression of women's rights, the play climaxes when the central character, Nora, rejects a smothering marriage and life in "a doll's house." A selection of the Common Core State Standards Initiative. 80pp.
0-486-27062-9

DOOMED SHIPS: Great Ocean Liner Disasters, William H. Miller, Jr. Nearly 200 photographs, many from private collections, highlight tales of some of the vessels whose pleasure cruises ended in catastrophe: the *Morro Castle, Normandie, Andrea Doria, Europa,* and many others. 128pp.   0-486-45366-9

THE DORÉ BIBLE ILLUSTRATIONS, Gustave Doré. Detailed plates from the Bible: the Creation scenes, Adam and Eve, horrifying visions of the Flood, the battle sequences with their monumental crowds, depictions of the life of Jesus, 241 plates in all. 241pp.   0-486-23004-X

DUBLINERS, James Joyce. A fine and accessible introduction to the work of one of the 20th century's most influential writers, this collection features 15 tales, including a masterpiece of the short-story genre, "The Dead." 160pp. 0-486-26870-5

THE EARLY SCIENCE FICTION OF PHILIP K. DICK, Philip K. Dick. This anthology presents short stories and novellas that originally appeared in pulp magazines of the early 1950s, including "The Variable Man," "Second Variety," "Beyond the Door," "The Defenders," and more. 272pp. 0-486-49733-X

THE EARLY SHORT STORIES OF F. SCOTT FITZGERALD, F. Scott Fitzgerald. These tales offer insights into many themes, characters, and techniques that emerged in Fitzgerald's later works. Selections include "The Curious Case of Benjamin Button," "Babes in the Woods," and a dozen others. 256pp. 0-486-79465-2

EASY BUTTERFLY ORIGAMI, Tammy Yee. Thirty full-color designs to fold include simple instructions and fun facts about each species. Patterns are perforated for easy removal and offer accurate portrayals of variations in insects' top and bottom sides. 64pp. 0-486-78457-6

EASY SPANISH PHRASE BOOK NEW EDITION: Over 700 Phrases for Everyday Use, Pablo Garcia Loaeza, Ph.D. Up-to-date volume, organized for quick access to phrases related to greetings, transportation, shopping, emergencies, other common circumstances. Over 700 entries include terms for modern telecommunications, idioms, slang. Phonetic pronunciations accompany phrases. 96pp. 0-486-49905-7

EINSTEIN'S ESSAYS IN SCIENCE, Albert Einstein. Speeches and essays in accessible, everyday language profile influential physicists such as Niels Bohr and Isaac Newton. They also explore areas of physics to which the author made major contributions. 128pp. 0-486-47011-3

EL DORADO: Further Adventures of the Scarlet Pimpernel, Baroness Orczy. A popular sequel to *The Scarlet Pimpernel*, this suspenseful story recounts the Pimpernel's attempts to rescue the Dauphin from imprisonment during the French Revolution. An irresistible blend of intrigue, period detail, and vibrant characterizations. 352pp. 0-486-44026-5

ELEGANT SMALL HOMES OF THE TWENTIES: 99 Designs from a Competition, Chicago Tribune. Nearly 100 designs for five- and six-room houses feature New England and Southern colonials, Normandy cottages, stately Italianate dwellings, and other fascinating snapshots of American domestic architecture of the 1920s. 112pp. 0-486-46910-7

THE ELUSIVE PIMPERNEL, Baroness Orczy. Robespierre's revolutionaries find their wicked schemes thwarted by the heroic Pimpernel — Sir Percival Blakeney. In this thrilling sequel, Chauvelin devises a plot to eliminate the Pimpernel and his wife. 272pp. 0-486-45464-9

ERIC SLOANE'S WEATHER BOOK, Eric Sloane. A beautifully illustrated book of enlightening lore for outdoorsmen, farmers, sailors, and anyone who has ever wondered whether to take an umbrella when leaving the house. 87 illustrations. 96pp. 0-486-44357-4

ETHAN FROME, Edith Wharton. Classic story of wasted lives, set against a bleak New England background. Superbly delineated characters in a hauntingly grim tale of thwarted love. Considered by many to be Wharton's masterpiece. 96pp. 0-486-26690-7

THE FEDERALIST PAPERS, Alexander Hamilton, James Madison, John Jay. A collection of 85 articles and essays that were initially published anonymously in New York newspapers in 1787–1788, this volume reflects the intentions of the Constitution's framers and ratifiers. 448pp. 0-486-49636-8

FINDING YOUR WAY WITHOUT MAP OR COMPASS, Harold Gatty. Useful, instructive manual shows would-be explorers, hikers, bikers, scouts, sailors, and survivalists how to find their way outdoors by observing animals, weather patterns, shifting sands, and other elements of nature. 288pp. 0-486-40613-X

FIRST SPANISH READER: A Beginner's Dual-Language Book, Edited by Angel Flores. Delightful stories, other material based on works of Don Juan Manuel, Luis Taboada, Ricardo Palma, other noted writers. Complete faithful English translations on facing pages. Exercises. 176pp. 0-486-25810-6

FIVE ACRES AND INDEPENDENCE, M. G. Kains. This classic of the back-to-the-land movement is packed with solid, timeless information. Written by a renowned horticulturist, it has taught generations how to make their land self-sufficient. 95 figures. 397pp. 0-486-20974-1

FLATLAND: A Romance of Many Dimensions, Edwin A. Abbott. Classic of science (and mathematical) fiction — charmingly illustrated by the author — describes the adventures of A. Square, a resident of Flatland, in Spaceland (three dimensions), Lineland (one dimension), and Pointland (no dimensions). 96pp. 0-486-27263-X

FRANKENSTEIN, Mary Shelley. The story of Victor Frankenstein's monstrous creation and the havoc it caused has enthralled generations of readers and inspired countless writers of horror and suspense. With the author's own 1831 introduction. 176pp. 0-486-28211-2

THE GARGOYLE BOOK: 572 Examples from Gothic Architecture, Lester Burbank Bridaham. Dispelling the conventional wisdom that French Gothic architectural flourishes were born of despair or gloom, Bridaham reveals the whimsical nature of these creations and the ingenious artisans who made them. 572 illustrations. 224pp. 0-486-44754-5

THE GIFT OF THE MAGI AND OTHER SHORT STORIES, O. Henry. Sixteen captivating stories by one of America's most popular storytellers. Included are such classics as "The Gift of the Magi," "The Last Leaf," and "The Ransom of Red Chief." Publisher's Note. A selection of the Common Core State Standards Initiative. 96pp. 0-486-27061-0

THE GÖDELIAN PUZZLE BOOK: Puzzles, Paradoxes and Proofs, Raymond M. Smullyan. These logic puzzles provide entertaining variations on Gödel's incompleteness theorems, offering ingenious challenges related to infinity, truth and provability, undecidability, and other concepts. No background in formal logic is necessary. 288pp. 0-486-49705-4

THE GOETHE TREASURY: Selected Prose and Poetry, Johann Wolfgang von Goethe. Edited, Selected, and with an Introduction by Thomas Mann. In addition to his lyric poetry, Goethe wrote travel sketches, autobiographical studies, essays, letters, and proverbs in rhyme and prose. This collection presents outstanding examples from each genre. 368pp. 0-486-44780-4

GREAT EXPECTATIONS, Charles Dickens. Orphaned Pip is apprenticed to the dirty work of the forge but dreams of becoming a gentleman — and one day finds himself in possession of "great expectations." Dickens' finest novel. 384pp. 0-486-41586-4

GREAT ILLUSTRATIONS BY N. C. WYETH, N. C. Wyeth. Edited and with an Introduction by Jeff A. Menges. This full-color collection focuses on the artist's early and most popular illustrations, featuring more than 100 images from *The Mysterious Stranger, Robin Hood, Robinson Crusoe, The Boy's King Arthur*, and other classics. 128pp. 0-486-47295-7

Browse over 10,000 books at www.doverpublications.com

CATALOG OF DOVER BOOKS

HAMLET, William Shakespeare. The quintessential Shakespearean tragedy, whose highly charged confrontations and anguished soliloquies probe depths of human feeling rarely sounded in any art. Reprinted from an authoritative British edition complete with illuminating footnotes. A selection of the Common Core State Standards Initiative. 128pp. 0-486-27278-8

THE HAUNTED HOUSE, Charles Dickens. A Yuletide gathering in an eerie country retreat provides the backdrop for Dickens and his friends — including Elizabeth Gaskell and Wilkie Collins — who take turns spinning supernatural yarns. 144pp. 0-486-46309-5

THE HEADS OF CERBERUS, Francis Stevens. Illustrated by Ric Binkley. A trio of time-travelers land in Philadelphia's brutal totalitarian state of 2118. Loaded with action and humor, this 1919 classic was the first alternate-world fantasy. "A much-sought rarity." — *Analog.* 192pp. 0-486-79026-6

HEART OF DARKNESS, Joseph Conrad. Dark allegory of a journey up the Congo River and the narrator's encounter with the mysterious Mr. Kurtz. Masterly blend of adventure, character study, psychological penetration. For many, Conrad's finest, most enigmatic story. 80pp. 0-486-26464-5

HISTORIC COSTUMES AND HOW TO MAKE THEM, Mary Fernald and E. Shenton. Practical, informative guidebook shows how to create everything from short tunics worn by Saxon men in the fifth century to a lady's bustle dress of the late 1800s. 81 illustrations. 176pp. 0-486-44906-8

THE HOUND OF THE BASKERVILLES, Sir Arthur Conan Doyle. A deadly curse in the form of a legendary ferocious beast continues to claim its victims from the Baskerville family until Holmes and Watson intervene. Often called the best detective story ever written. 128pp. 0-486-28214-7

THE HOUSE BEHIND THE CEDARS, Charles W. Chesnutt. Originally published in 1900, this groundbreaking novel by a distinguished African-American author recounts the drama of a brother and sister who "pass for white" during the dangerous days of Reconstruction. 208pp. 0-486-46144-0

HOW THE OTHER HALF LIVES, Jacob Riis. This famous journalistic record of the filth and degradation of New York's slums at the turn of the 20th century is a classic in social thought and of early American photography. Over 100 photographs. 256pp. 0-486-22012-5

HOW TO DRAW NEARLY EVERYTHING, Victor Perard. Beginners of all ages can learn to draw figures, faces, landscapes, trees, flowers, and animals of all kinds. Well-illustrated guide offers suggestions for pencil, pen, and brush techniques plus composition, shading, and perspective. 160pp. 0-486-49848-4

HOW TO MAKE SUPER POP-UPS, Joan Irvine. Illustrated by Linda Hendry. Super pop-ups extend the element of surprise with three-dimensional designs that slide, turn, spring, and snap. More than 30 patterns and 475 illustrations include cards, stage props, and school projects. 96pp. 0-486-46589-6

THE IMITATION OF CHRIST, Thomas à Kempis. Translated by Aloysius Croft and Harold Bolton. This religious classic has brought understanding and comfort to millions for centuries. Written in a candid and conversational style, the topics include liberation from worldly inclinations, preparation and consolations of prayer, and eucharistic communion. 160pp. 0-486-43185-1

THE IMPORTANCE OF BEING EARNEST, Oscar Wilde. Wilde's witty and buoyant comedy of manners, filled with some of literature's most famous epigrams, reprinted from an authoritative British edition. Considered Wilde's most perfect work. A selection of the Common Core State Standards Initiative. 64pp. 0-486-26478-5

THE INFERNO, Dante Alighieri. Translated and with notes by Henry Wadsworth Longfellow. The first stop on Dante's famous journey from Hell to Purgatory to Paradise, this 14th-century allegorical poem blends vivid and shocking imagery with graceful lyricism. Translated by the beloved 19th-century poet, Henry Wadsworth Longfellow. 256pp. 0-486-44288-8

JANE EYRE, Charlotte Brontë. Written in 1847, *Jane Eyre* tells the tale of an orphan girl's progress from the custody of cruel relatives to an oppressive boarding school and its culmination in a troubled career as a governess. A selection of the Common Core State Standards Initiative. 448pp. 0-486-42449-9

JAPANESE WOODBLOCK BIRD PRINTS, Numata Kashû. These lifelike images of birds and flowers first appeared in a now-rare 1883 portfolio. A magnificent reproduction of a 1938 facsimile of the original publication, this exquisite edition features 150 color illustrations. 160pp. 0-486-47050-4

JULIUS CAESAR, William Shakespeare. Great tragedy based on Plutarch's account of the lives of Brutus, Julius Caesar, and Mark Antony. Evil plotting, ringing oratory, high tragedy with Shakespeare's incomparable insight, dramatic power. Explanatory footnotes. 96pp. 0-486-26876-4

THE JUNGLE, Upton Sinclair. 1906 bestseller shockingly reveals intolerable labor practices and working conditions in the Chicago stockyards as it tells the grim story of a Slavic family that emigrates to America full of optimism but soon faces despair. 304pp. 0-486-41923-1

JUST WHAT THE DOCTOR DISORDERED: Early Writings and Cartoons of Dr. Seuss, Dr. Seuss. Edited and with an Introduction by Rick Marschall. The Doctor's visual hilarity, nonsense language, and offbeat sense of humor illuminate this compilation of items from his early career, created for periodicals such as *Judge, Life, College Humor,* and *Liberty.* 144pp. 0-486-49846-8

KING LEAR, William Shakespeare. Powerful tragedy of an aging king, betrayed by his daughters, robbed of his kingdom, descending into madness. Perhaps the bleakest of Shakespeare's tragic dramas, complete with explanatory footnotes. 144pp. 0-486-28058-6

KNITTING FOR ANARCHISTS: The What, Why and How of Knitting, Anna Zilboorg. Every knitter takes a different approach, and this revolutionary guide encourages experimentation and self-expression. Suitable for active knitters and beginners alike, it offers illustrated patterns for sweaters, pullovers, and cardigans. 160pp. 0-486-79466-0

THE LADY OR THE TIGER?: and Other Logic Puzzles, Raymond M. Smullyan. Created by a renowned puzzle master, these whimsically themed challenges involve paradoxes about probability, time, and change; metapuzzles; and self-referentiality. Nineteen chapters advance in difficulty from relatively simple to highly complex. 1982 edition. 240pp. 0-486-47027-X

LEAVES OF GRASS: The Original 1855 Edition, Walt Whitman. Whitman's immortal collection includes some of the greatest poems of modern times, including his masterpiece, "Song of Myself." Shattering standard conventions, it stands as an unabashed celebration of body and nature. 128pp. 0-486-45676-5

LES MISÉRABLES, Victor Hugo. Translated by Charles E. Wilbour. Abridged by James K. Robinson. A convict's heroic struggle for justice and redemption plays out against a fiery backdrop of the Napoleonic wars. This edition features the excellent original translation and a sensitive abridgment. 304pp. 0-486-45789-3

Browse over 10,000 books at www.doverpublications.com

LIGHT FOR THE ARTIST, Ted Seth Jacobs. Intermediate and advanced art students receive a broad vocabulary of effects with this in-depth study of light. Diagrams and paintings illustrate applications of principles to figure, still life, and landscape paintings. 144pp. 0-486-49304-0

LILITH: A Romance, George MacDonald. In this novel by the father of fantasy literature, a man travels through time to meet Adam and Eve and to explore humanity's fall from grace and ultimate redemption. 240pp. 0-486-46818-6

LINE: An Art Study, Edmund J. Sullivan. Written by a noted artist and teacher, this well-illustrated guide introduces the basics of line drawing. Topics include third and fourth dimensions, formal perspective, shade and shadow, figure drawing, and other essentials. 208pp. 0-486-79484-9

THE LODGER, Marie Belloc Lowndes. Acclaimed by *The New York Times* as "one of the best suspense novels ever written," this novel recounts an English couple's doubts about their boarder, whom they suspect of being a serial killer. 240pp. 0-486-78809-1

"THE LOVELIEST HOME THAT EVER WAS": The Story of the Mark Twain House in Hartford, Steve Courtney. With an Introduction by Hal Holbrook. The official guide to The Mark Twain House & Museum, this volume tells the dramatic story of the author and his family and their Victorian mansion. Architectural drawings, period photos, plus modern color images. 144pp. 0-486-48634-6

MACBETH, William Shakespeare. A Scottish nobleman murders the king in order to succeed to the throne. Tortured by his conscience and fearful of discovery, he becomes tangled in a web of treachery and deceit that ultimately spells his doom. A selection of the Common Core State Standards Initiative. 96pp. 0-486-27802-6

MANHATTAN IN MAPS 1527–2014, Paul E. Cohen and Robert T. Augustyn. This handsome volume features 65 full-color maps charting Manhattan's development from the first Dutch settlement to the present. Each map is placed in context by an accompanying essay. 176pp. 0-486-77991-2

MANHATTAN MOVES UPTOWN: An Illustrated History, Charles Lockwood. Compiled from newspaper archives and richly illustrated with historic images, this fascinating chronicle traces the city's growth from Wall Street to Harlem during the period between 1783 and the early 20th century. 368pp. 0-486-78120-8

MATHEMATICS FOR THE NONMATHEMATICIAN, Morris Kline. Erudite and entertaining overview follows development of mathematics from ancient Greeks to present. Topics include logic and mathematics, the fundamental concept, differential calculus, probability theory, much more. Exercises and problems. 672pp. 0-486-24823-2

MEDEA, Euripides. One of the most powerful and enduring of Greek tragedies, masterfully portraying the fierce motives driving Medea's pursuit of vengeance for her husband's insult and betrayal. Authoritative Rex Warner translation. 64pp. 0-486-27548-5

THE MERCHANT BANKERS, Joseph Wechsberg. With a new Foreword by Christopher Kobrak. Fascinating chronicle of the world's great financial families profiles the personalities behind seven legendary banking houses: Hambros, Barings, the Rothschilds, the Warburgs, Deutsche Bank, Lehman Brothers, and Banca Commerciale Italiana. 384pp. 0-486-78118-6

THE METAMORPHOSIS AND OTHER STORIES, Franz Kafka. Excellent new English translations of title story (considered by many critics Kafka's most perfect work), plus "The Judgment," "In the Penal Colony," "A Country Doctor," and "A Report to an Academy." A selection of the Common Core State Standards Initiative. 96pp. 0-486-29030-1

METROPOLIS, Thea von Harbou. This Weimar-era novel of a futuristic society, written by the screenwriter for the iconic 1927 film, was hailed by noted science-fiction authority Forrest J. Ackerman as "a work of genius." 224pp. 0-486-79567-5

MICHAEL PEARSON'S TRADITIONAL KNITTING: Aran, Fair Isle and Fisher Ganseys, New & Expanded Edition, Michael Pearson. This extensive record of unique patterns from the remote fishing villages of Scotland and England combines a social history of the regions with detailed patterns and practical instructions for knitters. Includes new pattern charts and knitting instructions. 264pp. 0-486-46053-3

A MIDSUMMER NIGHT'S DREAM, William Shakespeare. Among the most popular of Shakespeare's comedies, this enchanting play humorously celebrates the vagaries of love as it focuses upon the intertwined romances of several pairs of lovers. Explanatory footnotes. 80pp. 0-486-27067-X

MODULAR CROCHET: The Revolutionary Method for Creating Custom-Designed Pullovers, Judith Copeland. This guide ranks among the most revolutionary and revered books on freeform and improvisational crochet. Even beginners can use its innovative but simple method to make perfect-fit pullovers, turtlenecks, vests, and other garments. 192pp. 0-486-79687-6

THE MONEY CHANGERS, Upton Sinclair. Originally published in 1908, this cautionary novel from the author of *The Jungle* explores corruption within the American system as a group of power brokers joins forces for personal gain, triggering a crash on Wall Street. 192pp. 0-486-46917-4

THE MOST POPULAR HOMES OF THE TWENTIES, William A. Radford. With a New Introduction by Daniel D. Reiff. Based on a rare 1925 catalog, this architectural showcase features floor plans, construction details, and photos of 26 homes, plus articles on entrances, porches, garages, and more. 250 illustrations, 21 color plates. 176pp. 0-486-47028-8

THE MYSTERIOUS MICKEY FINN, Elliot Paul. A multimillionaire's disappearance incites a maelstrom of kidnapping, murder, and a plot to restore the French monarchy. "One of the funniest books we've read in a long time." — *The New York Times*. 256pp. 0-486-24751-1

MYSTICISM: A Study in the Nature and Development of Spiritual Consciousness, Evelyn Underhill. Classic introduction to mysticism and mystical consciousness: awakening of the self, purification, voices and visions, ecstasy and rapture, dark night of the soul, much more. 544pp. 0-486-42238-0

NARRATIVE OF THE LIFE OF FREDERICK DOUGLASS, Frederick Douglass. The impassioned abolitionist and eloquent orator provides graphic descriptions of his childhood and horrifying experiences as a slave as well as a harrowing record of his dramatic escape to the North and eventual freedom. A selection of the Common Core State Standards Initiative. 96pp. 0-486-28499-9

NEW YORK'S FABULOUS LUXURY APARTMENTS: with Original Floor Plans from the Dakota, River House, Olympic Tower and Other Great Buildings, Andrew Alpern. Magnificently illustrated directory of 73 of Manhattan's most splendid addresses includes mini-histories of each building, noting the architect, builder, date of construction, and more. 221 photographs and drawings. 176pp. 0-486-25318-X

THE NIGHT OF THE LONG KNIVES, Fritz Leiber. Deathland's residents are consumed by the urge to murder each other, making partnership of any sort a lethal risk. Novel-length magazine story from the Cold War era by an influential science-fiction author. 112pp. 0-486-79801-1